Making the World Safe for Tourism

To Patricia, Bob, Daniel and Samantha —

all the time I was writing this book,
I had a note taped to my refrigerator—
" The essence of travel is coming home."
You are what I think of when I
think of home.

Love to you all,
Patricia

Making the World Safe for Tourism

Patricia Goldstone

Yale University Press

New Haven and London

Designed by and set in Janson type by Bessas & Ackerman,
Guilford, Connecticut.

Printed in the United States of America by Thomson-Shore, Dexter, Michigan.

Library of Congress Cataloging-in-Publication Data
Goldstone, Patricia, 1951–
Making the world safe for tourism / Patricia Goldstone.
p. cm.
Includes bibliographical references (p.).
ISBN 0–300–08763–2 (cloth : alk. paper)
1. Tourism—Economic aspects. 2. Tourism—Social aspects. 3. Civilization,
Modern—20th century. 4. Cultural relativism. I. Title.
G155.A1 G644 2001
338.4'791—dc21   00–011676

A catalogue record for this book is available from the British Library.

The paper in this book meets the guidelines for permanence and durability of
the Committee on Production Guidelines for Book Longevity of the Council
on Library Resources.

10 9 8 7 6 5 4 3 2 1

This book is affectionately dedicated to the memories of two remarkable women: Helen Maguire Muller, who gave me my first good look at the world, and my grandmother Florence Lewis Theil Herrscher, who belongs in the league of great adventuresses.

Armed neutrality is ineffectual at best. The world must be made safe for democracy.

Woodrow Wilson,
address to the Joint Session
of Congress, April 2, 1912,
requesting that Congress declare war

Contents

Preface
The Glasnost Junket,
or How I Learned to Say "Shit!" in Finnish

IT IS MIDSUMMER 1990, seven months after the Berlin Wall came down, and I am shivering in an oversized red T-shirt with an inner tube girding my waist in the company of 215 churchgoing teenagers stationed at strategic intervals around the border of an arctic lake in Joensuu, Finland. The glasnost industry has spun off a peculiar satellite: summer camp for itinerant American artists insufficiently recognized in their own land. It follows conventional wisdom in other industries by exporting shoddy goods to the Third World, where, it is presumed, the natives will not recognize their lack of quality. There are supposed to be about 300 teenagers participating in this performance art symbolizing the breaking-down of boundaries, but a third have sensibly opted to stay home, and I have been drafted in the hope that the national television cameras covering the event will be far enough away not to pick up on the fact that I am middle-aged.

Joensuu is a raw and bustling border town about an hour by train from the former USSR. Twenty-five years ago it looked like its Russian counterpart, Sortavalla, a Chekhovian jumble of gabled timber houses and unpaved streets. But largely owing to the efforts of one contractor, Sudo Tervo, who bulldozed through the distinctive Karelian architecture to make way for jerry-built housing for workers in the local paper and timber industries, the town expanded outward into a maze of suburbs and busy highways that provide the connective tissue for most of Karelia (eastern Finland). Then, in order to draw a professional population of scientists, academics, and educated youth away from Helsinki (and the summer population of tourists away from the circuit of jazz festivals that necklaces western Finland) the municipal powers that be, including Tervo, built a university and promoted the hell out of culture.

The glasnost junket was born out of the political ambition of a deputy mayor who, with her round blue eyes fixed unblinkingly on the mayoralty, staked her bid on the publicity she hoped to garner with a glitzy media event dramatizing recent events in Western Europe— thereby proving that politicians' taste in art is at least as questionable as that of the peer review panel of the National Endowment for the Arts. At a cost of $100,000 to the taxpayers of Joensuu, American know-how was imported to produce a pen-pal exchange, a swim meet, and our own inexplicable exercise, in which we took meetings in the rural marketplace, lay down, and had our bodies outlined in chalk to symbolize the breaking-up of boundaries all over the world. (The young men of Joensuu, ever hopeful, seized on the opportunity to simulate sex with us.) The team of consultants hired by the ambitious mayor-in-waiting—whose name, according to her culture-happy aides, signified "village chief"—included one of the fathers of the 1960s "happening" and his protégée, the dean of a small college in northern California which specializes in performance art. According to these two, we were creating "extramarket art," which is defined by its frame (context to larger political events) rather than its content. Whatever inanities it might produce can be justified by its affordability: art can and should be free. In fact, most of the adult citizens of Joensuu were happy to turn their backs on our performances and pay thirty dollars a pop to hear the Leningrad Symphony instead.

There is a school of thought that holds, if Stalin had had a different personality, the Cold War would never have happened. If this is true, the glasnost movement should have picked its emissaries more carefully. The festival director, a stiff-backed blonde who favored jodhpurs, was happiest when she addressed the masses from an elevation, through her walkie-talkie. Occasionally she would make a gracious effort to be part of the proletariat. A grim chuckle erupted from an audience of Finnish students when she blandly substituted the Finnish word signifying *pigsty* for *changing area* in one of her countless orientations. It wasn't so amusing to watch dull distrust freeze lively young faces as they were led over and over through the boring and humiliating "rituals" they were being organized to perform. Or to watch her cut short her "interview" with a musician who had kept up her studies during World War II even after her sister starved to death by holding up signs reading, "Enough of that!" and "Talk about politics now!"

I ached at the sheer badness, monotony, and trivia of what we were required to do, which combined the relentless organization of a summit conference on global widget making with the worst features of summer camp, an experience I had loathed. The happening headquarters, commandeered from the local high school, was a maze of flow charts, schedules, and diagrams. The summit of artistic expression was the orientation meeting. We were mercilessly oriented every evening between five and six. Our marching orders included maps indicating the times and places we had to do our readings of postcards sharing people's "boundary" experiences; letters with the hours when we would read written in the lower right-hand corner; response cards we had to fill out and return the following day; a clipboard, also to be returned; sticks of yellow chalk; and, of course, our company logo T-shirt.

We were to begin each reading exactly on the hour, no matter where we were. We were to read in an intimate style which did not resemble acting in any way, but no mumbling, please. We were to allow time and space for audience response. (Response to what? What audience?) We were to listen to said response and then fill out the response card with our personal experience of reading the story. We were allowed to fill out these cards at our own convenience but had to return them to the school the next day, with a notation of the time, place, and attendance of each reading. We were to report back to the director our observations concerning our surroundings, presumably to further her own research.

The bureaucratic trappings of the happening quickly developed an odor of the police state. Most of the readers were students, imported at their own cost in exchange for three units of course credit—a plan designed, I was told as we knotted a 5,500-foot length of rope for the swim meet, to prepare them for the eventuality that they might never be paid for their labors as artists. To enhance their feelings of authenticity, they were kept at Sisyphean tasks in a workhouse atmosphere, housed in hovels, and left to scrounge for meals while the director and her cohorts lived luxuriously at the expense of the citizens of Joensuu. Participants were charged with examining their own feelings about private versus public motives in creating art, in an atmosphere which resembled the criticism–self-criticism of a Marxist cadre. They were encouraged to rat on one another for grades.

Lest I become fuel for the fires of NEA opponents or reclassified as a performance artist, I will say that there were advantages in being at the Joensuu Song Festival. There was much fine music in the white nights, which brought hundreds of people together to dance in a natural amphitheater under the sky. There were the nights themselves, mysteries of translucent violet in which the body floats free of the need for sleep; I used to meet an Australian bacchante every morning in the marketplace, still dancing on bloody feet like a princess in a fairy tale. There was a trip to Sortavalla, just over the Russian border, a small jewel of a town closed to travel since Stalin's time. Lacking television, it still maintained an official magician, a sad little man in rusty black polyester and white bow tie with a cold sore on his lip who matched hocus-pocus with two young Swedes in our entourage.

It is hard to remember these things when the police whistle blows. At the first blast from our director, who monitors us via her walkie-talkie while dressed snugly in a down vest, we parade like medieval penitents, carrying flags under our arms to the doleful tolling of a bell. At the second blast, we spread our lipstick-red flags (there has been much impassioned debate over whether making the flags red is *too* political), then dip them earthward. At a third blast we fling our flags over our shoulders, trying to avoid putting out our neighbors' eye, and race to the rim of the lagoon known as Illosaari. At the next blast we are supposed to jump into the lagoon, which is fed directly from the polar icecap, yelling "Vapaus!"—the Finnish word for "freedom." But when the whistle screams and the television cameras turn upon us, the clever teenagers all yell "Paska!"—"Shit!"—and many race away from the lagoon instead. As the numbing waters of Illosaari close over my head, my last thought is, "What am I doing here?"

This book attempts to answer that question.

Acronyms and Abbreviations

The acronyms and abbreviations listed here all appear in more than one chapter.

Amex	American Express
BCCI	Bank of Credit and Commerce International
CEO	Chief executive officer
CIAA	Coordinator for Inter-American Affairs
EcoSoc	(U.N.) Economic and Social Council
EEC	European Economic Community
E.U.	European Union
GATT	General Agreement on Tariffs and Trade
GDP	Gross domestic product
IFC	International Finance Corporation
IMF	International Monetary Fund
I2D2	Intragovernmental agency
LDC	Less-developed country
MEMTA	Middle Eastern and Mediterranean Travel and Tourism Association
NAFTA	North American Free Trade Agreement
NATO	North Atlantic Treaty Organization
MIGA	Multilateral Investment Guarantee Agency
PR	public relations
U.N.	United Nations
UNESCO	United Nations Educational, Scientific, and Cultural Organization
UNICEF	United Nations International Children's Emergency Fund
WTO	World Tourism Organization
WTTC	World Travel and Tourism Council
USIA	United States Information Agency

Making the World Safe for Tourism

The Democratization of Travel and the Rise of American Express

Hannibal encamped on the ridge, sweeping it clear of snow, and next set the soldiers to work to build up the path along the cliff, a most toilsome task. In one day he had made a passage sufficiently wide for the pack-train and horses; so he at once took those across and encamping on ground free of snow, sent them out to pasture, and then took the Numidians in relays to work at building up the path, so that with great difficulty in three days he managed to get the elephants across. . . .

Hannibal having now got all his forces together continued the descent, and in three days' march from the precipice just described reached flat country. He had lost many of his men by the hands of the enemy in the crossing of rivers and on the march in general, and the precipices and difficulties of the Alps had cost him not only many men, but a far greater number of horses and sumpter-animals. The whole march from New Carthage had taken him five months, and he had spent fifteen days in crossing the Alps, and now, when he thus boldly descended into the plains of the Po and the territory of the Insubres, his surviving forces numbered twelve thousand African and eight thousand Iberian foot, and not more than six thousand horse in all.

Polybius, The Histories, *trans. W. R. Paton*

IN THE BEGINNING, people traveled for necessity, not pleasure. They traveled for conquest, for gain, or for fear of their lives when threatened by plague, famine, or invasion. Travelers were, by definition, soldiers, privateers, merchants, diplomats, spies, or rogues. Travel was difficult, time-consuming, and dangerous, and not to be lightly undertaken. Traveling with an army was often the only way to go because armies built roads: Hannibal's invasion of Italy in 218 B.C. is remembered today chiefly for providing the first passageway through the Alps.

Today's travelers go cocooned in safe, packaged environments which generally insulate them from the very thing they wish to encounter; yet they too are an army, albeit of a different sort. Since the middle of the twentieth century, they have been praised as the foot soldiers of democracy for merely spending their vacations in countries that need hard currency. Since the fall of the former Soviet Union in particular, travelers have been marshaled by the forces of public relations to take those vacations in previously inaccessible and often still dangerous places in the interests of "opening" them to Western ways and Western trade. Governments, in conjunction with banking and financial institutions, travel companies, and the international lending institutions which traditionally sponsor foreign aid, are working overtime to reengineer former and even current trouble spots as tourist paradises. Tourism is now the world's biggest business; yet given the ambiguous boundaries that exist between finance, corporate power, national policy, and the tourism industry, it is almost impossible to tell whether our millennial rush toward global peace created the tourist boom—or whether the tourist boom created the peace.

The hardship and general inaccessibility of early travel created their own peculiar romance. The *Odyssey*, one of the foundation stones of Western literature, is a masterpiece of travel writing as well as an epic of conquest. The first great work of Western history, Herodotus' narrative of the Persian Wars (500–449 B.C.) describes the march of Alexander the Great through the exotic lands of Asia Minor: like many a traveler before and after him, Alexander became so enamored of the sights that he married the daughter of a local chieftain and stayed there.

From the far-flung legions of the Roman Empire to the far-flung legions of the British Empire, men went off to fight wars in order to escape their wives and children, their creditors, and their social class. Some, like the British merchant seamen of the sixteenth, seventeenth, eighteenth, and nineteenth centuries, made their fortunes. But rich or poor, they saw the world.

Merchants, among the most intrepid early travelers, often crossed entire continents to procure exotic goods, pricing them accordingly. Such men were not infrequently gifted storytellers, and the fabulous tales they brought back with them added to the value of their merchandise. The journal of the legendary Venetian trader Marco Polo (1254–1324), whose name remains synonymous with exploration, was throughout the Renaissance and well into the nineteenth century the only source of European information on many parts of central Asia. Polo, whose famous journey was the result of an accident—his father, Niccolò, and his uncle Maffeo established trading relations with the Mongol emperor

Kublai Khan when a war blocked their return to Venice from the Crimea—also became a diplomat by default. Brought by Niccolò and Maffeo to the court of the khan at the age of seventeen, Marco became a favorite of the despotic ruler, who employed him on business in central and northern China, southeast Asia, and south India; and for three years he apparently ruled the Chinese city of Yangchow.

As the borders of the world known to western Europeans expanded rapidly from the end of the Crusades to the beginning of the Industrial Revolution in what has become known as the Age of Discovery (the fifteenth to mid-eighteenth centuries), diplomats became the third great class of traveler. Often they were recruited from the ranks of poets and, later, novelists, for their skills in dispatch writing. Sometimes one function won out over the other, as in the case of Giles Fletcher, a British poet who led an embassy to Russia in 1588 to negotiate trading concessions for British merchants. His memoir of the experience, *Of the Russe Common Wealth* (1591) was suppressed by the British crown for fear it might give offense to the czar. The reason why is evident in Fletcher's description of Russians in the bath:

> You shall see them sometimes (to season their bodies) come out of their bathstoves all on a froth, and fuming as hoat almost as a pigge at a spit, and presently to leap into the river stark naked, or to powre cold water all over their bodies, and that in the coldest of all the winter time. The women to mend the bad hue of their skinnes, use to paint their faces with white and red colours, so visibly, that every man may perceive it. Which is made no matter, because it is common and liked well by their husbands: who make their wives and daughters an ordinary allowance to buy them colours to paint their faces withall, and delight themselves much to see them of fowle women become such fair images.[1]

Yet another great class of travelers were adventurers. These included writers and other artists hungry for experience like Byron and Shelley, who embroiled themselves in foreign wars, but also common or garden rogues like William Lithgow, also known as "Cut-Lugged Willie." Born in Lanark, Scotland, Willie left precipitately when four brothers cut off his ears, or lugs, after discovering him in bed with their sister. This appears to have left him with a taste for being tortured, as revealed in his *Totall Discourse, or Rayre Adventure and Painfull Peregrinations of Nineteene Yeares* (1632), written to support his claim of having walked more than 36,000 miles throughout Europe, Asia, and Africa between 1610 and 1629.

Women formed a surprisingly large subset of this group. From such wealthy aristocrats as Lady Mary Wortley Montagu (1689–1762) to poor convicts like the many unfortunates on whom Daniel Defoe patterned his Moll Flanders, women used travel to burst the bonds of convention and better their chances in life. Lady Mary's account of her visit to the Turkish bath at Sofia is almost identical to one written a century earlier by one Thomas Dallam, an organ builder who took one of his instruments as a gift from Queen Elizabeth of England to Sultan Mehmed III of Constantinople.

> I was here convinced of the truth of a reflection I had often made, that if it was the fashion to go naked, the face would be hardly observed. I perceived that the ladies with the finest skins and most delicate shapes had the greatest share of my admiration, though their faces were sometimes less beautiful than those of their companions. To tell you the truth, I had the wickedness enough to wish secretly that Mr. Jervas had been there invisible. I fancy it would very much have improved his art to see so many fine women naked, in different postures, some in conversation, some working, others drinking coffee or sherbert, and many negligently lying on their cushions, while their slaves (generally pretty girls of seventeen or eighteen) were employed in braiding their hair in several pretty fancies. In short, it is the women's coffee-house, where all the news is told, scandal invented, etc. . . . The lady that seemed most considerable among them entreated me to sit by her, and fain would have undresed me for the bath. I excused myself with difficulty. They all being so earnest in persuading me, I was at last forced to open my shirt, and shew them my stays; which satisfied them very well for, I saw, they believed I was so locked up in that machine that it was not in my power to open it, which contrivance they attributed to my husband.[2]

Both Lady Mary and Dallam write with the avid sexual curiosity of the born voyeur: the chief distinction between them is that Lady Mary, who eloped with her husband and accompanied him to the Turkish court, did not have to hide behind a screen with a eunuch in tow. But it was the contrivance of travel itself that unlocked Lady Mary's stays, not that of her husband. Some women, like Mrs. Christian Davies in the 1690s, disguised themselves as men and enlisted in the British army in order to see the world. "I cut off my hair and dressed me in a suit of my husband's having the precaution to quilt the waistcoat to preserve my breasts from hurt which were not large enough to betray my sex and putting on the wig and hat I had prepared I went out and bought me a silver-hilted sword and some Holland shirts."[3]

The ranks of Victorian ladies, famous for their social and sexual repression, produced some of the greatest travel adventuresses of all times. Mary Kingsley, Isabella Bird, Alexandra David, Dena Akeley,

Lady Duff Gordon, and Isabelle Eberhardt combined travel with exploring the farthest-flung reaches of empire, often competing with their soldier-husbands, fathers, or brothers. Kingsley, whose father was also an explorer, set out for Africa at the age of thirty in 1892. She traveled without male escort deep into the West African interior, something that was unheard-of at the time and would indeed be unusual in our own. Her game spirit and the knowledge she acquired of African societies and their rituals brought her celebrity on the lecture circuit, where she drew an enthusiastic audience of stay-at-home women who, eager to participate vicariously in her travels, financed her later adventures. Akeley, the wife of anthropologist Carl Akeley, accompanied her husband on his research trips to Africa and carried on his work after he died there of fever and dysentery. Lady Duff Gordon, dying of consumption, journeyed to Egypt alone to recover her health while her diplomat-husband stayed in Europe. She died while exploring the Nile but not before she wrote some of the most penetrating contemporary observations of Egyptian social structure in her diaries.

Other Victorian women, like Isabelle Eberhardt, went even further. Eberhardt, upon falling in love with an Arab chieftain, became a member of his harem, a romance epiphanized in Lesley Blanche's novel of pan-national sexual adventuring, *The Wilder Shores of Love* (1954). Later, the great gothic writer Isak Dinesen moved to Africa to run a coffee plantation when her chances ran out at home in Denmark: her adventures in her new world made her famous as an artist.

Adventurers came closest to traveling for travel's sake. But man or woman, rich or poor, soldier, sailor, organ builder, or spy, most found the idea of consuming experience with no tangible by-product foreign until the advances of the Industrial Revolution began to create that hotbed of modern anomie known as leisure time. It is no coincidence that by the mid-eighteenth century, when the concept of tourism as we know it today began to develop, the Age of Discovery was for the most part over. The great exception was the central and western regions of what is now the continental United States. The boundaries of the known world had settled into place, and so had the fortunes that exploration had created. People began traveling to see rather than to conquer.

It became fashionable for the young scions of new wealth (largely created by British shipping fortunes) to go to university. Those who managed to complete their curriculum without being "sent down" for unruly behavior were then expected to finish their education by traveling, in a suitably leisurely and opulent manner, about the world they were expected to rule. This advanced education took the form of the

Grand Tour, which generally lasted about two years and covered much of continental Europe, still exotic to most Britishers. While some took the educational aspect of their travels seriously enough to turn them into a minor ambassadorial mission, setting up diplomatic and commercial contacts to further their careers, many were seduced by life in the fashionable watering-spots, which accommodated the growing desire of the young to see and be seen as, half a century before, they had catered to the needs of overindulged courtiers. Although these spas were extremely luxurious, a vestigial nostalgia for the deprivations of exploratory travel can be glimpsed in the celebrated Madame de Sévigné's account of "taking the waters" at Vichy in 1696: "At length I have finished douching and exuding; in one week I have lost over thirty pints of water, and believe myself to be immune from the rheumatics for the rest of my life. There is little doubt the cure is a painful one, but a wonderful moment dawns at last when, empty and renewed, one sits relishing a cup of fresh chicken broth which joy is not to be despised, indeed I rank it very high: this is an adorable place."[4]

Although their ranks contained many gifted amateur writers and, undoubtedly, spies, for the most part the new wave of travelers were distinguished more by having the means to purchase sensations and experiences than by the peculiar talents associated with making those experiences valuable to others. By 1739 the English poet Thomas Gray, best known for *Elegy Written in a Country Churchyard*, could write in his *Letters* the following parody of those who traveled to explore their own prejudices rather than the conditions of the countries they visited.

> The Travels of T. G., Gent: which will consist of the following particulars
>
> CHAP. 1
>
> The Author arrives at Dover; his conversation with the Mayor of that Corporation; sets out in the Pacquet-Boat, grows very sick; the Author spews, a very minute account of all the circumstances thereof: his arrival at Calais; how the inhabitants of that country speak French and are said to be all Papishes; the Author's reflections thereupon.
>
> CHAP. 2
>
> How they feed him with Soupe; and what Soupe is. how he meets with a Capucin; & what a Capucin is. how they shut him up in a Post-Chaise and send him to Paris; he goes wondring along soe 6 days; & how there are Trees, & Houses just as in England. arrives in Paris without knowing it. . . .
>
> CHAP. 11
>
> Sets out the latter end of November to cross the Alps. he is devoured by a Wolf, & how it feels to be devoured by a Wolf. the 7th day he comes to the foot of Mount Cenis. how he is wrapped up in

Bear-Skins, and Beaver-Skins, Boots on his legs, Caps on his head, Muffs on his hands & Taffety over his eyes; he is placed on a Bier & is carried to Heaven by the savages blindfold. how he lights among a certain fat nation, called Clouds; how they are always in a Sweat, & never speak, but they fart. how they flock about him, & think him very odd for not doing so too. he falls flump into Italy. . . .

    CHAP. 15

Arrival at Florence. is of opinion, that the Venus of Medecis is a modern performance, & that a very indifferent one, & much inferiour to the K. Charles at Charing Cross. Account of the City, & Manners of the Inhabitants. a learned Dissertation on the true Situation of Gomorrah. . . .

And here will end the first part of these instructive & entertaining Voyages. the Subscribers are to pay 20 Guineas; 19 down, & the remainder upon delivery of the book. N.B. A few are printed on the softest Royal Brown Paper for the use of the curious.[5]

Gray, the son of a scrivener, traveled to Italy as the guest of the wealthy Horace Walpole (fourth earl of Orford and author of the gothic masterpiece *The Castle of Otranto*), whom he met at Eton. Without such aristocratic sponsorship, Gray would have had to wait at least another century to afford the trip; as it was, he quarreled mysteriously with his host and returned home to his mother. Gray identified the provinciality, credulity, and ignorance bordering on superstition that he satirized as peculiar to the British upper class, but the same strains would surface more than a century later, in Mark Twain's *Innocents Abroad* and Henry James's *Daisy Miller*. These describe the phenomenon of the New World meeting the Old as newly rich Americans re-created the Grand Tour in their own image, that of the Gilded Age. This was the fabulously vulgar era of the locomotion-driven thrust of America's great westward expansion—the settling of the last frontier, when rough men realized large fortunes in short lifetimes, leaving their wives and daughters to figure out how to spend them. To these socially ambitious women, the Grand Tour was simply a means to introduce themselves into Society, which viewed them with disdainful amusement not unmixed with alarm. The alarm proceeded from the newcomers' tranquil expectation that Society would adjust to them and, ultimately, it would be justified. As Henry James described his heroine in *Daisy Miller*,

It might have been said of this wandering maiden who had come and sat down beside him on a bench that she chattered. She was very quiet, she sat in a charming tranquil attitude; but her lips and her eyes were constantly moving. She had a soft slender agreeable voice, and her tone was distinctly sociable. She gave Winterbourne a report of her movements and intentions, and those of her mother and brother in Europe, and enumerated in particular the various hotels at which they had stopped. . . . She appeared to be in the very best humour with everything. She declared that the hotels were very good when once you got used to their ways and that Europe was perfectly entrancing. She wasn't disappointed—not a bit. Perhaps it was because she had heard so much about it before. She had ever so many friends who had been there ever so many times, and that way she had got thoroughly posted. And then she had had ever so many dresses and things from Paris. Whenever she put on a Paris dress she felt as if she were in Europe. . . .

"The only thing I don't like," she proceeded, "is the society. There ain't any society.—or if there is, I don't know where it keeps itself. Do you? I suppose there's some society somewhere, but I haven't seen anything of it. I'm very fond of society and I've always had plenty of it. I don't mean only in Schenectady, but in New York. In New York I had lots of society. Last winter I had seventeen dinners given me, and three of them were by gentlemen," added Daisy Miller. . . . She paused again for an instant: she was looking at Winterbourne with all her prettiness in her frank grey eyes and in her clear rather uniform smile. "I've always had," she said, "a great deal of gentlemen's society."[6]

Thomas Cook, the founder of Cook's Travel services, was quick to recognize that by the 1850s, Britain's more adventurous middle-class women were beginning to earn their own incomes and to covet travel, if not to West Africa, then at least to Germany. In order to safeguard their respectability, these women needed a tour chaperoned by an equally respectable male. Cook, who started his business organizing temperance tours for working-class men, realized the business potential of organized, or "package," tours for women after receiving a letter from four sisters in a middle-class temperance family. The Lincolne sisters of Suffolk had wages to spend and had read of the beauties of the Rhine, but how could they get there?

How could ladies alone and unprotected go 600 or 700 miles away from home? However, after many pros and cons, the idea gradually grew on us and we found ourselves consulting guides, hunting in guidebooks, reading descriptions, making notes, and corresponding with Mr. Cook. 'Tis true, we encountered some opposition—one friend declaring it was improper for ladies to go alone—the gentlemen thinking we were far too independent. But somehow or other one interview with Mr. Cook removed all our hesitation, and we forthwith placed ourselves under his care.

Many of our friends thought us too independent and adventurous to leave the shores of old England, and thus plunge into foreign lands not beneath Victoria's sway with no protecting relative, but we can only say that we hope this will not be our last Excursion of the kind. We would venture anywhere with such a guide and guardian as Mr. Cook.[7]

Travel remained a pleasure of the wealthy until the end of the nineteenth century, when an American captain of industry named J. C. Fargo was made to wait in line like any mortal to cash his banker's letter of credit on a visit to Paris. Fargo was the head of the American Express Company, whose story is inextricably tangled with the democratization of travel in the twentieth century. Ironically, he was closer kin to the dragons of the Old Guard in James's story than to the newly rich. A Tory by nature if ever there was one, J. C. referred to ordinary travelers as "rabble" and "loafers," but the inconvenience to his person made him consider theirs and demand that something be done about it.

That something turned out to be the creation of the American Express travelers cheque, which, more than any other previous development in travel history, revolutionized travel's demographics. The travelers cheque was, coincidentally, the only completely original innovation American Express has devised in all its corporate history, but it was sufficiently lucrative to support all the company's other endeavors. It turned the ordinary traveler back into a diplomat of sorts. It made the company into a formidably capitalized and totally unregulated bank, a player in world politics, and led it into a mystery of international intrigue which remains unsolved to the present day. Eventually, as American Express grew into a corporate colossus which bestrode the world, the company reinvented the nature of travel: instead of traveling to encounter the unknown, the traveler increasingly sought to encounter a world re-created in his or her own image. As the number of travelers expanded, the cocoon of packaged environments and other protections created around them by the travel business expanded as well, until they changed the nature of the world itself.

The express business began with lone post riders who plied the roads in the American colonies carrying goods, luggage, and, on occasion, money from village to scattered village. As the colonies expanded their boundaries into the mountain country, stagecoaches, pack riders, and wagons replaced the post rider. In the early nineteenth century, the jehu, a traveling agent who executed any kind of business, became popular. But it was the building of the railroad system that transformed the express business from a scrappy patchwork of independent operators into one of the titans of the robber baron era.

In 1826 the first U.S. railroad track was laid from Quincy, Massachusetts, to the Neponset River, about thirty-five miles away, for the haulage of minerals, primarily coal. Horse-drawn wagons traveled the tracks but carried no passengers. Several such short tracks were built to service coal mines over the next four years. Then, in 1829, the first successful locomotive run was made by an English import, the Stourbridge Lion, along the Delaware and Hudson Canal Company line from Honesdale, Pennsylvania, to Kingston, New York. Railroad building on a grand scale took off with the settlement of the Midwest in the 1830s and 1840s.

In 1834 two bank couriers, B. D. and L. B. Earle, created the first express company to carry money and packages by rail, on the new link between Boston and Providence. In 1839 a Bostonian, William Harnden, built on their success by establishing a Boston–New York service and, in 1840, a transatlantic service as well. Harnden employed a flamboyant misfit, Henry "Stuttering" Wells, who affected ruffled shirts and tasseled Basque caps to draw attention away from his chronic speech defect. When he couldn't talk Harnden into building an Albany–Buffalo express line, Wells did it himself, in partnership with George Pomeroy, and became Harnden's rival. In the 1840s, Wells and his subsequent partners, William George Fargo and Johnston Livingston, created the first widely networked express company in the northeastern United States by cornering the vital Hudson River shipping and rail services and then expanding their operations as far west as Chicago. Butterfield, Wasson and Company controlled virtually all the stagecoach lines in western New York (which still carried all of the freight and passengers to settlements that were not on a rail line), built the first telegraph (from Albany to Buffalo), and dominated traffic along Lake Ontario and the St. Lawrence River through their steamship operation. After a protracted price war, Wells and Company merged with Butterfield and Company, in a treaty as martial as any army's, and in 1850 the American Express Company was born.

Just as the express business was synonymous with the last great age of discovery in the Western world—the exploration and expansion of the western frontiers of the United States—so the expressmen were themselves relics of an earlier age. They were more feudal than democratic, robber barons like the railroad men on whose tracks they piggybacked their business. (The term "robber baron" originated in feudal times when territorial despots robbed travelers passing through their fiefdoms.) Although their wars were fought with price controls instead of swords, they were as ruthless, and in some cases as brutal: the excesses of Asa Whitney, Cornelius Vanderbilt, Jay Gould, and their ilk would become staples of muckraking journalism later in the century and initiate massive trustbusting action by the Supreme Court.

Although the express companies did not quite engage in the use of immigrants as feudal serfs, they did collude in fixing territories and prices at rates which mercilessly squeezed the consumers of their services, who were highly dependent because of their geographic isolation. In conjunction with the railroads, the companies formed not a monopoly but an oligopoly. If the railroad barons could have swallowed the express barons, they would have. But by the time the railroad barons realized just how much money the express business produced, it was too big to swallow. The large express companies had an inherent advantage in that they covered more territory than any individual railroad. By the time American Express opened its California route, it had become too large to be taken over unless all the railroads collaborated. Given the fact that the railroad companies were all warring fiefdoms, this didn't happen. An express company would use several railroad lines as well as steamships and even stagecoaches to reach particularly inaccessible territories. As a result, if a railroad overstepped the bounds of good host behavior, the express company could either play off its railroad carriers against one another or direct local traffic away from a particular one.

For the most part, the railroads and the express companies collaborated, developing interlocking relationships, which would be repeated later in the age of air travel. These monopoly marriages anticipated the modern megamerger. They were not quite "vertical integration" in the sense that oilman John D. Rockefeller was inventing the term. A fellow robber baron, John D., Sr., owned every step of the process that got his oil out of the ground, into his refineries, and through his pipelines into his tankers and to his customers (whom he fully believed he owned as well). But the express company–railroad mergers came close enough, owing to the ties forged early on between banking and express services. The banks loaned the expressmen easy money to build their companies, for the banks needed a permanent courier system in place to cut their own costs as the westward expansion gathered steam. Express companies, for their part, preferred bank business because they could charge according to the value of the financial instruments they carried. But the merger which created American Express in 1850 gave the new company a unique advantage over a bank: a joint-stock company with few legal obligations to its shareholders, it could operate in almost total secrecy.

Initially, American Express used this advantage to fix territories and rates in collusion with other express companies. To the extent that such collusion was known to the public, it was criticized, but monopoly practices of this type were not yet illegal. They would become so in 1890 and 1914, under the Sherman and Clayton Antitrust laws, respectively. Until then, a company like American Express gave considerable latitude to the more closely scrutinized railroads. They functioned as bankers to the capital-intensive business, which freely commingled private and public funds, using their abundant surpluses to buy railroad stocks and bonds. Off the books, they gave generous bribes to ensure favorable contracts. Eventually, they acquired considerable leverage over the railroads. By the 1860s expressmen sat on the boards of all the major railroads. Both John Butterfield and W. G. Fargo sat on the board of New York Central, which in turn acquired a huge chunk of American Express stock. This prominence would figure largely in the future of the company.

As investors, the express companies profited immensely from the expansion of the railway system at a minimum of risk: the Union Pacific and other transcontinental railroads were given vast tracts of public lands to develop their routes. This added fire to public outrage when price-rigging accusations came to a head. By the 1850s, the railroads dominated America's inland transportation and, because of the immense capital outlay required, the national economy as well. Overspeculation, overbuilding, and obstructive competition became commonplace. Growing regionalism and North-South conflict before the outset of the Civil War tended to block large-scale projects like the Lake Michigan–Pacific Ocean route proposed by Asa Whitney to Congress in 1845. The war itself gave the railroads the required political boost, for they were strategic necessities in troop transport, and Congress enacted Whitney's dream in 1862 and 1864. This became the Union Pacific Railroad in 1869. Like all the western railroads, the Union Pacific was built to help develop new territory. Promoters hired by the railroads induced farmers to settle the raw lands along the way. With the mass production of steel (1865), railway building actually became cost-efficient, but its gains were quickly swallowed by the excesses of the railway financiers, such as James Fisk and Jay Gould. These imbalances ushered in the Granger reform movement in the 1870s, resulting in the formation of the Interstate Commerce Commission in 1887. This regulatory entity finally caused the express companies to distance themselves from their railway holdings.

It was not only the decline of the railroad business after regulation but the U.S. Post Office that ultimately forced American Express to enable everyone to travel as freely as the rich. In 1860 the Post Office, which wanted the lucrative package- and money-carrying business for itself, began lobbying Congress to abolish express companies altogether, an effort which would persist for fifty years. Failing in that mission, the Post Office succeeded in pressuring Congress to create third-class mail, by which it broke the express monopoly on the transport of magazines and newspapers. Most important, the legislation also created the postal money order for the transmission of small amounts of money.

As insignificant as it may seem, the creation of the money order cannot be underestimated in terms of democratizing the business of travel. Part of what made travel inaccessible to large numbers of people was the difficulty of transporting money. Personal checking accounts existed only for the wealthy. But with business booming on the western frontier of the United States, more people had more reason to send money than ever before. Before the money order was invented, the safest way to send cash was to sew it into envelopes, seal them shut with wax, and send them via express, which guaranteed safe delivery but was relatively expensive. The postal money order was a prepaid check which prevented postmen from stealing cash out of envelopes: at ten cents an order it was cheap enough to break the express monopoly. By 1880, the Post Office was selling $100 million in money orders a year.

One group of citizens was left out of the new convenience. Because a customer needed literacy in English to send and receive money orders, the process was beyond the grasp of many immigrants, who were arriving in the greatest wave the country had yet seen. An executive at American Express, Marcellus Fleming Berry, noted this with interest in a company report of around 1881: "Immigrants, as well as stupid persons, or persons who cannot read or write, have to blunder about (a post-office) until some outsider takes pity and writes out their application for them." Berry, who was lobbying his irascible boss J. C. Fargo for a way to undercut the rampant success of the Post Office's foray into express territory, pointed out another weakness in the cumbersome nature of the postal money order. To prevent forgery, it had to be cashed at a designated post office, which was advised separately that the order had been placed. Loss of orders was embarrassingly frequent, and fighting the red tape for refunds took weeks.[8]

Berry patented an ingeniously simple "protection margin" that became the model for the American Express travelers cheque. On the left of the money order were printed the five-cent denominations from one dollar to ten dollars, the maximum order at that time. When a customer purchased an order, the clerk wrote the name of the payee and the amount on two separate stubs and gave one to the buyer after cutting the protection margin at the designated sum. The customer thus could not fraudulently raise the value of the order, but, English-speaking or not, he could easily cash the order with the proper receipt in hand. Just as it had guaranteed safe delivery of funds by the express, American Express guaranteed the funds behind the order to the banker, building on its previous banking relationships and forging new ones which again made it easier to cash Amex's money order than the post office's.

J. C. Fargo was a typical expressman in that he detested the march of progress as much as he facilitated it. The doom, in the classical sense, of these bold and intuitive frontier businessmen was that their companies' success spelled the end of the frontier. Like Shakespeare's King Lear, they were fated to outlive their time. Perhaps J. C. foresaw a world made small by instant communication and didn't like it. He objected to the creation of the money order for a number of reasons—not least that he didn't think of it himself—but chiefly on the grounds that he didn't want travel made easier for the mob. But business was business. After an ad campaign costing five thousand dollars (exorbitant for those days), American Express money orders expanded to $3.5 million a year by 1899, creating what remains the financial engine of the company to this day.

Typically, a customer paid for a money order in cash, in full, on a no-interest basis. The money stayed in American Express coffers until the order was cashed, usually a period of some months, given the duration of travel in those days. The amount of surplus, or "float," fluctuated, but busy minds like Marcellus Berry's soon realized that they had an average positive balance awaiting redemption. As the volume of money orders grew, so did the float, until by 1891, at hundreds of thousands of dollars, investing it became an executive priority.

The immigrant population continued to provide the primary market for money orders, using them to send funds home to the families they left behind in Europe. By 1896 the volume was sufficient to propel American Express into the financial business abroad, where the company established a major European banking link between Kidder, Peabody in New York and Baring Brothers of London. Money orders became cashable in ten countries, and American Express suddenly had an enviable foreign banking network.

When J. C. Fargo had his famous temper tantrum in Paris, the ever-ingenious Marcellus Berry reinvented the money order as the now-familiar travelers cheque. In addition to the promise of simplicity and fraud protection, he added a sweeping guarantee of convertibility in the form of a band displayed on all checks which showed its value, based on a two-year average, in all major European currencies. American Express guaranteed the checks convertible to the sums as printed. In an age of stable exchange rates, this was a low-risk proposition. But not only did the company guarantee conversion rates to its customers, it also guaranteed losses on currency exchange as well as on forged, lost, or stolen checks. While this generosity made the company extremely vulnerable, it also made it the clearinghouse for an independent, unregulated, international currency, open to no scrutiny but that of its own executives. This was ultimately to place the company in an extraordinary position on the world stage, where, like Rockefeller's Standard Oil and its six sister oil companies, it could dictate foreign policy and serve as an ex-officio State Department.

American Express fortuitously created the travelers cheque just as the American middle class began to expropriate the Grand Tour. Americans in the 1890s possessed great wealth proportionate to the rest of the world and, if not a growing awareness of European culture, then a growing awareness that it could be acquired. From the awestruck gaucheries of *Daisy Miller* to the somewhat belligerent bravado of *The Innocents Abroad*, the fertile American imagination applied itself to jumping the barrier of social class, the only one remaining in the New World. As Twain marveled,

> A strange new sensation is a rare thing in this humdrum life, and I had it here. It seemed strange—stranger than I can tell—to think that the central figure in this cluster of men and women, chatting here under the trees like the most ordinary individual in the land, was a man who could open his lips and ships would fly through the waves, couriers would hurry from village to village, a hundred telegraphs would flash the word to the four corners of the [Russian] Empire that stretches over a seventh part of the habitable globe, and a countless multitude of men would spring to do his bidding. I had a sort of vague desire to examine his hands and see if they were made of flesh and blood like other men's. Here was a man [the tsar] who could do this wonderful thing and yet if I chose I could knock him down. If I could have stolen his coat, I would have done it. When I meet a man like that, I want something to remember him by.[9]

Newly rich Americans were determined to prove they were not colonial hayseeds. The World's Columbian Exposition, held in Chicago in 1893, gave tourism a massive international boost. Ironically, since it was held to commemorate the four-hundredth anniversary of the discovery of America by Christopher Columbus, the expo, nick-named "The White City," boasted 150 new buildings of pan-European architectural style, constructed entirely of a synthetic white marble. Probably the first theme park on these shores, it attracted thousands of Americans, largely Midwesterners, whose appetite for the real thing was whetted by the high, if phony, cultural tone of the exhibition.

Because American Express was the primary carrier from the port of New York, it became the carrier of choice for the Columbian Exhi-bition. A junior executive named William Dalliba supervised opera-tions and observed the boom in European trade relations that resulted. He lobbied to take on European operations himself and quietly went about building up the company's tourist business without consulting the aging J. C. Fargo, who refused to relinquish his earlier prejudices.

European travel, once the prerogative of the wealthy, was rapidly metamorphosing into a rite of passage for the young, as hordes of American college students began trooping over for their summers, the less well-off hiring on as tenders on cattle steamers to pay their pas-sage. Dalliba was shrewd enough to detect in them the beginnings of a lifelong travel habit. By the decade's end, American travelers were spending nearly a quarter of a billion dollars abroad annually, and this business was largely controlled by American Express. Sales of Ameri-can Express travelers cheques rose from $6.4 million in 1900 to $13.2 million in 1905 to $23 million in 1909, and the significance of the float grew exponentially as well. For a financial institution that was not even recognized as a bank, it had mind-boggling assets: in 1903, according to an in-house study, the company's capital and surplus, at $28 million, came in just behind National City Bank of New York, the nation's largest lending institution.[10]

War provided further opportunities for the company to function far beyond the purview of a travel agency, as it was to do at least twice more in the century. Although J. C. Fargo continued to allow as how he would not have "gangs of trippers setting off in charabancs" from the doors of his sacred offices, the company headquarters at 11, rue Scribe in Paris became a de facto embassy in 1914, when the banks of Europe slammed shut their doors to prevent runs following the assas-sination of Archduke Ferdinand in Sarajevo. Exchange rates soared almost immediately, and travel became perilous when not impossible. A hundred and fifty thousand Americans, stranded in Paris with no hard currency in their pockets, descended on 11, rue Scribe. Dalliba, antici-pating war, had accumulated 3 million French francs in gold and instructed other European offices to build up sufficient cash to pay off their own and everyone else's paper. Brandishing a pistol like a Pony Expressman from the middle of the nineteenth century, Dalliba personally supervised the orderly dispensation of currency, arranged passage home for thousands of Americans, and kept the office functioning around the clock as a post and telegraph office. The American Express cheque gained so much stature that hotel keepers hoarded it in preference to other paper money, while, at home, the newspapers hailed the company as one of the heroes of the hour.

One reason that American Express made much of its wartime role as the savior of the American traveler is that the company desperately needed to mend its public image. Beginning in the late 1880s, the populist and progressive reform movements had gradually built a consensus in the country regarding government intervention in business, particularly in the business of transportation. In 1888 Congress had created the Interstate Commerce Commission to end price gouging and other discriminatory practices by the railroads. Although the express companies managed to wriggle out of regulation on a technicality, they were not spared by muckraking journalists like Ida Tarbell and Upton Sinclair, who went after the robber barons like the Fargos and their future business partners the Rockefellers with vengeful pens. In 1910, American Express came under attack when a particularly nasty strike threw the limelight on some of the company's tyrannical labor practices. A heavy-duty public relations campaign like the one launched by American Express under the tony bannerline "Voyager être vivre" (To travel is to live) was the perfect way to reassure the little guy that big business was really on his side, protecting his inalienable right to see the world.

In 1913 the U.S. Post Office succeeded in its fifty-year offensive when Congress finally authorized a government parcel-post system which lopped the profit margin on express as effectively as the protection margin operated on its money orders. And in 1915 J. C. Fargo, sensing that his world was changing beyond his control and that his own executives were waiting in the wings to oust him, died of a cold. The Tory period was officially over. But democracy did not wear well with American Express, and for many years the company floundered under the weak leadership of lesser men under the blows that befell it.

In 1918 another government edict forced the company to divest itself of its railroad holdings. The independently run railroad companies lacked both the will and the way to coordinate their services for wartime demands; and in December 1917, President Woodrow Wilson seized the entire American railway system, appointing Treasury

Secretary William McAdoo director-general. After prolonged and bitter negotiations over an equitable compensation package, American Express spun off its express network to the government, in exchange for 40 percent of the stock of the new company, which carried a government-backed 5 percent dividend. American Express retained its large liquid surplus, or float, its corporate headquarters in New York, and of course, its high-profile travel business.

When the Post-War Planning Committee met at 65 Broadway in New York City to review the company's gutted state and plan its post-war expansion, it glumly concluded (as it would after another wrenching contraction in the 1980s) that American Express had to expand or die. There was little left that could be expanded but travel and banking, and from the postwar period through the Great Depression, the leadership fought over whether to turn the company into a legitimate bank. There was tremendous pressure to do so, for banking was where the money was, but the culture of secrecy militated against it. Although American Express continued to engage in foreign-exchange trading, currency hedging, and other banking activities, it did so unsupported by the men at the top, who feared the loss of the company's tax status as an unincorporated stock association. This definition spared it from what its lawyers called the "annoyance or interference of disgruntled stockholders," and government regulation of its banking activities.[11]

The turmoil of war again created opportunities for profit. Before World War I, exchange rates, based on a virtually invariable gold standard, were constant. But monetary instability continued to plague Europe after the war ended, as governments trashed their own currencies by printing too much paper money. Exchange rates swung wildly, not only by the day but by the hour. The strength of the U.S. dollar against all other foreign currencies created unusual profit opportunities for companies that sold dollar-based foreign remittances. Currency traders sold futures and spot contracts to exporters, importers, and financial institutions who needed to protect themselves against currency swings. American Express dominated this market.

But doing good again gave the company its greatest opportunity to do well. After the war, America's newly prosperous immigrant population sent money home in unprecedented amounts to relatives in ravaged Europe. People literally needed the money to keep from starving, and the company was able to parlay its role into a kind of dollar diplomacy in its public-relations campaigns. Quite aside from the PR value, the company profited in three ways from every immigrant who came in to buy money orders to save his or her family: first, on the currency

swing in covering the initial sale, something the operator was understandably slow to do; second, on the initial conversion rate, which
favored the seller; and third, on the service charge paid by the customer for each remittance.

From 1918 to 1920, American Express handled at least a half a billion dollars a year in money orders alone. A company record states that
no one ever knew exactly how much profit was made in remittances,
because the books were so poorly kept. Legend has it that, when a senior vice-president was asked how much the company was earning from
exchange operations, his answer was "How much do you want?"

This answer was certainly the one that Albert Wiggin wanted.
Wiggin was chairman and chief executive officer of the Chase National
Bank, aka "the Rockefeller bank" because of the shareholder position
of John D. Rockefeller, Jr., who needed a bank to look after his family's
interests. As American Express went through a flat period from 1923 to
1928 under the uninspired leadership of the aptly named F. P. Small,
Wiggin looked at the balance sheet and saw that it was good. Wiggin
was a cunning and untiring predator with enormous resources at his
command. From 1918 to 1928, he expanded Chase from a bank with
less capital and surplus than American Express to an institution six
times its size, largely by cannibalizing weaker banks and other financial institutions. He deployed his gains in an aggressive stock-invest-
ment strategy that ultimately led to his own downfall.

In 1928 and 1929, Wiggin, who coveted American Express' international office network and enormous cash float for his bank- and stock-
market reserves, stealthily acquired a controlling share of company stock
by identifying and purchasing several large chunks belonging to its former railroad partners. (In 1928, before the Securities and Exchange
Commission was invented, a raider did not have to declare his intentions
by reporting a 5 percent holding. Typically, he would buy shares on the
market through several different accounts so activity could not be traced
to a single source. Often a company would not know it was under siege
until its stock price soared.) After trying unsuccessfully to buy all outstanding shares of stock and packing the American Express board with
his puppets, Wiggin made Small a tender offer which the latter had no
choice but to accept. On July 1, 1929, American Express became a subsidiary of the Chase Securities Corporation.

Three months later, on October 24, the market crashed. Instead
of pulling in his horns, Wiggin went on a buying spree, using American Express' cash reserves to buy up failing stocks, apparently with no
resistance from the friendly board of directors. He also set up the long-

heralded American Express bank, to be known as American Express Bank and Trust. He had further plans to absorb American Express completely into Chase, but these were cut short by the Pecora Hearings on securities dealings before the crash in February 1933. Under the prodding of Senate Banking and Currency Committee chief counsel Ferdinand Pecora, it was revealed that Wiggin, along with most leading New York bankers, had participated in market-manipulation "pools," using the funds of wealthy investors to bid up stock prices but selling short when outside investors piled on. This forced the stock price down and gave the wealthy pool players a profit on both ends of the deal but left the little guy to bear the loss. Wiggin, it appeared, had made a $4 million profit selling short the stock of his own bank. This disclosure was so exquisitely embarrassing to the Rockefellers that they gave Wiggin American Express instead of a gold watch, and promptly showed him the door.

Although Wiggin had succeeded in milking American Express of all but $3 million, its lowest level of cash reserves since the mid-nineteenth century, this ignominious period was not a complete debacle. The company's extraordinary resources were finally harnessed to a legitimate banking enterprise. It had also formed a symbiotic relationship with the Rockefellers, which could be called a marriage of like minds. Even though Winthrop Aldrich Rockefeller, brother-in-law to John D. and successor to Wiggin at Chase, paid over American Express as the price of getting Wiggin off the Chase board, the bank tried twice to repossess its former subsidiary. Both attempts were unsuccessful because of the malice of Wiggin, who refused to sell his shares, but the Rockefellers maintained close ties with American Express, using both its talent and its travel business in the creation of their own brand of dollar diplomacy. Although it is not a matter of company record whether J. C. Fargo and John D. Rockefeller, Sr., ever met in the flesh, it is likely that they blessed the union from whatever boardroom in which they eternally sit. The disdainful pursuit of the "loafers" and "rabble" were now not only big business, they were about to become big government as well.

"Little Rockiefeller"

CHAPTER 2

What's good for General Bullmoose is good for the U.S.A.

Al Capp

ON MARCH 30, 1996, three days before his death on a Croatian mountainside in a mysterious plane crash that also killed thirty-four top-ranking businessmen to whom he was promoting the virtues of investing in the former Yugoslavia, Ron Brown addressed a roomful of executives at the Union League Club in New York. Brown's keynote, exhorting American big business to help the wounded economies of the post–Cold War world help themselves by investing in them, was almost identical to plans devised more than half the century previously to make business into the foot soldier of democracy—or vice-versa. As Brown spoke enthusiastically of minuscule Northern Ireland as one of the ten most important emerging markets in the world, it became more and more tempting to stretch out, look up at the gilded ceiling, and imagine he was Nelson Rockefeller.

In 1938, as America dug in its isolationist heels, top American Express executives looked forward to the beginning of World War II. Like the rest of the country, the company was at the end of a flat five-year period following the trauma of its near-demise in the economic hysteria of the Depression. Although it had reestablished relative stability and consistent earnings, its top command almost welcomed the onset of hostilities because of the precedent set by the post–World War I travel boom. Speculating (correctly, as it turned out) that the post–World War II period would surpass even that record because of the development of fast, safe air travel, executives projected elaborate plans to mobilize people, papers, and money once war began. And, building on its World War I role as auxiliary embassy, American Express prepared itself to become a private-sector State Department, instructing personnel in place in Europe to file detailed reports on larger political and economic happenings as well as local office affairs. Once war broke out, several top American Express executives would go on loan to the real State Department—and some to Nelson Rockefeller.

In 1938 Nelson Aldrich Rockefeller turned thirty years old and began looking for ways to evade his father's control.[1] A handsome, affable athlete whose regular-guy charm hid reserves of ambition as deep as any Standard Oil well, Nelson was the third generation in one of the top ten American fortunes. Along with Asa Whitney, E. L. Harriman, Cornelius Vanderbilt, and Henry Flagler (an early business partner), Nelson's grandfather John D. Rockefeller, Sr., epitomized the term "robber baron." It was a title which was to both drive Nelson to achieve and frustrate him in the pursuit of his ambitions. Though these were enormous, as befitted the grandson of John D. Rockefeller, Nelson, too, was born out of his time.

In his grandfather's day, the frontier would have made good use of Nelson's boundless energies and impatience with rules. As it was, he came of age at a time when the speculative excesses of the 1920s had reawakened the specters of gross capitalist monsters for the public, the press, and the politicians with whom he found himself competing. Driven by the compulsion to distinguish himself from his family, Nelson went into politics, where he found himself checked on every side by suspicion, envy, and regulatory prudence. But, being a true Rockefeller, he barreled on regardless, with the interesting result that every time he failed (which he did frequently), he found a way to boost his schemes into bigger and bigger programs. Tourism and popular culture, two of his pet hobbyhorses, became part of the Roosevelt administration's Big Government. What was good for Nelson Rockefeller was good for the USA.

John D. Rockefeller, Sr., was the son of a lumber trader and amiable rogue in upstate New York. In 1845, when Rockefeller père abandoned his family to enter into a bigamous second marriage, the sixteen-year-old John D. became the man of the house and went to work as a bookkeeper. Four years later, he was running his own produce company. By 1863 he had established his first oil refinery near Cleveland, Ohio, where the infant oil industry was booming. By 1870, in association with Henry and William Flagler, he had set up Standard Oil, which would become synonymous with the Gilded Age itself as described by Mark Twain and Charles Dudley Warner in their novel of the same name, a time of "the manufacture of giant schemes, of speculations of all sorts . . . [and of] inflamed desire for sudden wealth"—in other words, a time not unlike our own.[2]

Yet while many of the other robber barons built their fortunes on speculation, financial manipulation, and fraud, Rockefeller became the wealthiest of them all by legitimately transforming a wildcat industry into a highly organized international business. By rigidly enforced economy and efficiency, by merging with his more able competitors while ruthlessly crushing those less able, and by accumulating large capital reserves, he dominated the American oil industry. Using far-flung agreements with railroads and control of pipeline distribution, he invented the concept of "vertical integration" as well, a strategy William E. Boeing would imitate in the next century to make his air-line company into the Standard Oil of aerospace.

In 1882 Rockefeller bundled his diverse holdings into the Standard Oil Trust, roiling the flames of public opinion, which had flared against combination and monopoly. Eventually, antitrust suits forced him to restructure his empire into the Standard Oil Company of New Jersey, a holding company capitalized at the (then) fabulous sum of $110 million. In 1911, the Supreme Court dissolved this company in a trustbusting decision.

In 1914 the oil titan became one of the first emperors of industry to employ the budding science of corporate public relations when several coal miners, their wives, and their children were slaughtered by deputy sheriffs breaking up a walkout at the Colorado Iron and Fuel Company, a Rockefeller subsidiary. Twenty thousand strikers camped outside the entrance to the mines when the Rockefeller management proved intransigent in negotiating a collective bargaining agreement, even defying President Woodrow Wilson's personal remonstrance. Violence surged after sheriffs lurched through the camp in a "Death Special," a crude approximation of a tank, spraying machine-gun fire and killing several strikers. Drunken guardsmen set the camp ablaze, and two women and eleven children suffocated in a pit where they had sought refuge.

In one of his rare accommodations to public opinion, Rockefeller hired Ivy Ledbetter Lee, one of the first PR men in American corporate history, when the U.S. Commission on Industrial Relations initiated an inquiry into the massacre. The Princeton-educated former journalist came to be known as "Poison" Ivy for his role in disseminating the Rockefeller family view in a series of bulletins, called "The Facts Concerning the Struggle in Colorado for Industrial Freedom," which were widely distributed to opinion makers and which contained deliberate disinformation. The ensuing outcry caused John D. Rockefeller, Jr., to initiate a public relations offensive to repudiate the bad old image of Standard Oil, even going to the extent of superficially democratizing labor relations and publicly embracing the legendary labor organizer Mary Harris Jones, better known as Mother Jones, whom Ivy Lee's bulletins had branded a whore.

It is often said that in America, the first generation creates wealth, the second enjoys it, and the third destroys it. In the Rockefeller family, the third generation was bred up with care neither to destroy nor dissipate the family wealth but to preserve it along with the family power by appearing to disperse it in the form of cultural or charitable endeavors. Like Franklin Roosevelt a generation earlier, or John F. Kennedy a generation later, "Junior's" son Nelson was a born communicator who concealed the fist of a ruler within the glove of accessibility. In his reign, the assets which had accumulated under the careful if uninspired stewardship of his father were deployed into the glittering new fields of media and travel. As Nelson sought political power, he used these "soft" businesses as public-relations shock troops to gain access to the U.S. president in the sphere of international relations. Consorting with the president was designed to get Nelson closer to an office he ultimately coveted for himself, but it had a commercial purpose as well. The Rockefellers had probably never forgotten how the Rothschilds had kept them from globalizing Standard Oil in the Middle East, and Nelson's public relations web served the secondary purpose of creating a Rockefeller cartel in the wide-open territory of Latin America. It took on a significance far beyond that of ordinary commerce, until ultimately it became part of the business of government itself.

By persistently enlarging his brief beyond media and travel into propaganda and foreign aid, Nelson not only leveraged himself into the position of diplomat but eventually acquired government funding for his pet programs, a rarity in the United States, where government is traditionally hostile to federal funding for private industry. (These patterns would repeat themselves with the Boeing Airplane Company, which overlapped military and commercial aerospace development in the postwar decades and won monies from the Kennedy and Johnson administrations to develop the SST.) When taxpayers reacted adversely, as they inevitably did at the thought of their dollars subsidizing a Rockefeller, the programs were killed but rose again, ever larger, in such government agencies as the United States Information Agency (USIA) and the Foreign Operation Administration. But though Nelson Rockefeller fought hard throughout his political life to escape his heritage, in the end the apple did not fall far from the tree. Innovative and pragmatic though they might be, Nelson Rockefeller's programs were designed both to soften public attitudes toward the monopoly that bore him and to conceal its continuous working.

In 1938, with the administration focusing its attention on the coming war in Europe, Nelson looked on the foreign-policy void in Latin America, and saw that it was a good way out of Rockefeller Center. Still smarting from his father's bleak response to his enthusiastic patronage of some very left-of-center murals by revolutionary Mexican artist Diego Rivera (who insisted on painting a portrait of Lenin onto the walls of the holy of holies of American capitalism), Nelson used his Brain Trust contacts to wangle a meeting with President Roosevelt on the pretext of offering an impassioned support for the artistic activities of the Works Progress Administration.

It was a mutually advantageous encounter. Roosevelt had been persuaded to meet with young Rockefeller (whose family had contributed heavily to the campaign of his opponent, Alf Landon, in 1936) on the premise that he was ripe for seduction to the Democratic cause. Nelson, for his part, looked on FDR as a role model and, it was to be hoped, a mentor; living proof that a Hudson Valley aristocrat could capitalize on his background at the same time he transcended it in learning to out-wardheel the wardheelers. Rockefeller did not want to be fobbed off with a dilettante's brief for the arts, which FDR initially handed him. His real agenda was Latin America. He had developed hotel interests in Venezuela, intended, as he said, to use tourism to wean the country from its oil-dependent economy; and he wanted to present the president with a broad-based plan for government and business to work in concert to promote inter-American relations.

Roosevelt expressed interest, but Nelson's plan lay fallow until the summer of 1940, when blatant pro-Nazi support in Argentina suddenly brought Latin America to the forefront of U.S. strategic thinking. Roosevelt was as worried about the formation of a Nazi business cartel, the Germania Corporation, as he was about an all-out military war. The Latin American economy was very fragile, and with European markets cut off by hostilities, the threat of a Nazi takeover close to U.S. borders seemed all too imminent. He invited Nelson to the White House in June 1940, where "young Rockefeller" proposed fighting cartel with cartel; specifically, he suggested that the United States buy up all surplus Latin American commodities, eliminate tariffs on Latin American goods, encourage interhemisphere business investment, increase its diplomatic presence in the region, aid in the conversion of external debt to domestic currency obligations, and encourage a "vigorous program" of cultural, educational, and scientific exchange.

In the name of making Latin America safe for democracy, Rockefeller cagily laid the tracks for tourism development which would eventually benefit his own hotels. His plan bore a strong resemblance to Ron Brown's agenda in the 1990s and also dovetailed with the aims of American Express, which already dominated the currency market.

In what would become a familiar routine, Rockefeller created a job description for which he was obviously the ideal candidate, but he was bypassed in favor of James Forrestal, president of Dillon, Read, and Company. Forrestal placed Rockefeller's name at the top of the list for the embryonic job of coordinator of inter-American affairs. In a position that would describe much of Rockefeller's later career, the coordinator would work with, but outside of, existing departments and agencies like the Office of War Information, successor to the Center for Public Information, which had launched the young Edward Bernays in World War I. Rockefeller's function, boiled down to its essence, was to organize expatriate U.S. businessmen to wage a propaganda war against the Nazis. His office was to be called the Coordinator for Inter-American Affairs (CIAA), and would come to resemble the Central Intelligence Agency in more than its abbreviation.

The brash young man did not fit in with the mandarins of State, who referred to him derisively as "Little Rockiefeller." From his insistence on driving his staff to work every morning—which subjected them to his horrible driving habits—to his splendid suite of offices once occupied by Secretary of War Newton D. Baker, Nelson Rockefeller stood out from the run of dollar-a-year executives who volunteered their services to aid the war effort in Washington. The most important difference was a letter of credit from his father, instructing Chase that "Junior" would personally guarantee any loans that the bank gave to persons doing business with the coordinator's office. For the first time, a private individual was personally bonding a government agency—and not without expectations in return.

Rockefeller buddied up with another multimillionaire "dollar-a-year" man in the formation of his motion-picture division. Hollywood paid careful attention to John Hay "Jock" Whitney, scion of the railroad family, who had personally bankrolled *Gone with the Wind*. Rockefeller was keenly aware of the propaganda value of movies, and he and Whitney made a persuasive team in lobbying the studio heads to present positive images of Latin American characters and themes, even going so far as to set up a representative within the infamous Hays Office for movie censorship. Through the CIAA office, Whitney and Rockefeller guaranteed Walt Disney, RKO's David Sarnoff, and others of the Big Five major producers and distributors against potential losses: Disney accepted $150,000 for making *Saludos Amigos* and *Three Caballeros*, which turned out to be only moderately successful.

Movies were felt to be good advertisement for tourism: if people saw an exotic locale on film, it would make them want to go there. Along with the movies themselves, tourism and investment were promoted in glossy brochures. Pan American Airways flew holiday-makers to Havana and Managua, Nicaragua; construction of the Pan-American Highway was started. Nicaragua's ruler Anastasio Somoza was invited to the New York World's Fair to celebrate regional democracy and progress. Latin American movie stars replaced the marines as the guarantors of regional harmony.

The studios, anxious to offset the steep drop in their European markets caused by the onset of hostilities and afflicted with a paucity of fresh material, were for the most part receptive to the CIAA agenda to promote the Good Neighbor policy, combat pro-Axis sentiment, and spark both tourism and local employment by filming in Latin American locations. Even if these movies were not big moneymakers, the status-hungry moguls felt that any losses would be balanced by their new Washington cachet. Generally, however, the Rockefeller-Whitney team did better churning out anti-Axis newsreels than they did with features. Propaganda feature films as a group did not sell well and later created some fiascoes in the rapidly shifting postwar political climate. But their worst disaster was made with one of Hollywood's few true creative artists, Orson Welles.

Welles, arguably Hollywood's only bona fide genius, was as addicted to spending money as later directors would be to keeping cocaine in sugar bowls on the set. Like his mentors, the Irish actor-managers Micheal MacLiammoir and Hilton Edwards, Welles operated best within strict economic limits which kept in bounds his natural tendency toward excess. When Rockefeller, through the CIAA, offered Welles's studio, RKO, a $300,000 guarantee against losses for a Welles dream project which fit perfectly—or so it seemed—into the CIAA scenario, it was an invitation to run over budget.

The film was an anthology composed of a number of stories each set in a different Latin American country, and its high cost alone would not have fazed the coordinator until Welles stuck to his artistic principles over the propaganda value of the film and insisted on filming in the *favelas*, the infamous slums of Rio de Janeiro. The ensuing public relations firefight soon brought to light Welles's huge cost overruns, with which he habitually commingled his exorbitant personal expenses.

An outraged Rockefeller pulled the plug halfway through the picture. He also welshed on the guarantee against losses to RKO, claiming that Welles hadn't fulfilled his contract. Coupled with the disastrous previews of Welles's family saga *The Magnificent Ambersons*, this pull-out effectively torpedoed Welles's relationship with RKO, whose boss David Sarnoff occupied office space at Rockefeller Center, and left Welles a Hollywood minister without a portfolio.

Rockefeller's media ventures also included radio and print journalism. He created a *Life* magazine look-alike called *En Guardia*, which the Nazis soon imitated. He also built a radio empire composed of sixty-four stations, through Bill Paley, his buddy on the board of the Museum of Modern Art. The CIAA improved their shortwave transmission with a $200,000 development grant, receiving in return a guarantee of seven hundred hours a year in programming to "strengthen bonds between the American republics."[3] This became the foundation of the Voice of America when the Iron Curtain descended.

In addition, there was the more sinister Prencinradio. Incorporated in 1942, *Prencinradio* was a contraction of *prensa* (press), cinema, and radio. Prencinradio was a Delaware corporation, wholly owned by the U.S. government and staffed entirely by CIAA employees. Its existence was known only to a few top CIAA and State Department officials, and its purpose was to serve as a conduit for "confidential" CIAA investment in Latin American media for propaganda purposes.

Rockefeller's widest mandate was to "communicate," that is, disseminate cultural propaganda. The bulk of the CIAA's original $3.5 million appropriation was earmarked for radio and movie programming, publications, culture-based tourism like archaeological expeditions, academic and sports exchanges, and art exhibits. Unlike his economic brief, where the coordinator was hamstrung by defense priorities and competing jurisdictions, culture and communications offered an open field. Rockefeller busily cultivated this field as an intelligence base: as one example, the famous "baseball spy," Moe Berg, got his start in the game from Rockefeller, who sent him on a tour of Latin America and then set him to filing confidential reports on the places he visited.

Rockefeller, in fact, utilized the CIAA as his own private intelligence service. He allied himself early on with J. Edgar Hoover, who had recently expanded the FBI's operations in Latin America, by proposing an information-sharing relationship between the two agencies. Hoover readily accepted. One of Rockefeller's first coups was to identify and ask for the removal of many Latin American agents for U.S.

businesses who were known Nazi sympathizers and who were slipping confidential trade information to the Germania Corporation. In addition, he kept files on all American diplomats in Latin America, which he made available to Hoover as well.

At the same time, Standard Oil of New Jersey was facing another damaging government investigation into a cartel of its own. This time, none other than Harry Truman was chairing a Senate committee on concentrations of economic power when he uncovered evidence that Standard Oil had engaged in a series of patent agreements with the German chemical consortium I. G. Farben, which persisted even after the United States entered the war. Although the full damage done by press revelations would not occur until after the war, Rockefeller's cooperation with Hoover may have been less than coincidental.

Little Rockiefeller's incursions into the lofty realm of intelligence operations riled his enemies in State even more than his habitual greeting of "Hi, fella!" They waited for him to put his foot in it, and he did not disappoint them. In a public relations campaign which prefigures the tourist boom of the 1990s, the CIAA, through its Inter-American Travel Committee, purchased huge amounts of advertising space in some 350 Latin American papers. Superficially, the ads were used to tout the pleasures of travel in the United States; but the real purpose of the campaign was to place U.S. propaganda in these papers and to dominate their advertising budgets. One of Rockefeller's chief advisers on tourism was Walter C. Rundle, a key American Express travel executive on loan to the coordinator to handle Latin American education travel. Rundle, who returned to American Express after the war to become head of its division of foreign travel, was later to play a role in helping Rockefeller save his Venezuelan hotel interests.

The newspaper campaign became a first-class fiasco. Diplomats fulminated at funneling dollars to Nazi-friendly publications (the ad folks thought they were making converts) and blanched at Rockefeller's mockery of wartime travel restrictions. Rockefeller's enemies in State saw him in conflict with their ambassadors. His octopus of monstrous business connections—General Electric, Standard Oil, Chase Bank and, of course, American Express—made him doubly dangerous, an invader from the privately held monopolies of his grandfather's era into the government sector with the ability to suck taxpayer money into his own projects. Worse yet, he actually had the resources to do things without waiting for the elephant to give birth, which, in the heat of war, gave him greater access to the president than they had. (Dealing with his own State Department, FDR is once said to have remarked, was "like watching an elephant become pregnant. Everything is done at a very high level, there's a lot of commotion, and nothing happens for eleven months.")

But, although FDR publicly supported Rockefeller and capitalized on his best ideas, the president was, for all his "accessibility," a genteel autocrat with a genius for playing his lieutenants against one another in order to prevent any of them from gaining too much power. If he supported Rockefeller, he gave equal support to Col. William "Wild Bill" Donovan, whose wartime intelligence agency, the OSS (or "Oh, So Secret," as it came to be called), duplicated many CIAA functions. Donovan—older, a seasoned army commander, and a wily Wall Street lawyer—eventually swallowed up the CIAA into what became the CIA after the war.

That Rockefeller also did a great deal of good in Latin America was undeniable even to his detractors. His $100 million public works program, while it supported a potential U.S. military presence, also built houses, roads, hospitals, and adequate water-supply and sanitation systems in places where these things were unknown. He also used the family charitable distribution arm, the Rockefeller Foundation, to bolster a literacy campaign. As Donovan and such others as the Office of War Information stripped away more and more of his propaganda functions, Rockefeller expanded the brief of the health institute far beyond the war effort, to a missionary role calculated to give economic aid to millions who, in his own words, "know only poverty and hardship, without security or even an adequate food supply."[4] In one of the farcical turns not uncommon to politics, Little Rockiefeller's many critics, after attacking his robber baron origins, next accused him of being a free-spending New Deal liberal.

But even this ultimate expression of the Good Neighbor policy was calculated to help Nelson Rockefeller. It created enormous dependency on Rockefeller's private enterprises through its *servicios*, semi-autonomous units set up within the government of the host country, staffed largely by nationals but directed by Rockefeller employees who reported directly to a government ministry. And Rockefeller used it, as always, to facilitate his intelligence-gathering operations.

With the war effort winding down, the CIAA's usefulness diminished. Rockefeller's mentor, Vice-President Henry Wallace, fell out with FDR and was ousted from the Democratic ticket in favor of Harry Truman, leaving Rockefeller shorn of his most important ally; his other protector, Undersecretary of State Sumner Welles, had been forced to resign the year before when his alcoholism and homosexuality became too obvious to ignore. Welles's boss, Secretary of State Cordell Hull, squeezed Rockefeller out by creating a new interdepartmental committee on hemispheric development in 1944. But then Hull himself resigned, out of frustration at FDR's constant undercutting. He was succeeded by Edward Stettinius, who, in purging the ranks of Hull's acolytes, appointed Rockefeller his new assistant secretary of state for Latin America.

The CIAA was not only preserved but expanded by Rockefeller's elevation, creating the phenomenon of a private state department within the Department of State. It seemed that big business had triumphed over the Brahmins at last. But Rockefeller's inherent tendency to overreach quickly eroded his winnings. For apparently no better reason than to prove himself a success, he put his propaganda machine to work backing the fascist state of Argentina, a disastrous public relations choice that jeopardized not only his own career yet again but the postwar peace as well. It became one of the many factors that influenced Stalin to renege on the treaty at Yalta and plunge the world into Cold War.

The headquarters of Germania Corporation, Argentina was the most militant as well as the most powerful of the Latin American countries, with a right-wing junta so deeply entrenched that nothing short of all-out war would dislodge it. Like the CIAA, the Nazis subsidized the country's newspapers, magazines, books, and movies; they also used Argentine corporations as shells to hold dollar assets in the United States. The friendly business climate made it easy for the country to function as a Nazi spy center as well, tracking Allied ship movements and infiltrating other countries. The high degree of Nazi support made it possible for Argentina's leaders to flout the United States with impunity. At a 1942 conference in Rio de Janeiro, they refused to join the rest of the hemisphere in breaking with Germany, so incensing Cordell Hull that he threatened President Pedro Ramirez with the seizure of all the country's assets in the United States if Ramirez did not comply. Ramirez caved and was booted out of office in a military coup, only to be replaced by Gen. Edelmo Farrell and his deputy, Col. Juan Perón.

Perhaps, like some of Bill Clinton's revisionist advisers later on, Rockefeller wished to épater the old guard and carve out his own niche in history. In any event, he completely broke with previous State Department policy in advocating the inclusion of Argentina in inter-American security discussions and the emergent charter for a United Nations. In exchange for Argentina's declaring war immediately on Germany and Japan and joining in the inter-American effort to combat subversion, Perón was to be "permitted" to remain in power and

offered a blank-check pledge of U.S. military enforcement. Rockefeller
succeeded in ramrodding this measure through despite congressional
and press protests, cheerily assuring all the dissenters that Perón would
live up to his commitments. (He was later accused of taking advantage
of FDR's failing health to get him to sign the memo approving the
measure on March 16, 1945, shortly before he died.) Argentina was
thus permitted to sign the United Nations charter declaration in San
Francisco on April 25, an action that reneged on a promise made by
FDR to Joseph Stalin at Yalta in February to bar the Argentinians
because of their persecution of Communists.

What FDR really intended was never known, for he fell into a
coma and died soon afterward, on April 12. The Argentinians immediately found ways to superficially comply with the agreement they had
signed while allowing Axis-controlled businesses to remain in place.
On April 14 Perón enacted a draconian decree against internal dissent
and rounded up opposition leaders in wholesale arrests. As soaring
inflation, commodity shortages, and stock-market contractions
wracked the country's already weakened economy, Rockefeller's
"engine of normalization" (in Cary Reich's phrase) continued to grind
out concessions to the regime, like supplying half a million tons of fuel
oil when America's own fuel supplies were still strictly rationed. In so
doing, he took the fuel away from Brazil, a far more loyal ally, causing
the Brazilian ambassador to the United States, Carlos Martins, to break
off relations after personally informing Rockefeller that State's word
was no good. Newspapers called for Rockefeller's head for preserving
the right-wing status quo in the interests of forging alliances with the
industrial class; but instead of offering his resignation, Rockefeller
threw a Hollywood-heavy party for the U.N. conferees in San Francisco, featuring entertainment by the "Brazilian Bombshell," Carmen
Miranda. (The record does not tell us whether the Brazilian ambassador was amused.)

Rockefeller changed his tune only after Perón issued a thinly
veiled threat to murder *New York Times* correspondent Arnaldo Cortesi
for reporting on his campaign of intimidation, which Cortesi described
as equal to anything he had seen in fascist Italy. Rockefeller planned
an expiatory speech in which he would serve as the voice of the State
Department in warning Perón to watch his step, but his new boss,
James Byrnes, told him that his resignation would be accepted instead.
(Stettinius had already been persuaded to resign over the debacle.)

After his dismissal and a characteristically brief period of self-
examination, Rockefeller, who was still considered a hero in Brazil

despite his pro-Argentine tilt, used the country as a base of operations to resurrect the CIAA in the private sector. Newly focused to meet the Soviet challenge instead of the Nazis, the agency took two corporate forms: one, a "Sunday" institution for philanthropic activity known as the American International Association for Economic and Social Development, or AIA; the other, a "weekday" business venture which again incorporated many existing private Rockefeller enterprises, called the International Basic Economy Corporation, or IBEC. But both, according to the articles of incorporation, had a missionary, or sub-U.N., charter, to "promote the economic development of various parts of the world," to "increase the production and availability of goods and services useful to the lives and livelihood of their peoples," and to "better their standards of living."[5]

Although the oil giants, including Rockefeller's home team Standard Oil, derided the idea behind his back when he hit them up for co-venture capital, they were quick to fall into partnership after Romulo Betancourt seized power in Venezuela in October 1945. Betancourt, head of the left-leaning Acción Democrática party, proposed punitive taxation for greedy foreign companies and even suggested setting up a government-owned oil company and refinery to drive them out of business. Rockefeller's enterprise now gave the oil companies a perfect forum in which to demonstrate that they had the good of the people at heart: four of the majors chipped in $15 million to create an efficient food-distribution system.

The largest single contributor was Creole Petroleum, the Venezuelan arm of Standard Oil. Creole was also the second-largest holder of stock in Hotel Avila, the luxury hotel Rockefeller had built with enormous cost overruns at the onset of the war, at the behest of the previous Venezuelan president, Loez Contreras. The hotel nearly went under during the war, but Creole bailed it out. The postwar travel boom that Rockefeller promoted through AIA and IBEC not only reversed its losses but put it solidly in the black.

The Avila's turnaround was due at least in part to another Rockefeller crony, Walter C. Rundle of American Express. After his wartime "loaner" to the CIAA, Rundle returned to head up Foreign Travel at American Express. In his new capacity, handling all groups and independent tour planning, sightseeing, and most particularly, lists of hotels, Rundle was able to steer a significant amount of business down Venezuela way.

American Express had begun an all-out travel offensive from almost the moment the Allies landed on the beaches at Normandy.

Two months later, their planned-for expansion began, when the U.S. military gave American Express both their banking business and the charter for setting up sightseeing tours for American servicemen and women on leave. (The south of France, where American Express set up its first exclusively military offices, was redesignated the "United States Riviera Recreation Area.") In 1945, the company launched a massive publicity campaign to invest tourism with the same missionary glow with which Rockefeller surrounded his business ventures in Latin America. Once the final overseas travel restrictions were lifted, American Express took out full-page ads in major newspapers across the country, selling tourism as an extension of the Marshall Plan. Otherwise known as the European Recovery Program, the Marshall Plan, enacted June 5, 1947, organized ways in which the United States could funnel goods and services to European countries to aid in their recovery from the ravages of war. Travel, American Express maintained in its ad campaign, was a "social, political, and economic force . . . a powerful instrument of helping foreign nations gain needed dollars." An in-house company history claimed even more stridently, "When dollar shortages are choking the arteries of international commerce, the American tourist plays a vital role in the economies of all free nations. . . . Money spent by American travellers in Europe in 1949 amounted to more than one-half the merchandise exports of western European countries to the U.S. . . . This forcefully indicates the great importance of the role which travel abroad plays in meeting the European dollar deficit and in easing the strain on the American taxpayer for Marshall Plan aid."[6]

The campaign sounded as if it had been ghostwritten by Nelson Rockefeller, and in a sense it was. From 1945 to 1950, Rockefeller's projects in Latin America became bigger and bigger, so big that not even Rockefeller money was enough. The only bank bigger than the Rockefellers, bigger than the oil giants, was the U.S. government. Rockefeller was spoiling for an opportunity to present the AIA to President Truman as the blueprint for an overarching government aid program, but was still a pariah in the eyes of the State Department for his share in almost sinking the United Nations over Argentina. He found a surprising advocate in the person of Truman's personal assistant, a bright young Washington attorney named Clark Clifford, who was to become infamous in his old age through his association with the rogue Bank of Credit and Commerce International (BCCI).[7]

In 1945 Clifford was short on ideas for Truman's inaugural address and wanted something bright and catchy from State that would turn the speech into a "democratic manifesto for all the peoples of the world," and an anti-Communist manifesto as well. A former CIAA employee and newsman named Benjamin Hardy offered Rockefeller's AIA agenda to Clifford. Clifford worked it into Point Four of Truman's speech under his own imprimatur, as a global aid program that would pick up where the Marshall Plan left off, and called for a cooperative effort between American business, private capital, agriculture, and labor "to help the peoples of the free world, through their own efforts, to produce more food, more clothing, more materials for housing, and more mechanical power to lighten their burdens." It was not to be, as Truman insisted, "the old imperialism," exploitation for foreign profit, "but a program based on the concepts of democratic fair dealing." Without the obnoxious Rockefeller name attached, the plan got a rousing ovation from State and was incorporated into the president's speech and the national budget, at a starting cost of $45 million.[8]

Unfortunately, the Rockefeller agenda bled money. Although the causes for failure were as diverse as the numerous enterprises in which IBEC and the Venezuelan Basic Economy Corporation (VBEC) were invested, there were some common threads. One was that Rockefeller's young, and for the most part untried, managers naively underestimated the importance of local corruption in their operating budgets. Another was hubris: the companies were undercapitalized to support the ambition of their undertakings. Chief among these were grandiose infrastructure developments, roadways, giant irrigation projects, and power plants, for which Rockefeller employed the talents of master builder (and master spender) Robert Moses. Moses, who built New York City's parkway system, pocketed his fees and left to map out the city's postwar transportation grid, leaving IBEC with a plan that was too expensive to implement. The food-distribution enterprise VBEC was picked clean by its rapacious middlemen: in 1949 the Venezuelan government pulled out for fear of default, even though the oil companies had agreed to pay their share. Local papers buzzed with the most delicious rumors—a Rockefeller going bankrupt? Even Junior turned down his son's request for more venture capital once the government well ran dry. This was the lowest blow of all for Little Rockefeller.

By the summer of 1950, Congress was castigating Point Four as an "international boondoggle" and "global WPA." In the face of continued hostility from the State Department, Rockefeller reinvented his Point Four manifesto as a bulwark against creeping communism. In this he was playing to the growing McCarthyite audience, but particularly to the anti-Kremlin prejudices of Truman's special assistant Averell Harriman.

Harriman was also the son of a robber baron, railroad magnate E. H. Harriman, but his achievements dwarfed Rockefeller's. Seventeen years his senior, with a list of glittering World War II appointments including ambassador to the Court of St. James, Harriman was also a brilliant entrepreneur who introduced high-speed trains to America, Western business practices to the Soviet Union, and the newly fashionable sport of skiing to the slopes of Sun Valley, Idaho, a resort he built himself. As ruthless as his father, Harriman listened amiably to Rockefeller's ideas for rolling his schemes together into an even bigger plan for a centralized worldwide economic offensive combining the administration of the Marshall Plan with several other agencies, including what was left of the CIAA, then engulfed them neatly within his own plans as head of the Mutual Security Administration, created in 1951 to control all U.S. foreign aid, military and economic.

Passed over for the leadership of the administration in favor of his erstwhile mentor and friend, Rockefeller had no choice but to resign from the federal government. He quietly washed himself clean of his Democratic spots and joined in the behind-the-scenes maneuvering to get Dwight D. Eisenhower on the Republican ticket in October 1951. Although the Republican Party could not refuse a Rockefeller readmission to the fold, Nelson's efforts to become a public player in the campaign were sternly rebuffed by Gov. Tom Dewey of New York, the campaign coordinator. When Eisenhower became president, he rewarded Rockefeller with a consolation prize, the chairmanship of a special committee on reorganizing the executive branch. As part of his brief, Rockefeller made sure that some of his old pet projects, as always, survived.

His propaganda empire became the new USIA with its now-famous radio network, the Voice of America. These would continue to promote tourism and culture as diplomatic tools throughout the Cold War era. His various economic programs became the Foreign Economic Operation Agency (later the Foreign Operation Administration), which administered foreign investment and trade, supervised export controls, and handled procurement of strategic material. Indeed, their outlines are still visible as the blueprints for the late Commerce Secretary Ron Brown's "trade versus aid" program, lending support to snide accusations among journalists that the Clinton administration had been truffling through FDR's yellowed memos in search of an original idea. But nowhere in the postwar era was the Rockefeller footprint more apparent than in the development of Boeing, the Standard Oil of aerospace.

When Betty Stettinius, the sister of Edward Stettinius, married Juan Trippe, head of Pan Am, the marriage celebrated more than the joining of two individuals. The worlds of diplomacy and commercial air travel were merging as well. Along with the Soviets' turn at Yalta and the slamming down of the Iron Curtain came another cold war: the former Allies turned into commercial enemies in competing for supremacy in this explosive new growth area. "The advent of jet travel made it clear that the airways were becoming the sea lanes of the twentieth century; the airports its docks; the planes its oceangoing craft. Control of the mechanics of world transport had been a European prerogative ever since the sixteenth century, and great wealth and empires had been founded on mastery of shipbuilding and seacraft. But as the sea lanes gave way to the airways, politicians and industrialists saw European mastery slipping away. It was not a sight they intended to witness with careless passivity."[9]

It was the British who developed the world's first passenger jet. The brilliant but ill-starred Comet was the brainchild of aerospace pioneer Geoffrey de Havilland, who developed it in the closing stage of World War II as his industry faced a rapid contraction from the military buildup. De Havilland felt that, by virtue of its concentration in transport and bombing aircraft, America would have a big lead when the inevitable competition for long-distance airlines began. If Britain was going to compete at all, the country would have to make a quantum leap.

The British, early masters of the sea, led the rest of the world in air travel for some years after the war, including the invention of the jet engine, developed by Frank Whittle and fitted to a Gloucester warplane. De Havilland witnessed one of the first flights and used the idea to create the Vampire jet fighter, which went into large-scale production for the Royal Air Force and took de Havilland's eponymous company to the forefront of the new technology: until 1959, development of jet travel was a strictly British affair.

De Havilland got further government assistance for his next step: to fit a conventional passenger air frame with four jet engines. The British government essentially paid for the plane, which de Havilland named the Comet, with grants and large orders. The Comet was first tested on July 27, 1949. After three more years of testing, it made its maiden flight, lasting 23 hours and 40 minutes, from London to Johannesberg, South Africa, via Rome, Khartoum, Entebbe, and Livingstone. De Havilland, and Britain, were cheered by a grateful world for inaugurating the jet age. But like its namesake, the Comet flamed up and out: after enormous fanfare, it crashed, not once but three times, killing all passengers on board each time. It was withdrawn from service after the third crash. After prolonged examination of the surviving wreckage and many theories, including international sabotage, the Comet's failure was attributed to metal fatigue.

De Havillands' fate was inextricably bound up with the Comet. From 1955 to 1959, the company was several times bailed out by the British government, which placed large orders for the RAF and advanced monies for further development. When these funds ran out, it intervened with a direct grant of £6.5 million to keep the company alive. In 1959, De Havillands threw in the towel and merged with Hawker Siddeley, but not before Bill Allen, chairman of Boeing, had seen the Comet and appropriated the idea for his own development.

The Boeing Airline Company, the Seattle-based brainchild of William E. Boeing, was on the brink of going under after World War I. Though the airplane had been invented in the United States, a serious industry was slow to emerge. The First World War gave it a tremendous boost, as it had done in Europe. But although Congress agreed in 1916 to follow the lead of the British (who had just won the Battle of the Somme in part by sending aircraft to attack enemy trenches) in allocating significant funds for army and navy planes, Boeing was beaten by his most significant competitor, Donald Willis Douglas of the Douglas Aircraft Company (later McDonnell-Douglas), in securing government contracts. Boeing, whose grasp of business resembled John D. Rockefeller's, hit on the idea of cornering the fledgling market in airmail service to create a market for the first civilian planes. With the U.S. Post Office tendering airmail contracts to private companies, Boeing underbid all its competitors and secured the franchise to carry the mail across the entire western half of the country. With the introduction of the five-cent airmail stamp and the growing reliability of the carriers, the plane became a serious competitor to the train. As the company boomed and went public in the feverish atmosphere of the late 1920s, it merged with a number of other companies to become the largest aerospace conglomerate in the world, United Aircraft and Transportation Corporation, assimilating the Boeing Airline Company, Boeing Transport, and the engine maker Pratt and Whitney, not to mention a propeller manufacturer and several young regional airlines. Like Standard Oil, United integrated every aspect of the business, from building airframes and engines to operating both passenger and mail carriers.

The 1930s were a dismal decade for Boeing, not so much because of the Depression, which did not affect the underlying growth in the airplane business (even though prices fell), but because of the same antitrust legislation which had served to hobble Standard Oil two decades earlier. The Boeing 247, which rolled off assembly lines in 1933, revolutionized standards of speed and comfort. With a top speed of 200 mph, it allowed United to introduce a coast-to-coast service in twenty hours, with seven stops along the way, thereby dominating the civilian market with 48 percent of share. Between 1929 and 1933, the conglomerate accounted for 48 percent of all army and navy sales as well. But in 1934, Congress began a highly publicized series of investigations into the endogamous networks of alliances between the military and manufacturers, and the manufacturers and the airlines. The Senate cried monopoly, and Boeing, which had profited so richly from underbidding the postal routes, suffered a stinging defeat. Bill Boeing sold his stock and broke up the conglomerate, just as John D. Rockefeller had done with Standard Oil.[10]

Like De Havillands, Boeing faced a postwar contraction. The war had lifted the American industry by an astounding 13,500 percent. As peace broke out, Boeing honed its edge by developing long-range bombers like the B-52 but still struggled to find its footing in the commercial market. The $15–$20 million required to build a prototype for a jet-engine passenger plane competitive with the Comet was beyond the budgets of either airlines or manufacturers without the kind of substantial government subsidy available in Europe. Chairman Allen, threatened by the Comet, gambled $13 million to build the 707, which Boeing first tested in May 1954.[11]

The crashes finished the Comet as a competitor, but the Boeing 707 was trumped by the Douglas DC-8, a larger, more comfortable plane for transatlantic hauls. Douglas, which had also beaten Boeing in manufacturing the DC-1 and DC-2, by now had a growing lead over the Seattle-based company. Realizing that he held the perfect hand to beat down manufacturing prices, Juan Trippe, the preeminent booster of new technology, played Douglas and Boeing against each other to make the largest, most advanced engine for Pan Am's transatlantic jets. In October 1955, Trippe announced an unprecedented order: $269 million for twenty 707s and twenty-five DC-8s, with the larger part of the order going to Douglas. Though it built the best engine through its Pratt and Whitney unit, Boeing actually lost money on the deal. It was prepared to gamble on the next big adventure in aerospace, the Concorde, in order to regain its lead.

In the Concorde, the first supersonic jet, the paths of geopolitics and geoindustrial rivalry not only cross but merge. Tracing its lineage back to the Comet, the Concorde became a "major element in the fight to keep independence and freedom in the face of American or Russian dominance" in the eyes of geoindustrialists, who did not hesitate to draw parallels to the ancient Greek and Roman empires. As aerospace, which had expanded exponentially during the war years, became the engine of choice to jump-start war-stalled economies, it absorbed downsizing military budgets into its research-and-development programs. In Europe, commercial air-travel development was folded almost immediately into government subsidies, which the United States eventually matched in order to compete. But increasing costliness made collaboration necessary not only between government and industry but between governments themselves.[12]

On November 29, 1962, Julian Amery, the British minister of aviation, met in London with the French ambassador, Geoffroy de Courcel, to sign an agreement to create the Concorde. Until the French launched the Caravelle in 1957, which was still in commercial service up to the 1990s, it seemed that the race to conquer the airways was between the British and the Americans. But the emergence of the French as aerospace players shifted the balance of power to a contest between America and Europe, with a bitterness that had not existed before, perhaps owing to the ill-disguised anti-Americanism of the French.

Nobody got along particularly well, for the most obvious cultural reasons (the Brits huffily insisted on anglicizing "Concorde" to "Concord" after Charles de Gaulle denied them entry to the European Economic Community). The British initially approached the Americans via the Ministry of Defence, but talks foundered because the Americans were only interested in a plane that could fly at Mach 3 whereas the British were convinced that Mach 2 was the fastest speed compatible with the existing technology. The British next approached the French, who had just aced them at the 1961 Paris Air Show with the Super Caravelle, the first public commitment to building a supersonic plane.

The British were looking for ways to deepen Anglo-French cooperation and prove their credentials as aspirant Europeans. But about the only thing that truly unified the British and the French was the threat of the Americans. In the British view, the Yanks were trying to subvert them by appointing Eugene Black, a former head of the World Bank who had lobbied aggressively against the Concord(e), as head of a high-level committee to pursue an American supersonic plane. This was sufficient to galvanize the French and British into uneasy collaboration in November 1962: production lurched ahead on a chimera with 60 percent of the plane's engine made in Britain and 60 percent of its airframe made in France.

At the same time, as early as 1963, both the British and the French were aware that the Soviets were feverishly at work on a plane which bore a remarkable resemblance to the Concord(e). In the mortal combat of the Cold War, the Western powers, who prided themselves on their superior technology, could not lose face by allowing the Russians to launch a supersonic plane ahead of them. But although competition with the Soviets might have provided political motivation for continuing with the unwieldy·Concord(e), it was competition with America that constituted the commercial spur.

Black, as head of the new American committee on supersonic flight, recommended that U.S. government funding be provided for development. Here, for the first time, the airline lobby proved more powerful than a president. John F. Kennedy was well aware of public and congressional hostility toward subsidizing private industry. When Trippe indicated his intention of buying the Anglo-Gallic product for Pan Am, Kennedy instructed Najeeb Halaby, head of the Federal Aviation Agency, to inform him that the president needed time and that Trippe was not to commit himself until Kennedy made up his mind whether to fund or not to fund. (To show how rapidly top airline executives were becoming a new form of royalty, Halaby's daughter, Lisa, later married King Hussein of Jordan, becoming Queen Noor.)

Trippe was not a man to take dictation from a mere president. He knew Kennedy's uncertainty, and also his ego. With Kennedy due to announce on a Monday, Trippe preempted him the night before by proclaiming his order for six Concordes. Kennedy was cornered: refusing now to back a U.S.-made supersonic jet would seem as if he were ceding the field to the Europeans. Since he had staked so much of his political profile on maintaining the United States's edge as the world's foremost technological power, he had no choice but to ratify government funding for an American Concorde, to be known as the SST.[13]

The SST would outlive the president. Despite demands on federal funds from the Vietnam War, President Lyndon Johnson ordered, and got, $198 million from Congress to continue its development. In time, geoindustrial politics would not only prove stronger than diplomacy, they would become diplomacy.

On August 17, 1993, only seven months into his presidency, Bill Clinton called King Fahd of Saudi Arabia to secure an order for sixty new planes, worth some $6 billion, from his national airline, Saudia. The Europeans had urged Saudi Arabia to split the deal with them at least fifty-fifty, but Clinton wanted the order for Boeing and McDonnell-Douglas and exerted heavy pressure, not least by sweetening his offer with substantial guarantees from the U.S. Export-Import Bank. (The bank finances sales by guaranteeing repayment of commercial loans. This guarantee lowers the rates of interest that commercial banks would normally charge. In theory, there is virtually no cost to U.S. taxpayers unless a creditor defaults, which is unlikely. Saudi Arabia, at the time, faced serious economic problems brought on by the worldwide glut in oil and accompanying drop in prices. Boeing was in trouble as well.) Clinton also reminded Fahd that the United States had saved his country from Saddam Hussein. For this he was both praised and damned as a "supersalesman" by journalists and members of Congress, while top officials like Secretary of State Warren Christopher, Ron Brown, and Transportation Secretary Federico Peña, who had lobbied with him, defended Clinton by pointing out that such sales efforts were common among European leaders of state. Fahd signaled assent; but after Clinton's Senate allies prematurely leaked the news of his "triumph," Fahd upped the ante by entertaining a counteroffer from Airbus, whose chief supersalesman was François Mitterrand.[14]

Airbus had been understandably incensed at the prospect of losing such an important order and launched a scathing attack on President Clinton, calling his role "blatant political interference and leverage" and suggesting that it violated Article Four of the General Agreement on Tariffs and Trade (GATT), which banned inducements related to defense and national-security issues in civil aircraft sales. Analysts speculated that, with Saudi Arabia suffering from a shortage of funds, an agreement by the United States to restructure $9.2 billion of Saudi defense spending had been the key to the order, an assumption supported by the comments of American officials. In a speech at the White House, Saudi Prince Bandur Bin Sultan acknowledged Saudi Arabia's responsibility to be a "strategic asset and not a strategic liability" for the United States and said that the country was ready to share the burden of supporting the U.S. aerospace industry. Airbus retorted that it was "keen to find out what arguments had been presented to the Saudis beyond the technical qualities of the aircraft under offer."[15]

Airbus may have had something even darker in mind than finagling arms deals. In his book *Birds of Prey*, Matthew Lynn gives an astonishing account of what happened behind the scenes. According to Lynn, who covered airline news for the London *Times*, Mitterrand offered Fahd E.U. aid to help the Palestinians establish self-rule in the Israeli-occupied West Bank and Gaza Strip, knowing full well that Clinton was unlikely to jeopardize his "special" relationship with Israel for $6 billion. Next, King Fahd received German Vice-Chancellor and

Foreign Affairs Minister Klaus Kinkel, who offered to mediate between Saudi Arabia and Iran, in addition to helping the Palestinians, in order to strengthen Airbus' hand. Even Prince Charles stopped by for a chat.

Most astonishing (and appalling) of all, according to Lynn, the ubiquitous Ron Brown then descended on the Gulf with a way around "the Jewish issue." Fahd was displeased at the lackadaisical European stance on the plight of Bosnian Muslims: the White House was prepared to weigh in with a firm plan to stop the war in Bosnia. Thus the deal was clinched for Boeing and McDonnell-Douglas, and, to show the manufacturers whom they had to thank, it was announced from the White House rather than from corporate headquarters. When I interviewed him over the telephone, Lynn, who now works part time for the London *Times* and writes suspense novels, reported that some of his information came from Airbus people, and some from newswires. In partial support of his story, a Lexis-Nexis search of the time frame involved turned up everything but the Bosnian Muslims as a deal-clincher, although Prince Bandur did make an elliptical reference to the "indispensable" nature of American leadership in Bosnia in his White House speech.[16]

"We have finally broken out of the shackles that have caused several decades' debate about the role of government," Ron Brown said at that White House ceremony. "Our international competitors figured out that role a long time ago, and that's why they are doing much better than they should be."[17]

Almost exactly a year later, Brown's plane crashed into a Croatian mountainside. Four years after that, in a neat role reversal, Israel announced plans to split an order for new planes for El Al between Boeing, once more in deep trouble, and Airbus. This occurred on the eve of Secretary of State Madeleine Albright's departure for Israel to discuss the troubled peace. Poetic justice? Or has the mouse learned to make the good doctor bring it cheese?

The story of Ron Brown's airline negotiations with the Saudis demonstrates a continuum with the alliance forged between government and business by Nelson Rockefeller a half-century ago. From his CIAA activities in Latin America to his involvement with Hollywood, Rockefeller provided a blueprint for the business-driven foreign policy of the Clinton administration and particularly for the massive promotion of tourism. As Standard Oil mutated into a multinational corporation which then networked with other multinational corporations like American Express, geoindustrial politics not only proved stronger than diplomacy, it became diplomacy. Unlike Clinton-era diplomats, Rockefeller had enemies in the State Department who were still conscious of the dangers of the invasion of privately held monopolies into the government sector, an awareness which appears to have vanished with the century. In fact, although Rockefeller's backing of the fascist state of Argentina bears a striking resemblance to the Clinton administration's backing of Croatian president Franjo Tudjman, the fates of the two efforts are very different.

Rockefeller first courted, then manipulated, government to facilitate, bankroll, and conceal the continuous workings of the family monopoly. Rockefeller's public-works program in Latin America is potent proof of the power of big business to do good; but as this beneficence was always motivated by self-interest, it is difficult to consider it a form of democracy, rather than a form of neocolonialism. Large corporations are seldom democratic institutions and tend to beat democratic swords into commercial plowshares.

This is particularly true of the post–World War II travel offensive launched by Rockefeller's ally, American Express, which sold tourism as an integral extension of the Marshall Plan. The resemblance of American Express' postwar advertising campaign to speeches made by James Robinson III and other American Express executives during the approach of glasnost is not accidental, for American Express has appropriated democracy as its global brand: as the official company history proudly declares, "When dollar shortages are choking the arteries of international commerce, the American tourist plays a vital role in the economies of all free nations."[18]

The Biggest Business
in the World

The role of multilateral development banks . . . goes far beyond that of promoting good policies or public investments. In a world of rapidly rising capital flows, they have a central part to play as investors who can unlock, expand and improve the quality and impact of these flows.

Amartya Sen, "Development Strategy and
Management of the Market Economy" (1972)

Reformism and sectarianism can happily coexist; they are not mutually antagonistic. This means that not only have the reforms not necessarily eradicated sectarian division, but they have often reconstituted that division in new and often more pervasive ways than before.

Bill Rolston, Reformism and Sectarianism:
The State of the Union After Civil Rights *(1983)*

WITH ITS EYE ON the nest eggs of retiring "baby-boomers," tourism today claims to be the world's biggest business. According to the 1995 World Travel and Tourism Report, it generates more than $4.4 trillion per annum, or over 10 percent of the world's gross domestic product. The business employs more than 200 million people, or one in nine workers worldwide. It contributes $65 billion to governments in direct and indirect taxes—11 percent of all tax payments—and is a major factor in international trade and the balance of payments.[1]

Other trade figures indicate that in the richer countries travel spending has increased at double or more the rate of GDP since 1945. These countries, with less than 25 percent of the world's population, account for nearly 85 percent of world tourist arrivals, which grew from 69 million in 1960 to 537.4 million in 1994. Europe, the world's most favored destination, accounted for 73 percent of all arrivals until 1990, the year after the Berlin Wall came down, when its share dropped abruptly to less than 62 percent.[2]

Why should tourism, more than any other business, claim such a large share of the world's resources? Part of the answer lies in the statistics on declining European travel after the official kick-off of the "peace process" in Eastern Europe. Although superficially we can attribute this shift to a lack of interest in "Western Civ." among this generation's Grand Tour graduates, on a deeper level it reflects an accumulation of changes that have been unfolding slowly since the 1940s, a process that accelerated sharply when the elaborate foreign-aid system that had supported the Cold War was abruptly dismantled.

The levers of "development economics" have been working overtime to redistribute the promotion and resources of tourism to developing countries. According to the United Nations Council on Trade and Development, "tourism is the only large sector of international trade in services where poor countries have consistently posted a surplus." Even in the perilous Asian downdraft of 1998, says the World Tourism Organization (WTO), international tourist arrivals increased 2.4 percent, matching growth in the previous year and "proving tourism has become a deeply rooted part of our culture." (Actually, the increase probably has a good deal to do with bargain-basement airfares and invitingly steep slides in local currencies.) In the aggressive public relations campaigns which, post–peace process, have replaced military ones, many of the problems plaguing developing countries have been ingeniously reinvented as "adventure travel" or "cultural tourism" aimed at the emerging boomer market.[3]

The domination of the United States in the postwar reconstruction era ensured that Nelson Rockefeller's vision would outlast his diplomatic career, surviving not at the U.S. State Department but in the United Nations and through the international lending institutions affiliated with it. The crusade to overcome poverty seemed a logical continuation of postwar reconstruction; but, as Rockefeller foresaw, the Cold War also made economic development a political big ticket. As decolonization swelled the number of independent countries from 55 in 1947 to more than 150 by the end of the 1980s, the Soviets and the West competed viciously over foreign aid because of its usefulness in proselytizing.

Development economics came into being as a means of dealing with the often uneasy transition period from colony to country and was adopted as a policy guide by the United Nations, the world forum for decolonized countries. At the United Nations, development economics became a platform for the World Bank, which in conjunction with the International Monetary Fund (IMF) came to stress market-oriented policies to boost foreign exchange and development in less-developed countries (LDCs), with particular emphasis on how such service-sector exports as tourism could be an important source of revenue. If Rockefeller's old ally, American Express, with its by now almost incalculable float, which could be used to develop tourism, had not piggybacked itself onto the Marshall Plan, however, it is possible that other solutions might have been found to treat the economic problems of developing countries.

These problems can be summarized as follows: less-developed countries generally have narrow, resource-based economies with limited manufacturing, and tend to be dependent on agricultural exports. Again generally, they suffer from a lack of capital and expertise to develop potential mining resources—which leaves them with vast stretches of pristine scenery, highly desirable for tourism. As major exporters of primary products (raw materials), they are vulnerable to export price-swings, accompanied by weak infrastructure, high unemployment, and high population growth. Their low level of development and need for development capital lead to severe deficits in the balance of payments, that is, they import more than they export. This in turn leads, chronically, to depreciating currency values and heavy reliance on foreign aid or loans. A large proportion of their export earnings must be used to pay foreign debt, rather than for new economic and social development.

Tourism is a natural fit for economies in this stage of development because it boosts hard currency receipts, which can then be used to pay off foreign loans in relatively short order. Tourism is also useful for teaching people service-sector skills. However, the heavy infrastructure investment required by tourism eats up resources which could be employed elsewhere (in housing, for instance). Often it simply replaces one single-crop economy with another, precluding, say, the development of a more broadly diversified array of agricultural commodities (as in Turkey) or heavy industry, such as mining, which would spoil the scenery for ecotourists (Panama).

Infrastructure investment in developing countries became the agenda of the World Bank at its creation at Bretton Woods in 1944 under the original title of the International Bank for Reconstruction and Development. Its basic mandate was to raise multilateral finance from the capital markets of developed nations to make long-term loans at favorable terms to the public sectors of developing countries, which would secure them by repayment guarantees. In a world where the patterns of international investment had been disrupted by the Great

Depression even before World War II began, the World Bank got capital flowing across borders again. It would cooperate closely with the International Monetary Fund as well as the United Nations.[4]

By the 1950s the bank had shifted its focus from the reconstruction of Europe to the development of what was termed the Third World. At the same time, tourism mushroomed with the advent of cheap travel and the awakened wanderlust of ex-G.I.s and became an important government weapon in the economic arsenal against poverty. Its earnings helped to erase chronic current-accounts deficits in non–oil exporting developing countries, to stimulate foreign exchange, and, most important in the view of the World Bank, to pay off war debt. Tourism's value as a quick economic fix was of paramount importance to creditor nations and wobbly governments alike, a pattern repeated in the post-perestroika 1990s when tourism was recast as a one-size-fits-all cure by the machinery of "globalization," which eerily came to resemble the Stalinist central planning it had just replaced.

After World War II, tourism was first deployed in government-supported marketing campaigns to attract foreign visitors. The American military colonized the French Riviera. The Swiss government provided funds to keep the country's hotel stock well-maintained. The British government funded the British Travel Association and also heavily subsidized the emerging aerospace industry. The intergovernmental Organization for European Economic Cooperation, established by Western European governments with generous U.S. aid through the Marshall Plan, removed travel constraints in the form of currency restrictions, customs, passports, and visas, much as the "borderless" European Union is trying to do now.

As Europe's former colonies broke away from their devastated colonizers, they began to join the newly formed United Nations. India, Israel, Indonesia, Algeria, Lebanon, Iran, Iraq, Bolivia, Brazil, Haiti, Honduras, Liberia, all boasted networks of roads, ports, and railways that had been maintained by the occupying powers but which now fell into disrepair—in many cases, they had been insufficient to begin with. The United Nations commissioned studies, which recommended development of these countries, and the World Bank stepped in because the developing countries could not mobilize sufficient resources to get the job done. When foreign investors did not disdain the low rates of return that were offered, their money was often rejected by prickly emerging nations as "colonialism." The work would be done by state-owned companies, which became the most visible embodiment of development economics, not only as engines of modernization and drivers of economic growth but as a way to break up oligopolies and to express the sovereignty, dignity, and birth of identity essential to nationhood. As Daniel Yergin and Joseph Stanislaw put it, "Taken as a whole, this change represents the process through which issues of national sovereignty were resolved, the residue of classic colonialism and imperialism was relegated to the past, and economics won precedence over politics."[5]

Whether the mass privatization of state-owned companies that began in the early 1990s is part of the globalization of democratization or simply colonial wine in corporate bottles is a good question. Because the state is not only a regulator of tourism but also in many cases a major operator, owning most public-transport systems as well as the majority of cultural, natural, and historic sites and such tourist facilities as sea- and airports, the privatization of tourism has been in many countries the most significant part of the privatization process. In the majority of instances this process has seamlessly incorporated the old elite into the new. In Cuba, for example, the military has marched into executive positions in Cubanacan and Gaviota, the two largest tourism-related companies. (Gaviota, which builds hotels and highways, still draws its labor from the armed forces.) In Russia, the old "nomenklatura," or Soviet ruling class, also perceives tourism as a "soft" posting, one with access to foreign contacts and the all-important dollar. The case for democratization-by-tourism of Cuba is not advanced by the fact that the current minister of tourism, Osmany Cienfuegos, described as a "longtime Marxist" by historian Robert Quirk, once commanded a death squad.

It is difficult to determine whether the rise of the school of development economics first buttressed the idea of economics-with-a-mission or vice versa, but the two had a mutually reinforcing effect. As development economists concluded that "natural" growth was inadequate to address the needs of developing countries, they advocated an urgent acceleration to achieve in a decade what had previously been left to a hundred-year cycle. Their fervor had the ring of other Cold War ideologies. The guru of the movement, Amartya K. Sen, challenged the position held by the World Bank, which concentrated on repayment of LDC debt, and emphasized human development and the restoration of personal income instead.

Sen began his career as an economist in a far more down-to-earth way than most, handing out rice during the 1943 famine in his native Bengal. His work during that famine, which killed more than three million people, led him to conclude that the famine had not resulted from unusually low food supplies but rather from a run-up in food prices spurred by, among other things, wartime panic and speculation. Unusual for an economist, Sen became a firm believer in the value of good publicity as a preemptive strike at laggard or indifferent government. In his 1981 book *Poverty and Famines*, he argued that famine was not just a consequence of nature but also a humanmade disaster resulting from inadequate political and economic responses to natural events. His research led him to conclude that government should take a more proactive role in alleviating human misery.[6]

Despite criticisms of superficiality, Sen's work has been enormously influential in guiding U.N. and World Bank policy to eschew traditional forms of aid. It also resembles the economic capstone of U.S. foreign policy in the Clinton administration: "trade versus aid," or internationalized workfare. Sen, who was awarded the Nobel Prize in economics in 1998, had this to say about the role of development banks:

> The development strategy of a poor country must depend on its opportunities for trade and the availability of other forms of support from other sources. As an outside player in repeated and long-term relationships with developing countries, a multilateral development bank can build trust and understanding and make a contribution far beyond the value of the resources provided. From the host-country perspective, there is a greater willingness to accept, and greater recognition of the potential contribution of, a multilateral development bank relative to a private investor or a single-country partner, since it is a party whose interest in a transaction extends beyond narrow self-interest. Moreover, because multilateral development banks are involved in multiple lending projects, they have an incentive to be worried about macroeconomic performance, and they have the ability to enforce, as part of their lending programmes, "conditionality," ensuring that a sound policy environment is maintained. . . .
>
> The role of multilateral development banks, however, goes far beyond that of promoting good policies or public investments. In a world of rapidly rising capital flows, they have a central part to play as investors who can unlock, expand, and improve the quality and impact of these flows. The fact that multilateral development banks are active partners may comfort other partners, who recognize that involvement of multilaterals enhances the strength and reliability of relationships with the host government. In turn, the host government will have more confidence in the private investor if multilaterals are involved, because private investors have valued long-term relationships with multilateral investment banks. They also value their own reputation. As a result of this greater comfort a variety of private projects may materialize that otherwise would fail to get off the ground and will function much better.[7]

In 1972 Robert McNamara, who became president of the World Bank Group following his stint as U.S. secretary of defense during the Vietnam War, recommended the encouragement of mass tourism for developing countries based on projections which showed vacation travel increasing by 45 percent, or 40 million travelers, over the next decade. The countries targeted by the World Bank included Yugoslavia, Morocco, Algeria, Egypt, Israel, Lebanon, Syria, Turkey, Cyprus, Colombia, Uganda, Ethiopia, Iran, Afghanistan, Ceylon (now Sri Lanka), Nepal, Thailand, and Indonesia; although a World Bank Tourism Sector working paper notes that "the growth of tourism in some of these countries has been hampered by the political situation."[8]

(Almost thirty years later, the 1999 list of places the Foreign Office in London adjudges it unsafe to visit because of terrorism or other criminal activity includes many of the same countries: Afghanistan, Algeria, Eritrea [because of tensions with Ethiopia], Sri Lanka, and Kosovo. The U.S. State Department also advises against visiting Iran, Colombia, Lebanon, and parts of Indonesia. In the Middle East, tourism stalled with the peace process in 1997. Economic conditions in the West Bank and Gaza Strip disintegrated after Israel closed its borders. In November a terrorist attack on tourists in Luxor, Egypt, dealt a severe blow to the rapidly expanding tourism sector in that country, as well as to that of neighbors like Jordan and Lebanon, all of whom were recipients of World Bank largess. Before the attack, tourism revenues in Egypt exceeded $3.5 billion in 1996–1997, and tourism and related activities provided employment for nearly four million Egyptians. Drastically reduced tourist arrivals following the attack hobbled the country's efforts to achieve a growth rate of higher than 5.3 percent for 1997.)[9]

Because of protectionism regarding cheap imports from develop- ing countries, and because tourism generated foreign exchange which could then be used to pay foreign debt, the World Bank targeted its expansion, particularly as a means of redressing "regional imbalances" in employment and income between urban and rural areas. The bank formed a department to deal with loans of about $404 million for forty-four tourism projects, which did not include tourism-related lending in air transport, highway construction, water and sewage, and vocational training. Previous to that time, total loans and investments made by the bank through its private-sector arm, the International Finance Corporation (IFC), totaled approximately $70 million.[10]

The World Bank disbanded its tourism department in the late 1970s, after it lent $16 million for an initially disastrous project to build a thousand-acre "tourist estate" at Nusa Dua, a remote location on the Bukit Peninsula of Bali. In 1968 the Indonesian government had requested the bank's assistance for tourism development, stressing the importance of international tourism in Indonesia's projected economic development and laying the foundations of a national tourism policy. Banking on Bali's reputation as a tourist paradise, dating from the colonial visits of artists and anthropologists, the government commissioned a French consulting firm, SCETO, to draw up a master plan for Bali, financed by the United Nations Development Program, with the World Bank as executive agency. The SCETO report green-lighted the resort but imposed many restrictions on its construction according to the dictates of "sustainable tourism," that is, the need to develop tourism in Bali without spoiling the famous Balinese culture. The consultants tried to strike a compromise, constructing resorts well away from residential areas but reached via routes through those areas so that tourists could "experience" Balinese life, as if they were visiting a zoo. Even SCETO seemed to have little confidence in the plan, evidenced by the report's conclusion that the resort was likely to cannibalize the very culture it was designed to protect.

Ian Christie, today the bank's lead sub-Saharan specialist, joined the tourism unit in 1972 and worked on the Nusa Dua project, which, he said, "took longer to gestate and become successful than we thought," eight or nine years, in fact. However, Christie noted that the Bank has a "100 percent repayment history" in tourism loans, and no bank loan ever went into default during the history of the tourism department. The department was disbanded because of mixed sentiments within the unit itself. "We didn't like the idea of financing temporary housing for rich cats from overseas," he said. "The local owners had very little say in what went on. The World Bank had no business being there. We all moved to the urban department, where we created housing for poor nations."[11]

Although the bank calculated that two jobs would be generated for every hotel room, the cost of construction averaged $70,000 per room, owing to massive overruns and delays. The report does not specifically mention corruption, but one assumes that that time-honored institution is represented somewhere in the $70,000 figure. ("Of course there was corruption," remarked one bank official. "It's in Asia, isn't it?")

To make matters worse, the horde of anticipated travelers who finally showed up turned out to be hippie backpackers rather than the high-end crowd so reverently anticipated by the bank and the Balinese government. After a four-year delay, the bank reaped a 6 percent return on its investment of $16 million, rather than the 19 percent expected. As the report noted in summation: "The economic viability of this type of an integrated tourist project is very sensitive to changes in the worldwide economic situation. In this connection, the Bank should have been more cautious in its demand projections, more conservative in project design, and obtained firmer assurances from private hotel investors before proceeding with such an ambitious project."[12]

A number of other tourism projects in Turkey and Latin America went sour at the same time, and the bank received a good deal of negative publicity, particularly for some of tourism's less attractive "image problems," such as child prostitution. The numbers of rich overseas investors who managed to finance recreational housing through World Bank initiatives while local landowners were closed out of the decision-making process did not win accolades, either.

Because of the bad press, the bank never formally regrouped its tourism unit. Today, sentiment regarding tourism at the upper levels of bank decision making is mixed, although the development at Nusa Dua is now accounted a success, for the loans have been paid back. Bank officials point proudly to their success in integrating culture with tourism in Bali as well by making the traditional Hindu religion a part of the tourist spectacle, although a growing body of contemporary work by anthropologists and local journalists complains that the spectacle is a degrading one.

Around the same time that the World Bank was trying to kick-start tourism through the IFC, the IFC was also trying to promote the flow of funds into the stock markets of developing countries. The great need of the capitalist world in the 1980s was to find new sources of money to fuel growth. Governments would not accept new debt, which was unavailable in any event because of continuing debt crises; instead, the reasoning went, capital would be attracted through local stock markets into private companies in developing countries. Thus, the developing countries could tap the savings—the mutual funds and pension funds—of the industrialized world. Again, according to dogma, countries would have to display stable currencies, encouraging prospects for growth, and a workable political climate. Tourism, and the kinds of government or intragovernment interventions that foster tourism (the promotion of human rights in Turkey, to name just one example) provided an excellent vehicle for facilitating these preconditions.

At the same time, the renewed perception that it was a force for democratization provided an excellent public relations vehicle for tourism, and particularly for the American Express Company, which had gotten into trouble with its investors in 1984 through misconceived investments in cable television and insurance. The cable venture, Warner-Amex, was viewed simply as a mistake. However, the insurance company, Firemen's Fund, created a major Wall Street scandal when the fact that it had covered its losses with funny bookkeeping came to light and broke American Express' thirty-six-year earnings streak.

A Dutch banker, Antoine van Agtmael, who had worked in Thailand in the late seventies when that country experienced its first bout of tulip-mania, joined the IFC and traveled to New York to raise investor interest in a "Third World investment fund," which would tap what he saw as the potential for rapid, exponential growth in LDCs. The catch phrase "emerging markets" was coined to entice Americans to part with their savings at the very moment when the debt crisis was casting a bright light on their economic peril. With unfortunate timing, the IFC helped get the Mexico Fund launched just as Mexico stumbled into bankruptcy. It did better with the Korea Fund. But the U.S. stock-market crash of 1987 put paid to such heroics, until the drumbeat of glasnost was heard in the land.

By the mid-1980s, the IFC didn't have much to show for its effort, although the need for relief was even more urgent as the debt crisis and a crashing halt to lending made it imperative to funnel money into the cash-starved economies of what continued to be a third and not an emerging world. In 1986 the IFC, in consort with the Capital Group, a money-management company, persuaded a group of major institutional investors to part with $50 million for an emerging-markets fund. With this and with the first public mutual fund for emerging markets offered by market guru Sir John Templeton, emerging markets began to, well, emerge. By 1996, assisted by feverish publicity, the capitalization was $2.2 trillion, exactly half of what the global tourist industry reports as its earnings.[13]

In a parallel development, James Robinson III, chief executive officer of American Express, was pushing for the establishment of an international agency to solve the problem of Third World nations that were indebted to the world banking system. American Express by 1986 had a potentially life-threatening exposure to loan defaults by less-developed countries through its subsidiary, the American Express Bank. The bank is described in Bryan Burrough's excellent book *Vendetta* as an "odd duck," cobbled together from a mélange of banking licenses accumulated by American Express from before World War I in order to conduct travelers cheque business in places like Pakistan; it operated without any of the normal regulatory oversight because of wrinkles in its charter and a strong executive desire to keep it free from inconvenient shareholder scrutiny. Backed by the enormous and largely unreported float from American Express travelers cheques, it fostered a cowboy culture that encompassed a lot of distinctly odd dealings (it was named, in conjunction with such unsavory partners as BCCI, as a possible money-launderer by the Justice Department in Operation Polar Cap, an investigation of how cocaine profits were transferred from U.S. banks to Latin America). At the time of Robinson's push for an intragovernmental agency, the bank had about $2.3 billion of LDC loans on its books, mostly to Mexico, Brazil, and Argentina. Repayment was uncertain at best; and although the parent company was able to survive without it, its equity was even more seriously damaged by this than by the Firemen's Fund mess of two years earlier.[14]

Exactly what American Express was doing understudying the IMF is a question which remains unanswered in the corporate literature; but Robinson's campaign for an intragovernmental body that could handle the American Express Company's problem was silent until March 1988, when he floated his own foreign-policy initiative in the form of an agency to be titled the Institute for International Debt and Development, or, with a nod to *Star Wars*, I2D2 for short. The plan for the agency, which would write off 40 percent of the existing $250 billion in developing-country debt, was met with contumely by bankers and the Washington establishment. John Reed, chairman of Citicorp, accused Robinson of trying to destroy the banking system with a reckless proposal. James Baker, who had resigned as Ronald Reagan's treasury secretary to head the George Bush campaign and had warned Robinson that Bush aides had their own plan, dressed him down for megalomania.[15]

Although Robinson's attempt, which perhaps foresaw his exit from American Express and a need to reinvent himself, proved ultimately unsuccessful, American Express became embedded in the World Bank through its subsidization of the World Monuments Fund. By the privatization-happy 1990s, some of Amex's former executives would be advising the United Nations. The Bush plan resurfaced in the Brady bond, which recast the troubled countries as emerging markets, and at the Madrid Summit in 1990, in a plan to bring democracy (and foreign-exchange earnings) to LDCs through the development of tourism.

After the Russian, Thailand, and Indonesian economies crashed between 1997 and 1998, the well of investors once again ran dry. Yet the World Bank's affiliates continued to promote the idea of emerging-market funds as the instrument to lean on when direct foreign investment in hotels and other tourist projects failed, no matter what the political cost in stock-market panic might be. According to economists, panic is simply part of a natural cycle in the rise of emerging markets, which they regard as entrenched and inevitable. Eventually, the theory goes, enough money will stick to make the periodic busts less catastrophic and provide a stable base to grow the economy; despite evidence in Russia and elsewhere that money usually vanishes into the black hole of corruption. The bank initiated an anticorruption campaign in 1999 when an audit by PricewaterhouseCoopers revealed misuses of bank funds in Haiti, Indonesia, and Thailand, among other countries. The bank tempered its introduction of measures for more transparent accounting with the caveat that too much bureaucratic control impairs the confidence of the business community.[16]

In the summer of 1999, the IMF and the United States held up a $640 million IMF loan to Russia because of allegations that foreign aid to Moscow might have been misused and funneled through accounts at the Bank of New York, the subject of a money-laundering investigation. An unpublished independent audit, also prepared by PricewaterhouseCoopers at the IMF's behest, concluded that the Russian Central Bank had indeed misled the IMF about important economic data regarding its use of offshore subsidiaries but hadn't actually stolen IMF money, thereby opening the way to give the bank the $640 million. However, the PricewaterhouseCoopers team did find evidence of misreporting of foreign-currency reserves in 1996 when the IMF and Russia were discussing a $10.1 billion loan that later fell apart. The auditors concluded that subsidiaries had invested in Russian assets, then asked the central bank to cover their investments. That meant that the money, somewhere between $100 million and $200 million, was no longer available to the central bank in case of an emergency.

In separate probes linked to the Russian money-laundering scandal, the World Bank investigated whether Leonid Grigoriev, a senior member of Russia's World Bank mission in Moscow from 1992 to 1997, provided Moscow-based Inkombank with tips on debt-market investment by leaking the intentions of the World Bank and the IMF. Grigoriev, director of a World Bank–funded think tank known as the Bureau of Economic Analysis, had predicted that Inkombank would make a 40 percent profit if it invested $10 million in defaulted Soviet-era debt, which at the time was fluctuating wildly because of speculations that the IMF was considering a restructuring deal. Two weeks after Grigoriev wrote his memo, Inkombank negotiated a buy option on $5 million, although it remains unclear whether that option was exercised.

Investigators also suspected Konstantin Kagalovsky, Russia's representative to the IMF from 1992 to 1995, when the Clinton administration was deeply involved in IMF lending to Russia, of engineering the diversion of millions of dollars through the Bank of New York accounts. Tendrils of the scandal reached close to Vice-President Al Gore, chairman of a joint commission on bilateral ties with former Russian Prime Minister Viktor Chernomyrdin, depriving Gore of a foreign-policy credential he had hoped would be an asset in his presidential campaign. The Bank of New York money-laundering probe included allegations that profits earned by Russia's international air carrier, Aeroflot, were skimmed off by a Swiss-based firm named Andava for the benefit of officials close to Russian president Boris Yeltsin.[17]

Tourism and emerging-market investment are strongly analogous if not interchangeable: tourism is used as a stimulus to emerging-market investment and is also a form of that investment. The World Bank continues to throw money at tourism on a region-by-region basis despite what officials other than Ian Christie describe as a "checkered" loan-repayment history, including a high percentage of reschedulings. Bank officials claim that no exact statistics are available. However, a search of the bank's library archive yielded some specific examples. (I arrived in Washington to use the library and conduct interviews around the time of the PricewaterhouseCoopers investigation. As I conducted my library search, the documents I was searching kept breaking up onscreen. A librarian explained that the "Image Bank" computer system in which all the documents were stored was being reconfigured. This did not explain why a character named Jeeves kept popping onscreen to ask me if I wanted to look at pictures of bare-naked ladies. I did not, and found a sympathetic librarian who retrieved some of the necessary documents on paper.)

In 1996 the bank signed off on $42 million for the reforestation of Croatia on the assurance that, because of the cease-fire, tourism would recover and the risk of "conflict-related damage" was small. In 1997 the bank loaned $600 million to finance the reconstruction of Lebanon, with hotels and other tourism-related projects a priority. The reconstruction of downtown Beirut alone, an area of almost a square mile, is one of the largest construction projects in the world and, like much of the rest of Beirut's new construction, was undertaken by Solidère, a company the World Bank called an "innovative partnership" between the public and private sectors. Most Lebanese consider Solidère to be the private property of Rafik Hariri, at that time the president of Lebanon. Hariri, who left office in 1998 in circumstances which are still unclear, is rated as one of the world's wealthiest men by *Forbes* magazine. A Solidère representative interviewed in Beirut denied that Solidère had been loaned any World Bank funds. "We are a private company," he said. At the time of my visit to Lebanon in May 1999, the government of the new Lebanese president, Emile Lahoud, had halted construction on the Solidère project because of a dispute over the misuse of government funds during Hariri's presidency. Hariri had been asked to give back monies missing from the treasury, and was litigating the matter.[18]

The World Bank also loaned $300 million to Thailand in 1998 for "social investment." Seventy-five million of the loan is earmarked for the Tourism Authority of Thailand. According to human-rights activists (UNICEF among them), the backbone of the Thai tourist industry is sex tourism, with as many as 2 million prostitutes estimated to be working in the country today. The World Bank loan targets $3.2 million for reeducating "disadvantaged women," funds which will reach approximately ten thousand women. Critics of World Bank policy say that the bank's support of tourism in Thailand really supports prostitution.

Bank officials counter that it is extremely difficult to get coordinated figures on the total level of World Bank support of tourism today. Ian Christie claimed that "less than 1 percent" of the World Bank's portfolio is currently invested in tourism. Carolyn Cain, an officer of the International Finance Corporation, estimates its current tourism portfolio at about $450 million, spread over eighty-five projects, or $50–$100 million over twelve to twenty projects a year. Potential projects are judged on both their "development impact"—whether they can create new jobs, become sources of tax revenues, or "pioneer new destinations"—and on their chances of commercial success. The bank acknowledges that the element of commercial risk is high. "It's a very risky business," Cain said. "Yes, it is recessionary. Yes, it gets hit hard by natural disasters, and other things we have no control over. We don't think it should be the only thing a country is invested in. But if natural advantages are all you have, that's all you can do."[19]

The bank also supports tourism through the World Monuments Fund. According to World Bank literature, the fund was set up in 1965 as a private, nonprofit organization for the conservation of cultural heritages. Currently, the fund is involved with sixty-two projects in forty-six countries, including the preservation of Angkor Wat, an enterprise that figured in the Cambodian dictator Hun Sen's decision to hold "free" elections. The World Monuments Watch, launched in 1995 to celebrate the fund's thirtieth anniversary (which fell fortuitously as the peace process gathered steam), identifies imperiled cultural sites and leverages financial and technical support for their preservation. The World Monuments Watch is heavily subsidized by American Express and carries the imprimatur of James Robinson's attempts in the mid-1980s to set up an intragovernmental agency to deal with the problem of Third World debt.

Other officials say that tourism projects are difficult to implement, because of both the familiar "image" problems of corruption, prostitution, and the like, and the difficulties in dealing with unfamiliar ministries and issues of defense, protectionism, and other matters. The IFC now hires "quantity surveyors" (a British term for an outside consultant who gives an independent opinion on costs) to combat corruption. By mandate, it is not allowed to invest in government partnerships, but in countries like Vietnam or Russia, where all land and other assets are still owned by the state, this is hard to avoid. The IFC makes an effort to fund "sustainable tourism" according to strict environmental guidelines. One recent hotel project in Fiji, for example, required the hotelier to run a new sewage line all the way from his hotel to a distant treatment plant, thereby hooking up all the villages along the way. But once a project is accepted, the IFC does not "micromanage." "It's up to them to pull it off," Cain said.

Tourism statistics are notoriously weak for a number of reasons. Governments, the principal suppliers of data, are slow to publish them and are apt, in Cuba for example, to inflate the numbers if they wish to stimulate growth. In addition, government figures, which specifically measure traffic and expenditure as they relate to transport, trade, and balance of payments, are often incompatible with industry figures, which reflect market information. There is little or no coordination between the public and the private sector except on an ad-hoc basis, usually through sampling bases that may or may not reflect instability, with the result that figures lag behind reality by a year or more.[20]

The porous nature of tourism figures leaves them open to abuse, and there is evidence to suggest that the World Bank's advocacy has contributed to its credibility problems. In 1999 the World Bank halted a $50 million loan for road construction in Haiti because of mismanagement and suspected corruption. (Transport infrastructure comes under the general heading of tourism according to Robert McNamara's working paper.) The loan program was quietly suspended after PricewaterhouseCoopers investigators uncovered major irregularities in awarding contracts, but by that time the bank had already disbursed about $23 million. Despite pledges for more openness by President

James Wolfensohn, the bank kept the embarrassing disclosures quiet for some time because of the additional pressure of revelations that it had overlooked or even encouraged mismanagement.

Although PricewaterhouseCoopers has focused its investigation on Haitian government officials, the company is also examining the bank's internal failures to follow its own guidelines, including approving a contract with a French engineering firm that more than quadrupled its fees. The U.S. Congress has brought intense pressure to bear on reforming both the World Bank and the IMF after these and other scandals such as failed lending programs in Russia and Ukraine. The suggested reforms involve phasing out loans to countries with access to private finance.[21]

(The hotel business offers an excellent vehicle for money-laundering to those who are so inclined. John le Carré, the doyen of the modern spy novel and possibly one of the best commentators on the postwar world, provides a highly entertaining description of exactly how this is done in his post-glasnost novel, *The Tailor of Panama*.

> "The hotel belongs to a certain consortium, which has its headquarters in Madrid, Andy."
>
> "So?"
>
> "*So*. Rumor has it that this consortium belongs to some Colombian gentleman not totally unconnected with the cocaine trade, doesn't it? This consortium is doing nicely, you'll be pleased to hear. A posh new place in Chitre, another going up in David, two in Boca del Toro, and Rafi Domingo hops between them in his plane like a cricket in a frying-pan."
>
> "Hell for?"
>
> "We may only guess, Andy. Rafi doesn't know the hotel business from his elbow, which is not a problem because, like I told you, the hotels don't take guests. They don't advertise and if you try to book a room, you'll be politely told they're full up."
>
> "Don't get it."
>
> "Each hotel banks five thousand dollars a day cash, right? A financial year or two from now, as soon as the hotels have notched up a healthy set of accounts, they'll be sold off to the highest bidder, who by coincidence will be Rafi Domingo wearing a different company hat. The hotels will be in excellent order throughout, which is not surprising seeing they haven't been slept in and there's not one hamburger been cooked in the kitchen. And they'll be legitimate businesses, because in Panama three-year-old money is not just respectable, it's antique."[22]

That this form of "encouraging prospects for growth," while perhaps not quite what the IFC had in mind, is not a figment of le Carré's imagination is documented in a 1995 article in the *Wall Street Journal* describing a luxurious complex of hotels on Zanzibar, one of the Spice Islands off the coast of Tanzania noted for the beauty of its architecture and its historical relationship to the Persian Gulf. The complex, complete down to the last extravagant detail, was also completely innocent of guests. The article noted the popularity of the hotel business to money-launderers, who use it to "smurf," that is, to break down large sums of money into small [or smallish] bank deposits. Today, the hotels are respectably booked, and Zanzibar has become a gem of African tourism.)

Sometimes it is difficult to avoid the impression that the bank is out of good development ideas. "We're owned by our [member] countries," said Cain. "That's what governments want. There's not a lot else you can do in some of these countries."

Many of "these countries" are in Africa, where tourism is considered essential in the evolutionary scale of development. This largely consists of *Roots*-style tourism for black American visitors to Senegal and Ghana, wildlife or ecotourism in eastern and southern Africa (notably Victoria Falls in Zimbabwe and Kruger National Park in South Africa), and "cultural" tourism in the archaeologically rich areas of northern Africa like Egypt, Tunisia, and Morocco. Bank officials are quick to say that "no way" can the bank directly finance tourism, but it does have up to $10 million on its books in loans for various hotel and infrastructure coventures in the region out of a total loan portfolio of approximately $20 billion. "The argument is to provide the right incentives, and private investors will follow," said Ian Christie, who wrote the bank's private-sector strategy for Africa, adding that tourism is only part of a diversified growth strategy, which encompasses mining, agroprocessing, local participation in infrastructure projects such as toll roads and railways, and manufacturing. "The big issue in Africa is, should African development be based on its own resource base or should we import manufacturing based on low wages?" In either event, Christie explained, the bank's concern is to support the country's overall growth strategy rather than to limit its options to tourism—although he is bullish on the latter and predicts that the bank will move back aggressively into the tourism sector. "When we come back into tourism, it will be in ecotourism, in second-generation reforms to get the costs down, in better infrastructure and attracting more private investment, projecting a better image of Africa as a good business address."

In 1999 Africa was heavily promoted as "the millennial tourism destination" by the African Travel Association and other travel groups: significantly, when the head of one of the world's most influential lobbying organizations, the World Travel and Tourism Council (WTTC), announced his resignation, it was to work in Africa. The executive's bad move may indicate crisis mode: unfortunately, African countries do not have the time to wait for a "diversified growth strategy" to take hold. Prices for their primary commodities—coffee, gold, oil, and other raw materials—have fallen 75 percent since the beginning of the 1990s and are likely to continue to remain there or even to slide farther as long as inflation rates remain low in the industrialized world. And at the same time that Africa is being promoted as the world's millennial tourism destination, social unrest that will inevitably affect tourism earnings appears to be increasing.

The steep drop in gold prices has provoked heavy if organized protest in areas like Ghana, where goldmining has been a way of life for centuries: top officials of Anglo-American Gold, the world's largest gold producer and the most important player in the region, lobbied Washington to stop the IMF from selling its gold reserves to fund debt relief in Africa and other countries that have difficulty in meeting their repayment schedules, on the grounds that sales would prompt a further slide in gold prices and thus hurt the very people they were intended to help. A heavy police presence is already evident in high-end tourist spots like the Ritz-Carlton in downtown Johannesburg, where there have been sporadic outbursts of violence directed at tourists. Tourists have been attacked on the beaches of Mombasa, Kenya, and murdered in Bwindi National Park, Uganda, where, although rebel Hutus took responsibility for the slaying, local resentment over having been forced out of traditional farming and timbering industries by tourism appears to be part of the problem.

Officials say that the best control is "information management," their term for belaboring the local population with the obvious fact that if the tourists go home, so will their incomes. But it can be difficult to convince hungry and resentful people of the value of good public relations, despite the conviction of bank officials that tourism, like emerging markets, is here to stay. And tourism, like so many of the big economic bets of the 1990s, is dependent on the health of the U.S. stock market, which in turn depends at least in part on low commodities prices. When asked if the First World was buying its heady stock-market gains at the expense of the Third World and its commodities exports, Christie replied, "Well . . . yes."

Politicians come and go like the wind, but there will always be virgins.

John Sayles, Los Gusanos

While sex may not be the first thing that springs to mind at the words *World Bank*, one form of tourism that is downturn-proof is sex tourism. It is evident that as public-sector funds have accrued to build the business of tourism worldwide, the business of sex tourism, also worldwide, has ridden on its back, so to speak. The international sex industry is today estimated at $20 billion on the low end, including everything from prostitution to virtual sex on the Internet, which is, interestingly, both a rival and an accessory to physical sex tourism. Sex tourism makes up a large part of the tourism industry. Because sex tourism is illegal in many places, there are no precise estimates on the number of "tourist arrivals," the workers who service them, or the amount of money changing hands. But the business is ubiquitous, growing as rapidly as legitimate tourism and fed by many of the same sources. Like AIDS, it has spread from regions where histories of colonial oppression and poverty make a tolerable excuse for it to infect prosperous First World countries, where younger and younger children of both sexes are now being bartered.

The development of sex tourism into a multibillion-dollar international industry follows roughly the same trajectory as that of legitimate tourism. Although the historical connection between military bases and prostitution goes back to the late eighteenth century, the emergence of large-scale sex tourism coincided with the establishment of "rest and recreation" facilities for American G.I.s during World War II, the Korean War, and the Vietnam War. Cheap airfares and the opening of airports in Indonesia and other Asian destinations made longer excursions more popular in the 1970s, which in turn made Thailand, South Korea, Sri Lanka, and the Philippines the world's premier sex tourism destinations, with Vietnam, Cambodia, and Cuba now entering the competition.

Thailand in particular has become known as the world's sexual Disneyland. Figures range wildly because prostitution is technically illegal there: however, a deputy minister is on record as a booster. In 1990 police figures indicated that 100,000 underage girls were involved in the flesh trade; the Center for the Protection of Children's Rights in Bangkok estimated their number at 800,000. The Ecumenical Council for Third World Tourism cited a figure of two million for total sex-industry workers, including children of both sexes and adults. Some Thai social workers say female prostitutes alone number two million, or 13 percent of the total female labor force. End Child Prostitution, Child Pornography, and Trafficking in Children for Sexual Purposes (ECPAT), another human rights advocate, claims that more recent figures are unavailable because governments do not fund such research. The high-end figures are probably closest to the mark: as one World Health Organization official (who preferred to remain anonymous) remarked to me, "It's really very difficult to present a convincing argument to a rural mother whose annual income is eight thousand baht that selling her daughter to a brothel recruiter will leave the girl any worse off than she would be at home."[23]

As the former Soviet Union opened up and became a fashionable visiting place in the late 1980s, it flooded the world with desperate "Natashas," willing to do anything to get out of their miserable circumstances. In 1990, when I took the hydrofoil from Helsinki to Taillinn after finishing my glasnost junket, the bars in the business hotels built by crafty Finns who had also built Estonia's offshore banking system were already filled with half-starved fourteen-year-olds in thin white sleeveless dresses: when the black light in the bars hit the white dresses, the edges of their underwear lit up in a beacon of advertisement. Today, the beautiful medieval city of Taillinn is known as one of the world's underage sex capitals. "Russian prostitute" is almost a tautology, and the Russian "mafiyeh," with its worldwide dominance of the flesh trade, has replaced the Evil Empire.

Many, particularly those in academic circles, see a direct linkage between Robert McNamara, the World Bank, and the globalization of the sex biz. McNamara, of course, unilaterally detested by Vietnam antiwar activists, was secretary of defense when the U.S. military signed an "R & R" contract with Thailand in 1967, and flotillas of troopships hove into Thai ports in search of the brothels, bars, and massage parlors that sprang up like mushrooms on demand. McNamara subsequently moved on to the presidency of the World Bank, where he "urged Thailand to supplement its export activities with an all-out effort to attract rich foreigners to the country's various tourist facilities." Many commentators feel that McNamara must have been aware of the Thai sex industry, and that this awareness was a factor in the thinking of World Bank economists who assisted Thailand in creating a National Plan of Tourist Development in 1971 as way for the country to pay off its debts to the bank for agricultural loans. As one World Bank official, speaking under condition of anonymity, wondered, "Is that something the Bank should have been on top of, or just a social problem we can't do anything about? One culture getting to know another certainly is good. I remember a lot of young Tunisian men wanted to make contact with European women, back in the age of instant gratification in the 1970s. Now we're in the age of HIV, and the Thai Health minister has to wander around town tossing water-filled condoms right and left."[24]

Ironically, Japanese businessmen replaced U.S. servicemen as the next wave of sex tourists, taking advantage of bargain rates engineered by government design through the creation of package tours. As part of a major bid for the international tourist trade, according to the Ecumenical Coalition on Third World Tourism, Deputy Minister of Thailand Boonchoo Rojanasathian in a 1980 speech urged provincial governors "to consider the natural scenery in your provinces together with some forms of entertainment you might consider disgusting or shameful, because they are forms of sexual entertainment that attract tourists. We have to consider the jobs that will be created."[25]

It worked. In 1980, 1.8 million tourists spent a total of $700 million. By 1986 the number of tourists had increased more than 50 percent, to 2.8 million, and spending had almost doubled, to $1.5 billion. More than five million tourists visited Thailand in 1990, and spending increased to $4.5 billion. The sex industry by then accounted for 10 percent of Thailand's GDP, only $500 million less than all agricultural export income. (Most visitors to Thailand are men.) Tourist earnings, of course, became the largest foreign-exchange earner, reducing the trade deficit by almost half.[26]

In this sense, the effort to achieve democratization by growing the economy through tourism dollars has resulted in its opposite, a peculiarly ugly form of neocolonialism. As Prof. Prawase Wasi of the Ecumenical Council on Third World Tourism succinctly put it, "It is ironic that while Thailand is claiming to be a NIC (Newly Industrialized Country), it is also a PIC (Prostitution Industrialized Country)."[27]

The response from Third World recipients of World Bank and IMF planning has been in many instances, a resounding "No, thank you!" with country after country making a direct connection between mass development of tourism and prostitution, particularly and sadly, child prostitution. The following complaints are all taken from position papers given at the Ecumenical Coalition on Third World Tourism, held in Bangkok in 1990:

> The nature and character of modern tourism centers around the
> unquenchable thirst for profit and the sexual gratification of men from

the First World. As such, tourism cannot but breed and perpetuate the prostitution of deprived and dispossessed women and children of the Third World. The Philippine government has been pursuing a development program on tourism for more than twelve years. Because of this tourism drive, the Philippines exists as one of the flesh capitals in Asia, where even children are prostituted.

Philippines Steering Committee

Tourism is the main reason why prostitution is highlighted along with the name of Thailand. . . . The Thai government has been promoting tourism as the main foreign exchange earner for the country. There are two prongs to this policy: one, to sell the physical and cultural beauty of the country. The other, to sell the "service attraction" of the Thai people. The "service attraction" inescapably includes the sex-related services. The expansion to include children in the sex trade is possible because of the degeneration of adults who profit from such trade. The frightening thing is the fact that all the elements involved have cooperated with and, in some cases, become part of state power.

Thai Steering Committee

In the early halcyonic days of increasing tourist arrivals and the euphoria this brought with it, tourism was hailed as the liberator of the economy, which had been tied for more than a century to the tea export trade and the plantation industries. A time was visualized when tourism would replace tea as the main earner of foreign exchange for the country. The sensitivity of the industry, however, was well proven by its dramatic decrease from the time of the communal disturbances of 1983 until the present, when those disturbances have escalated almost to the proportions of civil war.

In those early days of tourism, too little thought was given to the expansion in the number of arrivals in the country. On legitimate tourist visas, a new brand of tourist became increasingly common, the homosexuals and paedophiles—a direct result of tourism growth in a global context.

Sri Lanka Steering Committee

And, from Amartya Sen's native India:

It is no great secret that the number of massage parlors and health clubs that have mushroomed in Goa hotels are only fronts for organized prostitution rackets, and that Middle Eastern tourists will visit Bombay in hordes largely for sexual gratification. A new development has been the influx of Japanese investment in the tourism sector, ostensibly for cultural tourism. But a recent advertisement in major Indian newspapers forces us to question the kind of cultural inputs for which the Japanese are looking.

Despite widespread evidence that mass recreational tourism fuels prostitution, our government has firmly set its sights on precisely this kind of tourism. Given the existence of a highly organized underground racket in prostitution there is little reason to blindly ignore future consequences.

For the government, however, the lure of the short-term foreign exchange gain seems far more promising than attempts to remedy the causative factors of poverty, inequality, and justice in our political economy.[28]

It is no coincidence that the rapid emergence of prostitution as a multinational growth industry has paralleled that of tourism in the 1990s. Sex, after all, is the original cheap vacation. Its industrialization fits altogether too neatly into the same problem set that created development economics: the single-crop economy. As more traditional commodities, such as sugar, rice, rubber, or even oil, prove unreliable sources of income in the global commodities market, it becomes increasingly tempting for governments to rely on the quick fix of tourist dollars by whatever means. (In 1999 the World Bank published a report indicating that global commodity prices may never fully recover from their historic lows of 1997–1998, with "far-reaching consequences for emerging economies." Although certain commodity prices, notably oil, had recovered by 30 percent at year's end, it is by no means certain whether they will continue to do so, or with what consequences for the U.S. stock market.)[29]

Absent a coherent business structure, as in post-glasnost Russia, organized crime may look better than no organization at all. In Thailand, observers say that the success of the sex industry is based on the shared interests of a network of military leaders, police officials, business-tour promoters, "godfathers," and pimps. In other countries, like Cuba, the military have doffed their uniforms and marched straight into executive positions in the tourist industry, considered a privilege because of its access to goods, dollars, foreigners, and free travel. The relationship of military power to prostitution is particularly easy to understand in Cuba, where, despite frequent roundups and Castro's protestations that socialism and prostitution do not mix, the hotels still teem with underage hookers. As one sex-industry worker remarked, "If he [Castro] really wanted to, he could close us all down tomorrow."

Castro's remarks on prostitution tend to vary with the state of Cuba's economy. Before 1991, when aid and oil were still flowing from the soon-to-be-former Soviet Union, Castro ran strident anti-vice campaigns that denounced prostitution as the tool of capitalism. In 1993, after the Soviet economy collapsed and the Cuban government worked round-the-clock to develop tourism as a replacement for the lost subsidies, Castro remarked, "Thanks to socialism, Cuban girls must make the cleanest and best-educated prostitutes in the world." In 1996, when it became clear that sex tourism would choke off higher-end tourism such as family groups in Cuba, prostitution once more became incompatible with socialism as President Castro asserted, "We don't want the image of a country of gambling, drugs, and prostitution."[30]

Other afflictions of developing countries, such as brushfire wars, the impoverishment of rural economies, and the migration of village youth to the cities, where they swell the supply of cheap, unskilled labor, all combine to make prostitution flourish in the same climate as tourism. In Cuba one male hustler told me that the war in Angola had created a shortage of Cuban men, making it easy for a man to have a wife and several mistresses or girlfriends, who, owing to the "economic need of the Revolution," would be better off fully employed as *jineteras* (literally, jockeys), or female hustlers, than remaining idle at home. Some commentators go so far as to blame national and international economic planning for intentionally prostituting entire nations by exacerbating these weaknesses, undermining traditional patterns of land ownership, implementing deforestation schemes, denying family farm credits, and manipulating water and irrigation policies.

Although this seems far-fetched, it is true that tourism has crowded out other traditional rural ways of earning a living, to the point where its overdevelopment may eventually threaten the world's food-gathering system. In Ireland, probably the most successful example of a tourism-driven economy, tourism has displaced agriculture as the country's leading industry since GATT farming subsidies have been steered toward large European Union (E.U.) members with more clout, such as France and Germany. Fishing, the agriculture of the sea and a way of life for centuries, has also been edged out largely due to E.U. politics: the tuna fishers of western Ireland have for years waged war with those of Spain. In the west, the displaced farmers are competing to operate bed-and-breakfasts, often with comic results, such as the woman who persists in speaking Gaelic to her Japanese guests. The locus of political power has shifted from the country to the city as the money in farming dries up and the young move to Dublin and Galway in search of jobs. Fifty percent of the population is now under twenty-five, and they are the first generation not to emigrate. It is the daunting task of the governments of both the North and the South to provide these young people with jobs. Not surprisingly, prostitution in Dublin is sharply on the rise.

Ireland is fortunate in that its highly educated, English-speaking population is attractive to legitimate businesses like banks and telemarketers, who can hire cut-rate MBAs for offshore outsourcing. For countries like Cuba, where there is a considerable language barrier and where service is still a foreign concept, tourism-fed prostitution is a crutch which will prove difficult if not impossible to lay aside. It is not far-fetched to assume that in countries, like Cuba, that tend to have machismo-driven cultures, dependence on prostitution exacerbates preexisting hostilities: in Sri Lanka, where sex tourists are predominantly not only pedophiles but homosexuals to boot, sex tourism may have something to do with the savagery of the attacks on tourists in recent years.

All of the countries in the study by the Ecumenical Council for Third World Tourism pointed the finger at the World Bank and the IMF for promoting the industry without a concern for how tourists spent their money as long as they spent it, for, in effect, taking from the rich to give to the poor so that they could acquire more foreign exchange to buy technology from the rich. In this view, governments of poor countries cannot afford not to take advantage of the money from tourism because they must earn ever more income to pay foreign debts, to feed their corrupt and inefficient bureaucracies, and to buy more war toys for their military. It is the perfect Schumpeterian Catch-22, nowhere more evident than in the fact that the United Nations, which created the mess in the first place (see Chapter 4), can now keep people permanently employed in cleaning it up.

Although the international community has paid increasing attention to the problem of sexual exploitation, particularly the sexual exploitation of children, advocates say that enforcement is still weak. The United Nations Convention on the Rights of the Child, adopted in 1989, explicitly prohibits the exploitation of children in prostitution and in other illegal sexual practices. The more recent Draft Optional Protocol to the United Nations Convention on the Rights of the Child Concerning the Elimination of Sexual Exploitation and Trafficking of Children, an Australian and French–sponsored protocol adopted in 1994, designates the crimes of child sexual exploitation that are so common in sex tourism as crimes against humanity. In 1990, ECPAT was formed in Thailand to influence the government to eliminate tourist-related prostitution and to comply with international conventions. But both ECPAT and UNICEF, the other nongovernmental organization most closely associated with anti–sex tourism educational and legislative campaigns, admit that they rely on the goodwill of the countries in which they operate and are thus relatively powerless. "The child has no political power," sighed Carole Smollensky, executive director of ECPAT-USA. The World Bank can take no punitive measures against countries that promote sex tourism: officials say this falls under the umbrella of "micromanagement."[31]

In the late 1990s several industrialized countries promulgated legal measures to prevent child-sex tourism and to make child-sex tourists, as well as those who operate sex tours, liable to prosecution on their home soil. Sweden has investigated a Swedish sex tourist under a law that allows the prosecution of Swedish citizens who engage in illegal activities abroad. Australia recently passed legislation directed at child-sex tourists. The United States passed similar legislation in 1994, when President Clinton signed into law the Violent Crime Control and Law Enforcement Act, which includes the Child Sex Abuse Prevention Act criminalizing travel to another country for the purpose of engaging in sexual intercourse with a minor. But most prosecuted sex tourists have thus far evaded punishment, and the Internet continues to teem with advertisements for sex tours featuring ever younger children.

Hotels in the Pacific Rim area (notably in Singapore, which is not mentioned in ECPAT's literature as a particular problem spot) have initiated training programs aimed at providing hotel employment for youths who might otherwise be attracted to prostitution. But they will have to offer wages commensurate with the wages of sin to make their argument a convincing one.

Following the collapse of the Iron Curtain, tourism played a major role in filling the vacuum left by cutbacks in defense spending. Its American advocates claim, as they have since the early years of the twentieth century, that it has become an important part in the complicated machinery of democratization itself. Because of the dominant role played by the United States in the postwar reconstruction era, tourism has become an all-purpose development tool for the United Nations, the World Bank, and the International Monetary Fund. The argument advanced in reams of minutes of the United Nation's Orwellian-sounding EcoSoc (Economic and Social Council) is that tourist money—meaning dollars—equals economic growth, and economic growth equals democracy. However, recipients of such largess often complain that it is nothing more than a quick fix for desperate or corrupt governments which don't have time to address such underlying economic factors as poverty and injustice. The real beneficiaries appear to be the international lending institutions themselves (who are eager for their debts to be paid off as quickly as possible) and the powerful multinational corporations, most notably American Express, who invest in tourism. These relationships are so intertwined that American Express is by now embedded in the World Bank.

Although the World Bank claims that tourism provides a useful way to diversify foreign-exchange earnings, there is ample evidence in Bali, Thailand, Cuba, and other parts of the Caribbean to suggest that because of its heavy consumption of often scant resources and labor, tourism simply replaces one single-crop economy with another. In traditional rural economies, tourism may even aggravate underlying causes of poverty by forcibly redistributing land use and displacing large populations from the country to the city, thus ultimately exaggerating the very inequalities it seeks to address. In Bwindi National Park, Uganda, where eight tourists and a guide were killed by tribesmen in 1999, a local who was driven off his family farm by the creation of a gorilla park that exacerbated tribal land disputes said that he would return to his original way of life if he had the choice. If diversification is truly the goal, it might make more sense to let him do so—to help him to become better at producing more of the commodities he's good at. (Another sensible diversification strategy would be to support the kind of heavy industry that the First World is less and less willing to do, such as mining; but that would spoil the landscape for eco-tourism—and for the·oligarchies of large landholders, who still control certain governments, such as Panama.)[32]

However, if the price of that farmer's commodities is allowed to rise, thus producing inflation, the U.S. stock market and other markets will fall, a connection that leads one to wonder whether the kind of democratization produced by tourism isn't just another form of neo-colonialism.

In the Clinton years, tourism, in the service of the peace process, has become the most powerful vehicle of trade versus aid. Its earnings, as ebullient as those of the stock market to which it is inexorably linked, have been used extensively by developing countries as an all-purpose panacea to service existing debt and facilitate new investment; to provide foreign exchange for international trade as well as convertible currency, not to mention jobs for the high proportion of unemployed youth. But whether economic growth equals political stability remains to be seen.

The negative argument, as Bill Rolston sets out in his excellent essay on the state of the "union" in Northern Ireland after the introduction of reforms initiated by the civil rights struggle of the late 1960s, is that reformism (tourism in the service of democratization) can and often does aggravate the antidemocratic elements in a preexisting structure. Thus legitimate housing reforms enacted to redress inequities between Protestant and Catholic public housing allocations in Northern Ireland are coopted by the Royal Ulster Constabulary to become a form of crowd control. Thus aid monies sent to Russia and Lebanon end up lining the pockets of billionaires; and thus gambling casinos are planned in "innovative" public-private partnerships. The success of the reform depends on which is stronger: the need for reform or the need of the entrenched power structure to remain entrenched. As the soldiers of democracy optimistically tackle previously nondemocratic countries with tourism and foreign aid as their heaviest artillery, the answer to that question is by no means certain.[33]

In places like Cuba, where foreign exchange is desperately needed, the government has supported sex tourism very much against the well-being of its citizens. In Cuba also, where food supplies are scarce, government support of tourism has reduced Cuban citizens to cadging meals from tourists. Naturally enough, with these manifestations of tourism comes crime, relatively unknown in Cuba until the 1990s. The heavy police, and in some instances military, presence needed to ensure the safety of tourists in the places that need tourists most—Cuba, southern Turkey, Cape Town, and Johannesburg—means that certain regimes may become less rather than more democratic in order to protect their tourist trade. The adaptability of tourism to various forms of money-laundering may mean the introduction of organized crime to countries without the means of fighting it. Even international banking institutions which support tourism, like the American Express Bank or the World Bank itself, may not be immune.

Despite widespread corruption and other flaws, there is still a good argument to be made in favor of investing aid money in the kind of insider-owned hard-currency earners that tourism represents. In the expansionary era of the nineteenth-century robber barons, the United States was rife with corruption; so were the Pacific Rim countries when they were held out to the world in the early 1980s as miracles of rapid progress. In both cases, great growth was made possible at the same time as great thievery because corrupt officials and businessmen invested in their own emerging markets; the close and corrupt relationship between government and business made such reinvestment more profitable than Swiss bank accounts. But in many if not most countries that have used tourism to "open up" in the 1990s, from Russia to Cuba to Lebanon, the profiteers have sent their profits to foreign banks. If tourism is truly to be an engine for growth and not just another colonial crop like sugar or bananas, some mechanism must be put in place to ensure that the money stays at home.

The best argument in favor of tourism as a development tool is undoubtedly its relative speed: Cuba did manage to turn itself back from the edge in three short years after the collapse of aid from the Soviet Union by opening its doors. "Tourism is part of a diversified growth strategy in many countries," said Ian Christie of the World Bank. More accurately: "In some countries, it is the only opportunity going." But a more varied menu of exit strategies is needed if tourism is not to become as much of a trap as sugar. To suggest, as do some of the economists in charge, that tourism is a springboard to the rapid growth promised by information technology is to ignore the fact that English is not the first language of most LDCs, which will not be lifted by the tide.

The dogma runs that, despite the "inevitability" of periodic set-backs (read: crashes), the rise of emerging markets is inexorable but their risk is extreme. "[The rise] has accelerated the shift towards reliance on market knowledge, tied economies together, become a force for change, and created a major counterbalance to traditional government intervention. Across the developing world, government decision makers now have to worry not only about the domestic impact of their decisions, but also about the reaction of foreign investors. Officials still can, and often do, intervene as they will; they can impose autarkic policies or put up barriers; they can pursue policies that stimulate inflation or create deficits. But they risk engendering a reaction— a speedy exit from their stock markets—that did not exist before."[34]

The business of tourism, integrally linked to that of emerging markets, is more vulnerable to a crash-induced recession than most, with the exception of sex tourism, which, as the Ecumenical Council on Third World Tourism dryly notes, is a safe investment because of the compulsive nature of pedophilia. In a bitter irony, the drop in the ages of child prostitutes only mirrors the drop in other worldwide commodities prices. Pity the country that needs child prostitutes as its heroes. If things get worse, the dependence of this administration on tourism to perform many foreign-policy functions, like its dependence on the stock market to perform many domestic-policy functions, could take its place in history as the Long-Term Capital Management of foreign aid: a Nobel Prize–winning one-way bet in the wrong direction.

CHAPTER 4

Have I Got a Country for You!

Propaganda is the executive arm of the invisible government.
Edward Bernays, Propaganda *(1928)*

IN APRIL 1994, as promises of peace were heard round the world, an article in a small scholarly journal called *Midstream* ignited a startling response from the global public relations firm of Ruder Finn. Written by Yohanan Ramati, director of the Jerusalem Institute for Western Defense, the article detailed what appeared to be an extraordinary effort by the PR giant to manipulate public opinion in order to dictate U.S. policy toward Croatia and Bosnia-Herzegovina. The firm's founding partner David Finn wrote a strenuous denial that not only, ironically, supports Ramati's allegations, it strongly suggests that Ruder Finn usurped the role of the U.S. State Department in these countries.

Such efforts find their source in the vision of Edward Bernays, founder of the modern art of public relations, who hymned the "ability of public relations to bring order out of confusion and social disarray." They also appear in the quest of Nelson Rockefeller, American Express, and others to make democracy the "mission statement" of big business: the bigger the business, the more "making the world safe for democracy" makes that business palatable to shareholders and voters alike. What is new in the Ruder Finn case is scale: the evidence of how powerful a handful of firms, assisted by strategically placed lobbyists and the machinery of globalization, have become in directing the flow of international news and in creating, or re-creating, a school of advocacy journalism resembling that of the nineteenth century, when monopolies ruled uncontested. While this fortified brand of PR is a product of the eminently pragmatic principle that prosperity brings peace, it is alarming in the aftermath of the war in Kosovo to realize how inflammatory such campaigns, driven by commercial concerns like tourism and waged with the skills of advertising rather than diplomacy, can be.

A regular contributor to *Midstream*, which is bankrolled by the Theodore Herzl Foundation and which publishes Daniel Pipes among other foreign policy experts, Ramati quoted an interview with James Harff, then director of Washington-based Ruder Finn Global Public Affairs, in which Harff claims that the firm was hired by the governments of Croatia and Bosnia-Herzegovina to cleanse the image of now-deceased Croatian president Franjo Tudjman of charges of antisemitism and to enlist the sympathy of the Jewish-American public for both the Croatian and Bosnian Islamic regimes. This was accomplished both by heavily lobbying Congress and Vice-President Al Gore and by a publicity campaign that used Holocaust imagery to equate the Serbs with the Nazis. Tudjman, who is on record in his *Wastelands of Historical Reality* as saying, "Genocide is a natural phenomenon; it is not only permitted, it is recommended by the Almighty," was rehabilitated in the eyes of Congress by the opportune discovery that the Nazis had put a price on his head in the murky years of World War II. The relentless drumbeat of propaganda, which ignored the fact that the Serbs actually saved many Jews during World War II while the Croats slaughtered some 30,000 in concentration camps, was accompanied by the gentle patter of touristic panegyrics extolling Croatia's beaches and culture.[1]

In Harff's interview, which originally appeared in a book by Jacques Merlino, he boasts of "outwitting" the B'nai B'rith Anti-Defamation League, the American Jewish Committee, and the American Jewish Congress (all Ruder Finn clients at one time or another). He says that the "game" was won in the former Yugoslavia by playing upon Jewish sensitivities about the Holocaust.

> Nobody understood what was happening in Yugoslavia. The great majority of Americans were probably asking themselves in what African country was Bosnia situated. But by a single move, we were able to present a simple story of good guys and bad guys, which would hereinafter play itself. We won by targeting the Jewish audience. Almost immediately there was a clear change of language in the press, with the use of words with high emotional content such as "ethnic cleansing," "concentration camps," etc., which evoked images of Nazi Germany and the gas chambers of Auschwitz. The emotional charge was so powerful nobody could go against it.[2]

In light of the high financial and diplomatic cost of the Balkan conflict, the possibility that the specter of the Holocaust might have been invoked by Ruder Finn's Global Public Affairs Division as a form of "global branding" is as deeply unsettling as the axiom that those who forget history are condemned to relive it. ("Global branding" is an industry buzzword for the creation of a universally recognized product through familiar imagery. Identifying Serbs with Nazis through images of the Holocaust—which, through overuse, have alas become generic—is a form of global branding.)

The fact that Serbia sheltered a large number of Jews in World War II while Croatia slaughtered tens of thousands in concentration camps, along with even greater numbers of Serbs, was overlooked by Harff's ahistorically minded staff of twenty-somethings, whom he characterized as youthful idealists under the unfamiliar pressure of enemy fire. It was not overlooked by the Israelis, who refrained from criticizing Serbia or supporting NATO when the bombing campaign began in March 1999 because those in senior diplomatic circles felt that the country owed the Serbs something for their behavior during World War II. (Foreign Minister Ariel Sharon, usually a hawk, led the retreat, raising the fear of a greater Albania, united under Islamic rule and supported by Iran. During this time, Sharon led a trade mission to Moscow, which cherishes pan-Slavic political ties to Serbia.)[3]

Following the publication of Ramati's article, David Finn protested that the Merlino interview was fabricated. Harff admitted that the interview had taken place but insisted that the "slant" was fabricated. Joel Carmichael, editor of *Midstream*, backed Ramati. Ruder Finn, which represents a number of Jewish organizations and has been in the vanguard of Holocaust-related PR, threatened legal action, which was never undertaken. However, in his response to *Midstream*, Finn acknowledged that after taking on the government of Croatia as a client in August 1991, his firm organized two congressional delegation visits to Zagreb, briefed President Tudjman on how to address the issue of his antisemitism with Congress, and conducted a "public information program to report to the American public [on] what was happening in Croatia." According to Ruder Finn's research, the genocide-friendly Tudjman actually had impeccable pro-Jewish credentials: not only had the Nazis put a price on his head, but a leading Jewish physician had entrusted him with the care of his son![4]

Finn also detailed his firm's relationship with Bosnia. In early 1992, Ruder Finn shepherded Foreign Minister Haris Silajdiz to emergency sessions of the Organization of Islamic Conference on Bosnia-Herzegovina in Istanbul, the Conference of Security and Cooperation in Helsinki, the London Conference on Former Yugoslavia, and the United Nations General Assembly. In the person of Harff, Ruder Finn helped draft policy statements and participated in private meetings between Silajdiz and former British prime minister Margaret Thatcher, U.S. vice-presidential candidate Senator Al Gore, Saudi Ambassador to the United States Prince Bandar (also a member of the late Ron Brown's Gulf excursion), President George Bush, and U.S. Secretary of State James Baker.

Ramati implies, but does not prove, that the governments of Bosnia-Herzegovina and Croatia were backed by Arab money, U.S. oil companies, or perhaps international banks with interests in Islamic countries. Harff, who left Ruder Finn in 1997 to open his own public relations firm in Washington, complained that he was paid less than $200,000 for several years of work because the campaign did not pay off as anticipated. David Finn described his firm's work for Croatia and Bosnia as "pro bono."

Finn, who worked for army counterintelligence during World War II, has handled many national accounts that have significant intelligence links. His first experience in the former Yugoslavia came during the 1950s, when he organized a peace conference in Belgrade for an outfit called the World Veterans Organization, which he discovered to his astonishment was a front for the CIA.

The number of "sensitive" projects Ruder Finn has handled over the years include engineering PR campaigns for President Kennedy's Nuclear Arms Treaty with the Soviet Union and for Israel during the Six Day War and after; creating a campaign to expand business in Thailand in the 1970s; and inaugurating a disaster-control campaign for United Brands (formerly United Fruit) when its strictly rabbinical CEO committed suicide after he was caught bribing the dictator of Honduras not to raise taxes on Chiquita bananas. National accounts also include the Bahamas during a drug-smuggling scandal, South Africa during apartheid, Zaire under Mobutu, and Iran under the shah.[5]

Today approaching eighty, with the wavy white hair and twinkly spectacles of a country doctor, Finn downplays his role as an éminence grise. "People are very suspicious of this business," he said in an interview in his white office decorated with his own life-size paperclip sculptures. "I've been in it fifty years. I'm aware of its limitations. I've read many books on the spin-doctors and image-making and most of them are silly. I don't know how to doctor a spin. I don't know how to make an image. Walk through our offices and you'll see that we're not the all-powerful people who manage behind the scenes to change the world. We do the best we can to help people articulate who they are, what they stand for and why. I've been arguing against the hidden persuader image of PR all my life, but it still keeps cropping up." ("Hidden persuader" is an allusion to the book of that name on the postwar PR boom by social anthropologist Vance Packard.)

As tourism has become increasingly globalized, with consortia of major airlines, credit card companies, insurers, hoteliers, and entertainment conglomerates, public relations firms have begun to compete fiercely for foreign national accounts in emerging markets such as the former Yugoslavia. In 1997 Porter Novelli International, the top earner among travel specialists, made $13 million from its travel-related accounts. The government of Mexico paid Burson-Marsteller close to $1 million to cleanse its tourism image of charges of corruption, civil unrest, violent crime, and drug trafficking, with a little promotion for the North American Free Trade Agreement (NAFTA) thrown in. Burson-Marsteller's other foreign accounts for 1998 included the government of post-crash Indonesia, the Israel Economic Mission to North America, Saudi Arabia's King Faisal Foundation, and the governments of Norway and Finland, for a grand total of $1.9 million earned in the first quarter. Turkey's account at Fleishman-Hillard was worth $525,000 for the first quarter, until the government dropped the company after journalists worldwide criticized Turkey for imprisoning reporters. The government of New Zealand's tourism account at Saatchi and Saatchi was worth NZ$50 million, until the company was fired in a complicated political scandal.[6]

As a rule, firms are highly secretive about their foreign national accounts, sometimes because their PR tactics are profoundly anti-democratic. Campaigns PR firms have undertaken include burnishing the image of the brutal regime of Cambodian strongman Hun Sen (the Morey Group); promoting "free" elections in Nigeria (Ruder Finn); and cleansing the Bahamas' tourism image of stains accruing from government drug-running scandals (Ruder Finn).

After Hun Sen muscled his way into the 1993 "free" election in Cambodia only to lose his budding tourist trade (not to mention his IMF funding) in a 1997 coup, he hired David Morey, who came recommended by Kim Dae Jung, the leader of South Korea. For the sum of $550,000, Morey and his team of Washington-based lawyer-lobbyists advised Hun Sen to hold another free election. During this election, in August 1998, international observers took note of the killings of opposition-party activists, the bribery, the voter intimidation, and Hun Sen's control of the news media.

The observers approved the election anyway so as not to embarrass the United Nations, which had spent $2 billion to organize elections there after moving in with a massive peace-keeping force in 1991. A spate of articles encouraging travel to Cambodia accompanied the election. "What the coup did was to bring Cambodia to people's attention as a tourist destination," one tour operator said.[7]

In another example of peace-process PR, during the week in August 1994 that the Irish peace was somewhat prematurely declared, a major financial scandal disappeared from the Irish headlines and, to all intents and purposes, was never reported in the United States either, in spite of the fact that it had far-reaching policy implications. Prime Minister Albert Reynolds was under investigation in the Irish courts for accepting a $1 million private loan from the rogue bank BCCI in exchange for granting Irish passports, much prized in certain circles for their neutrality, to eight senior BCCI senior executives. Hill and Knowlton, which handled the BCCI account, did not return my phone call. Reynolds, who with his family has made a handsome living out of suing newspapers and has almost singlehandedly tightened libel law in Ireland so that it is even more draconian than in Great Britain, survived the crisis to be credited with being one of the architects of the peace. Instead of scandal, the newspapers were deluged with rosy reports of Irish culture and tourism.[8]

More recently, in March 1999, the public relations company of Saatchi and Saatchi was fired from a lucrative tourism promotion campaign for New Zealand after the accusation that Minister for Tourism Murray McCully, himself a former public relations expert, had paid more than half a million dollars to remove board members and staff of the national Tourism Board who were hostile to his hidden agenda of ensuring the reelection of the government of Prime Minister Jenny Shipley. The opposition Labor Party claimed that the entire tourism campaign engineered by Saatchi and Saatchi's international chief, Kevin Roberts, was designed to promote the government's reelection through "feel-good" advertising featuring a series of sporting events, including the America's Cup.

Although tourism is in itself a form of public relations in which countries attempt to put their best faces forward for foreign visitors, the "peace process" has politicized travel. As journalist Dan Burstein aptly remarked in his excellent book *Euroquake* on the "battle of the capitalisms" after 1992,

> Travel is integral to European unification. Airline deregulation, high-speed train service linking European downtowns, the "Chunnel" connecting England to the Continent, the Danube Canal project, the end of customs red tape, and the abolition of physical frontiers within the EC are all bolstering the concept of the "free movement of people" enshrined first in the Treaty of Rome and now in the 1992 program.

The explosion in Eastern Europe actually began with "tourism"—East German vacationers using their holidays in Czechoslovakia to escape to Hungary and from there to West Germany. A central demand of East Germany's peaceful revolution was freedom of travel, symbolically epitomized by the right to walk freely across the city of Berlin.[9]

Countries with war-shattered economies now fight for tourist dollars: some travel agencies even justify inflated prices as a form of foreign aid. Many political propaganda blitzes have been tied into tourism campaigns, both as a means of delivery and because tourism has been promoted as a growth business by commercial interests and policymakers alike.

Movies are increasingly regarded as an advertising tool by tourist boards, who see them as a slam-dunk means of popularizing or "branding" their cultures, particularly through historical epics like *Braveheart* (for Scotland) or *Michael Collins* (for Ireland), which also deliver a contemporary political message. "Walk down any street in Santa Monica and people can identify Ireland and Australia through their movies and their movie stars," said Gregg Anderson of the New Zealand Tourist Board, which is launching a "significant effort" to develop the New Zealand entertainment industry. Ireland and Australia (and Canada and Britain) have developed their film industries through munificent tax breaks similar to those enjoyed by the tourist industry. In Ireland, where the government essentially has script control through the highly politicized Irish Film Board, this has led to the films' having a decidedly Republican slant.[10]

From the standpoint of realpolitik, tourism helps advance deeper agendas. Tourism has been heavily supported by financial incentives in the Republic of Ireland and in Croatia, for example, on the principle that the prosperity it brings will encourage combatants to drop their weapons. The relentless drumbeat of anti-Serb propaganda was accompanied by the gentle patter of touristic panegyrics extolling Croatia's beaches and culture. Ironically, the World Bank spent $42 million to reforest Croatia in 1996—right before war broke out again.

In Croatia, Harff worked side by side with Nazli Weiss of the Rebuild Dubrovnik Fund, a pro bono client of Ruder Finn's. The Rebuild Dubrovnik Fund, whose board members include both David Finn and American Express executives, was formed by the American Association of Travel Agents in conjunction with Atlas Travel, the largest travel agency in Croatia, to revive tourism in Dubrovnik. (A $5 billion industry in Dubrovnik before the war, tourism saw its receipts plunge to zero in 1991.) Geoffrey Lipman, current president of the

World Travel and Tourism Council, itself a creation of American Express, is an honorary member of the board of Rebuild Dubrovnik.

Dubrovnik, for centuries the gateway to the East for caravans to Constantinople and for ships all over the world, was beloved of the novelist Rebecca West, who urged, "For an ideal first visit the traveller should go into the city and find the light just faintly blue in the open space that lies inside the gate."[11] Rebuilding the city is noble work, but even in realpolitik terms to misjudge the toxic life of the conflict is to doom a sizable investment. It is also probably a bad call to favor one side (Croatia) of a nasty tribal conflict over another (Serbia) in a seemingly arbitrary fashion.

Harff calls Rebuild Dubrovnik "one of the first collaborations between the preservationists and the travel industry working side by side." This may be true. But it is also true that the campaign made Croatia, whose World War II history is far less noble than Serbia's, into a tourist enclave with World Bank largess at the same time that NATO was attempting to bomb Serbia into good behavior. The logic was similar to that of the reconstruction of Ireland: if the malcontents in Northern Ireland saw the Republic of Ireland's economy take off, its success might induce them to give up their belligerent ways. As Slobodon Milosević's response to NATO bombings illustrated, it was not a pill the Serbs (who in fact identify with the Northern Irish Protestants) could swallow peacefully.

The politics of the situation become even murkier in light of U.S. Sen. Jesse Helms's attack on Richard Holbrooke's nomination to be ambassador to the United Nations. Helms, chairman of the Senate Foreign Relations Committee, accused Holbrooke of having conflicts of interest during his tenure as both a private businessman and a government adviser. Holbrooke was managing director of the New York investment bank Lehman Brothers from 1985 to 1992 when it was owned by American Express. American Express was also deeply involved in loan programs to LDCs at this time, attempting to salvage them by developing an intragovernmental agency, or I2D2. American Express invested in Croatia through Rebuild Dubrovnik and the World Monuments Fund around the time that Holbrooke became a roaming ambassador for the Clinton administration and a central figure in Balkan negotiations.

The mission of Rebuild Dubrovnik was to restore war-damaged buildings and bring back tourism to the Croatian coast. Weiss claims that the fund completed thirteen projects, including rebuilding the main street of Dubrovnik, where the fund restored the facades along the street as well as an elementary school, a synagogue, and, ecumenically, the library of the Franciscan monastery. Weiss says that all of this was accomplished with a mere $450,000 raised through grassroots efforts. Other funding was supplied by "government organizations," American Express, and UNESCO.[12]

The funds of Rebuild Dubrovnik have now been transferred to the World Monuments Fund, American Express' direct line to the World Bank. The founding sponsor of the program, American Express, committed $5 million, with the objective of raising the same amount in matching grants. The goal: to develop cultural tourism, which President James D. Wolfensohn of the World Bank has identified as a method of empowering inhabitants of developing countries who feel overwhelmed by the forces of globalization.

But culture in this context is being used as a blunt weapon. Lipman, who helped Weiss organize her travel program, wrote a letter to the *Washington Post* advocating that the bombers of world heritage sites be tried as war criminals; he also lobbied for legislation to that effect. One of the stated goals of the WTTC is to be instated on the agenda of international governments, but this particular effort, perhaps seen as too patently self-serving, has so far met with no success.

Weiss, who organized tourist travel to Dubrovnik during the heightened tension of the early 1990s, explains that she overcame a negative news image of "all those shells exploding on CNN!" by ferrying journalists over on junkets. The goal was to create positive press about how people carried on in spite of the shelling and used culture to keep their souls alive.

Now Weiss says that the fund's mission has been accomplished and tourism has returned to about 75 percent of its prewar levels. Official figures from the Ministry of Tourism estimate the rise at 27 percent of prewar levels. In the same week that Rebuild Dubrovnik completed its transfer to the World Monuments Fund, NATO commenced hostilities against Serbia. Soon afterward, Weiss returned to her employer of the past ten years, Atlas Travel.

The belief of PR practitioners in their own ability to bring order out of confusion and social disarray began in 1917, when a young journalist turned press agent joined the army of publicists at the Committee on Public Information (CPI) to concentrate on wartime propaganda aimed at Latin American business interests. Pleasant-faced if nondescript, with the sleek bowlered look of twentieth-century man as envisioned by Belgian surrealist René Magritte, his name was Edward L. Bernays, and he was well acquainted with the Rockefellers through his work in the theater. The family's early discovery of the uses of the fledgling business of public relations in distracting people from the brutal labor practices of Standard Oil was a further bond, as were the Rockefeller holdings in Latin America.

Bernays, born in Vienna in 1891, was Sigmund Freud's nephew through both his father and his mother (his mother was Freud's sister, his father Freud's wife's brother). It was therefore no accident that he should have been fascinated by human psychology, albeit in the most manipulative sense. Along with Walter Lippmann, Bernays is credited with being one of the fathers of the modern science of public relations and owns the dubious distinction of being the only Austrian Jew admired by Nazi propaganda minister Joseph Goebbels.

Bernays created the first linkage between corporate sales campaigns and popular social causes when, in the 1920s, he persuaded suffragists to use the product of his employer, the American Tobacco Company, as a symbol of their liberation. But his legacy is greater by far than Virginia Slims.

The CPI was an American propaganda juggernaut, mobilized in 1917 to package, advertise, and sell World War I as "making the world safe for democracy." Anticipating Nelson Rockefeller's interests, the CPI launched an unprecedented campaign to deploy the persuasive new medium of movies as a weapon of war. The CPI did not directly produce movies, but it did maintain a "scenario department," which drafted general story outlines on such issues as the necessity for civilians to conserve rubber to promote the war effort. Often less than scintillating, these "scenarios" were then passed along to commercial producers, whose job it was to besprinkle them with the fairydust of entertainment. (During World War II, the Office of War Information carried on the good work, using Hollywood producers.) To further ensure that the sugar pill of propaganda was swallowed by a mass audience, the CPI originated the modern concept of "bundling," a practice common in film distribution and syndication today. A producer "bundles" inventory by tying a number of duds in with a commercial success in a single sales package. Buyers take the duds to get the one good product. The Hollywood producers had to agree that no American entertainment films would be sold to foreign exhibitors who refused to show the committee's mostly soporific war pictures.

Briefly a journalist following his graduation from Cornell in 1913, Bernays entered the arena of opinion engineering by using a controversial play called *Damaged Goods* to help the medical profession broadcast the necessity of treating syphilis. Written by Eugène Brieux, *Damaged Goods* is a homily about a syphilitic young man who marries against the advice of his physician and produces an infected child. (Ibsen wrote a much better play on the same subject entitled *Ghosts*.)

In his meticulous book *PR: A Social History of Spin*, communications professor Stuart Ewen describes how Bernays overcame the dramatic deficiencies of *Damaged Goods* by promoting it as a cause. In order to circumvent the New York Society for the Suppression of Vice, which expressed the limits of contemporary social tolerance by closing down similar shows the organization thought too daring, Bernays became the first publicist to operate by staging an "event" that the press would consider a legitimate source of news. In his capacity as editor of a medical journal, he announced the formation of a new, not-for-profit organization for the advancement of education on venereal diseases. No mention was made of *Damaged Goods*, but not by coincidence the first project of the newly established Sociological Fund Committee, whose members included not only staff of the prestigious Rockefeller Institute but John D. Rockefeller, Jr., himself, was to back the play.

The enlistment of high society inoculated the play against the vice patrol. Instead of lousy reviews, the play opened to loud huzzahs. With His Eminence John D. Rockefeller, Jr., proclaiming in print that the play broke down the "harmful reserve which stands in the way of popular entertainment," lesser social luminaries could not help but follow suit. President Woodrow Wilson and other political nabobs ordered a command performance in Washington. Touring companies and a film soon followed.[13]

Damaged Goods has long since vanished without a trace, but Bernays' career as a publicist was made. As a theatrical press agent, he represented Serge Diaghilev's Ballets Russes, as well as Vaslav Nijinsky, Enrico Caruso, and other stars. But the glamour of entertainment soon paled beside the steely glint of power.

Bernays believed that a modern, large-scale society such as that in the United States required the services of an elite corps of experts trained in the care and feeding of public opinion, which he regarded as an irrational beast: "In place of thoughts it has impulses, habits, and emotions. In making up its mind, its first impulse is usually to follow the example of a trusted leader. This is one of the most firmly established principles of mass psychology."[14]

Bernays, who like most people in the entertainment business craved legitimacy, envisioned the reengineering of public relations as a potent social instrument to organize chaos and bring order out of confusion. He saw the role of public relations within the modern architecture of power as an instrument with which the elite could govern the masses while allowing the masses to believe they were governing themselves. In this view the flack, previously an object of intellectual scorn, was elevated to the role of "counsel on public relations," a quasi-legal wise man, one of the "intelligent few" who could successfully navigate a course between the Scylla of the Rights of Man and the Charybdis of an elite power structure increasingly personified by monopolistic corporate entities such as Standard Oil.

This transformation would be accomplished by creating the century's first rendering of virtual reality, a parallel universe in which seemingly spontaneous events that were in fact carefully manipulated by the invisible wire pullers of public relations could subconsciously persuade the Little Guy to see the Big Guy's vision of the world. But, instead of the rich muck of sex and mythology out of which Freud fashioned his idea of the human psyche, Bernays reduced his symbols to the intellectual equivalents of generic road signs for food, gas, and shelter. In the words of his colleague Walter Lippmann, "The signs must be of such a character that they can be recognized without any substantial insight into the substance of a problem. . . . They must be signs which tell the members of a public where they can best align themselves so as to promote the solution. In short, they must be guides to reasonable action for the uses of uninformed people."[15]

Eager as ever to leave his stamp on history, Bernays taught one of the first courses in public relations at New York University in 1923. He saw the image as an instrument of persuasion—a concept that was freely adapted by the Nazis—focusing on the importance of symbols and their capacity, when systematically applied, to set off unconscious chains of mental association. The aim was, in Lippmann's unapologetic phrase, "to manufacture consent."[16]

Fast forward, as they say in the motion picture business which Bernays assiduously followed, to 1995. I am sitting in Ireland House at New York University, which has recently purchased the New School of Social Research's travel and tourism program, whose dean is a former American Express executive. A sampling of ambassadors, academics, journalists, and editors from august policy publications discuss a foreign policy that is gaining currency in the Clinton administration. It is a doctrine entitled "preemptive peace": declaring a peace before the combatants have actually stopped fighting in the hope that businesses, that is, direct foreign investors, will rush to take advantage of the opportunity to realize rapid growth, thereby providing employment at a level which will in turn prevent fighting from breaking out again.

It is almost a century since Bernays taught here, and yet his presence is palpable. The gist of the argument being advanced is that there are certain circumstances that are equivalent to war in the "moral demands" they place on journalists to forget objectivity. In the face of the opportunities presented by the breakdown of the former Soviet Union to end the century in a blaze of brotherhood, journalists are urged to drop their traditional antipathy toward public relations and join with big government and big business in printing only positive stories about the peace. Journalists, it is claimed, actually inspire genocidal violence by their insistence on remaining above the fray as professional bystanders. "Scientists" (meaning people in PR) know that facts do not exist in the outside world but are produced by the interaction of events. In the fashionable postmodernist world, media no longer reflect reality, they produce it, or, rather, they produce "hyperreality," a state in which truth, reality, and fiction lose their distinction (this is also a clinical definition of psychosis). As the playwright Jean Girardoux, himself a diplomat, remarked in *The Madwoman of Chaillot*, "If you wear false pearls long enough, they become real."

If journalism is to survive, it is argued, journalists must "feminize" themselves, turning from a conception of fairness ("male") to a conception of caring ("female"). Never mind if beatings and the odd pub bomb or two continue in the back alleys of Belfast. Never mind if Muslims and Christians still slaughter one another in the hills of Kosovo. Never mind if the occasional tourist is kidnapped or raped or blown up or hacked to death with machetes. The more people who come, the more people who will come, until the gritty, grimy truth is smoothed and whitened by the nacre of forgetfulness. The study of history is for depressives; centuries-old blood feuds are ripe for the power of positive thinking. When people come, the money comes, and in the closing years of the twentieth century one thing we can be sure of is that economics, not politics or tribalism or the Jurassic swamp of human nature, is what moves the big ball of human events.

Nobody in the room laughs at this concoction of tripe smothered in Bernays sauce. The profit motive in such cheerleading has become irresistibly powerful as the forces of globalization have transformed recreational industries into political lobbying tools.

In 1990, a year before President George Bush mentioned tourism as a force for peace in the first open series of peace talks in Madrid, a group of high-ranking tourist industry executives formed the World Travel and Tourism Council to make the world safe for tourism, that is, for the airlines, credit-card companies, and hoteliers that form its chief constituency. One of the WTTC's primary objectives throughout the decade was to move tourism onto government agendas. In part by claiming a "symbiotic" relationship between tourism and the peace process, it succeeded.

In the best Bernays tradition, the WTTC and offshoots such as the Middle Eastern and Mediterranean Travel and Tourism Association (MEMTA) claim a strong ideological identification with democratic rights like free assembly. "Freedom of assembly is more critical than freedom of speech," says Cord Hansen-Sturm, a former Cold Warrior and American Express executive who now heads MEMTA. "What America has done since the Cold War is to prevent people from going to those countries so they couldn't be used as spies. Europe did just the opposite: it just pushed up against the USSR with travel and information."[17] One of MEMTA's objectives is to create a "stake" in tourism in order to keep the peace process going, using the lure of Year 2000 tourism as a prize for good behavior. As we shall see in Chapter 7, its success has been limited.

Does this type of fortified public relations usurp the role of the State Department? The department states "categorically" that no consideration other than the safety of U.S. citizens factors into its decisions: not tourism, not commerce, not the importance of bilateral good feelings, not the lobbying efforts of powerful industry groups such as airlines or any other branch of government can sway its decisions.

On the day that NATO attacked Serbia, Croatia, which has been heavily redeveloped for tourism by several organizations, remained on the department's Public Announcement list rather than being issued a Travel Warning, even though the country was badly shelled in the last round of hostilities and seemed to be in the flight path of many of the NATO plane deployments. (A Public Announcement disseminates information about terrorist threats and other "relatively short-term and/or trans-national conditions posing significant risks to the security of American travelers such as coups, bomb threats to airlines, violence by terrorists, and anniversary dates of specific terrorist events." A Travel Warning recommends that Americans avoid certain countries altogether. Press reports, together with information submitted by embassies, American travelers, government officials from other U.S. agencies, host governments, and third party governments are all used to determine how to advise Americans about travel risks.) As the bombing campaign intensified, a representative of the Croatian embassy in Washington assured me on the telephone that there was no problem traveling to Croatia for tourism "because it's relatively far from the problem and the situation can only get better."

Although Nazli Weiss denies that any lobbying of the State Department to lift the advisories on Croatia took place in 1994, other travel agents admit that they lobby to change advisories all the time and accuse the State Department of excessive caution. Interviewed two days before Hutu militants kidnapped fourteen Western tourists and eventually slaughtered eight of them in Uganda's Bwindi National Park, a travel PR executive who preferred to remain anonymous said that the "upscale" clientele, that is, "older, sophisticated baby-boomers," traveling to eastern and southern Africa were "not scared off" by accounts of violence in the region. Like many in the travel business, she was less than candid about whether the jeep-driving, mountain-trekking, gorilla-chasing set which gets its information on the "real" Africa via the Internet has more money than sense. "Sophisticated people know that bad news makes headlines," she said, adding that "long-haul adventure travelers" (who used to be called safari travelers or Great White Hunters in the era before political correctness) "don't even think in terms of genocide." The same executive, contacted three days later, would merely state, "We don't handle Uganda," and declined to comment further.

Public relations professionals pass the safety buck to tour operators and tourism boards, who pass it back to the tourist. "We tell people to take the same precautions as they would in New York, or any major city in the world," said Peggy Bendel, senior vice-president in charge of travel for DCI, the public relations firm for SATOUR, the South African Tourist Board. But military police don't patrol downtown New York in search of terrorists, as they do in Johannesburg.[18]

Ultimately, travel PR professionals say, it is up to the individual countries to solve their own problems. At the same time, hungry for exotic "long-haul" destinations and impatient with the slowness of diplomatic solutions for the political problems that beset most of them, the industry has created the WTTC.

While lobbying to have tourism put on government agendas as a major generator of employment, the WTTC also hoped to transform the traditionally loose relationships between governments, tour operators, and tourists to create a "global network." This sounds like a monopoly 1990s-style, with international "uniform rules" that will even out all the old state-owned competitive disadvantages.[19]

One of the founders and chairman of the WTTC was James (Jim) Robinson III, then chairman of American Express, who formed a core group with Robert L. Crandall of American Airlines and Robert Marshall of British Airways. At least part of what motivated Robinson may have been his company's long fall from grace during the 1980s. Although industry sources say that the failure of American Express to catch the wave of frequent-flier programs precipitated its tumble and Robinson's subsequent ouster in 1993, it is probably more realistic to say that a long series of executive missteps, including the opprobrious investigation of Edmond Safra and unanticipated losses at Shearson-Lehmann and Optima (which left Wall Street analysts questioning Robinson's ability to recognize internal problems before they blew up in his face), were at the bottom of it. What better way to restore legitimacy than with a cause that, like the campaign to educate the public about venereal disease that saved *Damaged Goods*, was impossible to fault?

In addition to being socially responsible, the formation of the WTTC also served the interests of American Express. Largely because of the vast international exposure of the company, Robinson saw his CEO's role as that of "corporate statesman" and, along with the International Finance Corporation, spent an increasing amount of his time in the 1980s trying to devise a solution to the problem of Third World nations being indebted to the world banking system. If Robinson could broker a solution, he would flood the company with business. His pet project was the ad hoc group I2D2, the outlines of which can be seen today in the WTTC, formed to brainstorm the problem.

The agenda of the WTTC is set forth in what its members call their Millennial Vision, formulated by president Geoffrey Lipman. The Vision contains four strategic prongs: making tourism a priority in government economic development and employment programs; enlarging the markets for tourism through "open skies" airlines agreements; privatization of state-owned tourism facilities; and deregulation. The last also applies to the telecommunications industry, which the WTTC regards as part of its brief because the industry facilitates the transfer of information, thus reducing costs for travel-related businesses in developing countries. "It's better for business and therefore better for their economies," MEMTA's Hansen-Sturm said.

The WTTC also advocates "sustainable tourism" as set forth in the guidelines of the United Nations Earth Summit. Its final priority is to eliminate such barriers to growth as taxation of tourism products, that is, hotel taxes, which ordinarily pay for convention halls, stadiums, and other amenities for local taxpayers. As we have seen, one of the projects sponsored by the WTTC in conjunction with American Express and the World Monuments Fund was the Rebuild Dubrovnik Fund.

The WTTC is a throwback, albeit on an international scale, to the National Association of Manufacturers (NAM), which came to prominence during the Depression. Between 1929 and 1933, the American gross national product fell from $103.1 billion to $55.6 billion. More than 100,000 American businesses failed. Total industrial productivity dropped 51 percent. The value of both American exports and American imports declined by two-thirds. The public, not entirely irrationally, blamed big business for its sufferings. The corporate view of the customer changed from that of an irrational beast to a beast that was raging as well. At the same time, businesses grew increasingly desperate to keep customers in the market, and the new science of market research took on the ideological fervor of wartime espionage. Added to the trend of newspaper consolidation and the ubiquitous and insidious presence of radio in the American home, public relations and advertising increasingly took on aspects of social control that are more commonly attributed to totalitarian states.

From the mid-1930s onward, particularly in the wake of Franklin Roosevelt's overwhelming reelection in 1936, American corporations sought to improve their image by allying themselves in public relations efforts which reached beyond their own parochial interests. Chief among these efforts was the National Association of Manufacturers, an umbrella trade association founded in 1895 to curb the power of government and protect the privileges of private wealth. Between 1935 and 1941, NAM's membership swelled from 2,500 to 8,000, including such drivers of American industry as General Motors, Chrysler, U.S. Steel, Dupont, General Electric, and General Foods. Over the next two decades, NAM became obsessed with the idea of "educating" the American public on several fronts, in particular in linking the idea of free enterprise with free speech, free press, and free religion as a requisite of democracy.

As America emerged from Depression, it embroiled itself in war. The evolving apparatus of social control was incorporated into the propaganda machine of World War II, which allowed the whole apparatus to become even bigger. The need for corporate involvement in the production of weapons and other war matériel offered American business a heaven-sent opportunity to put its brutal repression of labor protest in the 1930s behind it. Addressing a NAM meeting in Philadelphia in 1943, J. Howard Pew, of the Philadelphia Pews, founders of Sun Oil, announced that, "slandered and vilified as it was in the thirties, subjected to crushing regulations and restrictions," corporate America was now deservedly seen as the savior of both the nation and the world.[20]

This time Hollywood contributed its own Propaganda Corps to the war effort, and its recruits were given formal military status as officers. The army of writers, flacks, broadcasters, moviemakers, and other media mavens was organized through the Office of War Information under the direction of a radio journalist, Elmer Rice. Once again, war supplied the synergy needed to create a state-of-the-art laboratory where business and government could learn from each other in experimenting with the tools of ideological command.

One American corporation whose image had not been burnished by the war was the Rockefellers' Standard Oil. In 1942 a Senate committee chaired by none other than Harry S. Truman discovered a series of patent and process-exchange agreements for synthetic rubber between Standard Oil of New Jersey and the German chemical cartel I. G. Farben, which became infamous after the discovery that it had set up a subsidiary next to Auschwitz-Birkenau in order to avail itself of concentration-camp labor at ten cents a day. Standard Oil retained the agreements even after the United States entered the war, a proceeding that created a scandal in 1943 sufficient to justify creating its own public relations department. Earl Newsom, who had helped rehabilitate Henry Ford after the auto magnate embarrassed himself as the advance man for the antisemitic counterfeit conspiracy document known as the *Protocols of the Elders of Zion*, was brought on board as the corporation's "general counsel on public relations" to reinvent its image in a human light.

But the sense of unification against a common enemy that had imbued the American labor movement during the 1930s was to a great extent neutralized by the balm of consumer products, many of them luxuries that had been far beyond the reach of the ordinary working family before the war. The penetration of television into the American home permitted advertising to "bundle" with entertainment in images that were even more potent than radio messages. The threat of communism helped sustain the ideological body fat of the Office of War Information, and corporate public relations grew along with the rest of the military-industrial complex.

The patron saint of virtual reality emerged in the postwar era when Ronald Reagan became public relations spokesperson for General Electric. Reagan's new job, for which he was paid considerably better than he had been as an actor, was to put his own affable, Midwestern Everyman's face on the corporate behemoth of G.E. This he did for eight years, hosting the company's weekly coopting of culture on television, *General Electric Theater*, while roaming the nation for face-to-face meetings with G.E. employees at which he tried to convince them of their personal importance to private enterprise. It was the perfect grooming for his further political career. At the same time, Reagan became a regular speaker for NAM.

In the 1960s and 1970s, in his new capacity as governor of California, Reagan tried to squelch the voices of the civil rights and antiwar movements in the state university system. But the student movement,

which also incorporated women's rights, gay rights, and environmental-
ism, represented an enormous market, which began to command enormous affluence after its members shed the Counterculture and got jobs.

A new generation of "opinion engineers" emerged. Among them
was David Finn, one of the first to perceive the value of the new market and to decree that the man in the gray flannel suit must shed his
corporate image. Finn used the theme of culture to command the student market at the same time that it provided a "soft" cover for strategic interests.

The good-cop, bad-cop routine played by culture and strategic
interests is neatly illustrated in Ruder Finn's business relationship with
the Shah of Iran, who retained the firm to promote cultural exchanges
through Marion Javits, wife of the senator—who was involved in arms
procurement for the shah at the time. When a *Village Voice* reporter
discovered that Marion Javits had registered as a foreign agent in order
to work as a consultant on the deal, the ensuing public opinion storm
severely dented Ruder Finn's relations with Israel, to the extent that
Lew Wasserman, head of the Music Corporation of America (MCA),
fired the company for walking both sides of the street. (The firm was
later rehired.)[21]

While it may provide opportunities for artists, the use of culture to
advance other interests inevitably debases culture itself. This is most
evident in movies, where "branding" has overlapped the conventions
of both genre and the tried-and-true story approaches recognized by
studio executives. One of the more egregious examples is the
Nazification of the British in recent American and Irish films. (The
Irish film industry has strong links to the Irish Tourist Board, and the
Irish government has blessed foreign film companies with the
munificent tax breaks also enjoyed by tourism.) Like the identification
of the Serbs with Nazis, this propaganda represents a reversal of history: the British were among the staunchest opponents of Germany in
World War II while Ireland stayed neutral because of its anti-British
sentiments and, in fact, allowed German U-boats to land in the North.
British and Irish commentators both remarked that the Republican-
leaning films *Michael Collins* and *Nothing Personal* probably intensified
passions during the highly volatile "marching season" between Good
Friday and mid-July, when Ulster Unionists traditionally commemorate their victories by marching through Catholic neighborhoods.

While not all "Holocaust" campaigns can be laid at Ruder Finn's
doorstep, it is possible that their ubiquitousness has much to do with
the sincerest form of flattery. The "success" of campaigns like the

Croatian one is highly debatable, particularly from an ethical point of view, but public awareness of the Holocaust is undeniably higher because of the number of Jewish clients Ruder Finn has handled over the years. These include the United Jewish Appeal, which employed Ruder Finn to help it "convince" the American public that it had nothing to do with politics following a $20 million drop in donations because of Reform and Conservative outrage over their exclusion from Israeli politics by Orthodox Jews. The firm also represents such groups as the American Jewish Committee, Hebrew University, and the Anti-Defamation League, which were also caught up in the Croatia campaign of Holocaust identification. In 1998 the government of Switzerland hired Ruder Finn for the sum of $207,500 to deal with the issue of Holocaust gold. Ruder Finn assisted the Conference of Major Jewish Organizations to "formulate a response" to the 1997 Eisenstadt report analyzing Swiss handling of Nazi gold. Switzerland dropped Ruder Finn from the account after discovering the name of a Ruder Finn employee on a press release saying that the World Jewish Restitution Organization planned a class-action suit against Swiss banks "anywhere in the world where Holocaust survivors reside or where Swiss banks maintain branches." The release was written on the letterhead of the Jewish Agency, another Ruder Finn client. Ruder Finn's brief was to "mediate" between the Jews and the Swiss, but the conflict, perhaps unsurprisingly, escalated.[22]

Today, Ruder Finn also counts the United Nations among its "pro bono" clients. David Finn describes Secretary-General Kofi Annan as a close personal friend. On Annan's recommendation, the firm did a study of Nigeria in 1998, the year before the first "democratic" election was held there. "They thought hiring a PR firm would change their image, like so many countries," Finn said.

> They can't change their image without changing themselves. We interviewed journalists, politicians, and others who know most about the country, and presented a report to the government. Now Nigeria is democratic. That's very heartening, very encouraging. It's exactly what Kofi Annan encouraged them to do. But it was not our doing that made this happen. The dictator died. A new head of state assumed power, and he created a democratic government. It gives us too much power to say that we can achieve such results. If a government wants to know what its PR problem is, all we can do is conduct responsible research and report our findings to the proper authorities. That's exactly what we did.

(After a landslide victory on March 1, 1999, swept General Olusegun Obasanjo into power against ex-finance minister Olu Falae, the election was widely held to be fraudulent.)

The Walt Disney Company quoted Kofi Annan, David Finn's close personal friend, in a shareholders' report announcing that the United Nations would be an official participant in Disney's resort-wide Millennium Celebration. As the special adviser to the secretary general, John Ruggie, explained, "Sure, it's unusual for us to lend our name to a quintessentially commercial venture. But we have an unusual Secretary General." (Annan is unique for his interest in forming partnerships with nongovernmental organizations and with the international business community as well as for his keen interest in PR.) Annan canceled his own anticipated appearance at the celebration when a public relations furor erupted over Disney's insistence on characterizing Jerusalem as the "capital of Israel" in the planned exhibit, thus infuriating the Muslim world at a delicate stage in the painfully resuscitated peace negotiations. "We actually decided to cancel before that happened," Ruggie said. "It just didn't work out with his schedule."[23]

The price exacted by big business from big government may be a high one: the most efficient way to make the world safe for tourism—that is, the management of public relations—is profoundly antidemocratic. Salesmanship may have its place, but not in the halls of diplomacy. Salesmanship is by definition one-sided. In the case of tribal conflicts like those taking place in Kosovo, Northern Ireland, and the Gaza Strip, where atrocities have been committed by both sides, often for centuries, employing salesmanship at the expense of diplomacy is to commit a grave injustice for which understandable resentment may exact a terrible price. How is it possible to convince people who have reason to believe they have been unfairly treated that they are witnessing a new, democratic dawn? In contemplating the mass graves of Kosovo, it is sobering to remember that false pearls may become real in more ways than one: the demonization of Germany by Europe and the United States following World War I did much to create Adolf Hitler.

CHAPTER 5

Tourism Under Castro
A Talent to Amuse

"EVERYWHERE YOU GO in Cuba, you will be welcomed and received with open arms. . . . We are confident that tourism will become the largest and most prosperous industry in the country." The speaker is Fidel Castro, addressing the American Society of Tourist Agents at their annual convention in Havana. The year is 1959. In 1999, "celebrating" forty years of Castro's rule, the Cuban government projected earnings of $1.8 billion from tourism, out of a total economy valued at $2.5 billion.

The explosion of tourism, while it still nominally excludes U.S. visitors because of the U.S. embargo, has been hailed as the harbinger of a "new" Cuba, a "Club Red" in which sexual liberation foreshadows political liberalism and Fidel, defender of the Communist faithful, becomes the Santa Claus of *capitolismo frío*. But after Castro's strident anti-vice campaigns of the 1970s and 1980s, which scapegoated tourism, the Cuban tourist industry seems more like a cynical theme-park re-creation of the bad old, good old days when dictator Fulgencio Batista and American mobster Meyer Lansky ruled Cuba as the sun-and-sin destination of choice. Today, Castro trumpets that the sexual smorgasbord that makes Cuba the freest of markets will be "cleaned up" in order to make the place palatable to "high-end," or family, tourism. But as long as the Cuban economy remains at its present level, it is difficult to see how prostitution can be regulated without losing Cuba's main attraction to couch-potatoes who think they are *conquistadores*.

The fact that after forty years the Cuban economy remains more than two-thirds dependent on one of the most recession-prone of all modern industries is nothing to celebrate. It is a sad commentary on both the failure of the "revolution" and the failure of the United States to come to terms with the Castro government. As tourism visibly diverts scant resources away from the Cuban people, it has also become a recipe for social unrest and a reason for soldier turned tourism minister Osmany Cienfuegos to hang on to his uniform.

Few of the 1.3 million visitors anticipated for 2000 know that Cuba's minister of tourism commanded a death squad in the not-so-distant past, a piece of information that captures the many paradoxes of tourism in a country that wants tourists but not foreigners, a country where IRA-inspired plaques commemorating a history of common struggle mark the addresses of Christmas shops and hotel investors are advised to anticipate government confiscation. Cienfuegos, who fought alongside Castro in his earliest days in the Sierra Maestra, is one of a small circle of old comrades still on the preferred list for top government positions. Described variously as a "longtime Marxist" by historian Robert Quirk and as a *prostático* (old fart) by rude Cubans, Osmany Cienfuegos was emissary to Russia in 1962, when Premier Nikita Khrushchev started shipping vast amounts of military matériel to Cuba so he could use the island as a base against the United States.

An IRA-inspired plaque on the Calle O'Reilly in Havana marks a history of common struggle shared by Cuba and Ireland.

In his *Against All Hope*, Armando Valladares, a noted poet and leader of the Cuban-American right, identifies Cienfuegos as the commander responsible for the deaths by asphyxiation of nine political prisoners shortly after the Bay of Pigs invasion in 1962.

> "We're going to suffocate in there," one of the prisoners said.
> "Good. Then we won't have to waste ammunition shooting you," Cienfuegos answered.

Minister Cienfuegos declined my repeated requests for interviews.

"He's a political appointee," explained John Kavulich, whose New York–based U.S.-Cuba Trade and Economic Council offers information to U.S. companies about investment opportunities in Cuba. "In Cuba's political reality, age has its benefits."[1]

While younger men such as Vice-President Carlos Lage strive to mend Cuba's fences with the Paris Club, Cienfuegos sits securely astride the cash cow for what is left of the Revolution, in charge of an infrastructure investment of some $500 million made during the "Special Period" from 1991 to 1994 when Cuba was stony broke after aid from the former Soviet Union dried up. But that infrastructure is a Potemkin village, an elaborate facade hiding dire shortages.[2]

The Cubana Air flight I took from Nassau to Cuba when I began the research for this book is a good example of the triumph of marketing over essentials. As we taxi down the runway in our vintage Soviet VAK-420, a thick white smoke from the air-conditioning vents fills the interior like the fog in a 1950s film noir. We are due to arrive in Havana at 5:15 P.M. Five o'clock goes by, then 5:15, then 5:30. We are still flying at the same altitude, into the skirts of Hurricane Mitch, a soggy, sullen mass of cloud that hangs over Cuba like nine administrations of embargo.

"Welcome to Cuba," says the glossy in-flight magazine in both English and Spanish. "When you arrive, the entire archipelago is yours to fulfill your fondest dreams and desires at beaches that are truly beaches, on deserted cays, breathing pure mountain air as you walk through green-robed woods, getting to know friendly, lively people."

My fondest desire is to get my feet on terra firma. I overhear a flight attendant say we are going to make an emergency landing at Varadero, Cuba's premier beach resort, where the island's largest airport is only a two-hour bus ride from Havana. But 5:45 rolls by, and we haven't started our descent. The flight attendants disappear to huddle with the military in first class, leaving us passengers, a motley crew of Bahamians traveling on business and Americans traveling on monkey-business, completely in the dark. My translator and I are the only two females on board. We earn a lot of bleak looks, particularly from a bevy of men in black. Travel in Cuba is still a guy thing, and we are spoiling their game.

The man seated across the aisle from us appears to be having a very bad time.

"Look!" I say brightly. "I see lights!"

"Shut up!" he says, still glued to the window. "I'm a pilot!"

Patrick, our newfound friend, turns out to be an RAF-trained pilot for British Airways. He explains that the antique we are flying has no radar and no reverse engines to slow us down before landing. The pilot must make the landing by eyesight, which is impossible if the cloud cover sits too close to the land, or by intercepting a radio signal, which allows very little room for divergence. Even fifty feet is too much, he says, not to mention the danger of catching a tailwind going down which would hammer us into the ground like a nail, or of flying smack into an embedded thunderhead, a lethal cone of electricity which has wrapped itself in nimbus and is undetectable without radar.

Six o'clock. Even the men in black are peeing in their Polos. We have now been in the air two and a half hours, almost the same amount of time (the in-flight magazine tells me) it took to make the first flight from Key West to Havana in 1913. We make one, two, three circles over what appears to be a road.

"He can't lock into the signal," Patrick says. "He's going to have to take us to the Caymans . . . if he has enough gas."

I close my eyes, remembering what I've read about fuel shortages in Cuba.

The invisible hand waves a wand and we are lodged at a surrealistically luxurious purpose-built resort, courtesy of the state.

Suddenly, the plane flips halfway over and we hurtle down like a dive-bomber. But at the very last minute, just as it looks as if we are going to bury ourselves in the ground, the pilot pulls up the nose and we land on a small airstrip as smoothly as if the wind isn't blowing 65 miles an hour.

Welcome to Cuba, where the tourist's "right to satisfaction" is now a Revolutionary ukase, and where government officials, instead of disseminating propaganda, eagerly solicit market feedback. Having put us through the minor inconvenience of almost losing our lives, the invisible hand now waves a wand and all thirty or more of us are lodged and fed at a surrealistically luxurious purpose-built resort courtesy of the state.

We have landed at Cayo Largo, approximately 110 miles south of Havana. The long, elbow-shaped island is the last jumping-off point before the Caymans and a neighbor of Isla de la Juventud, site of the Bay of Pigs landing in 1961. Today Cayo Largo is a free port, and international travelers can arrive without visa or passport if they do not intend to visit the Cuban mainland. This is also true for arrivals by private yacht, and the island houses a world-class marina with twenty berths for people like my translator's husband, an aristocratic English money-manager.

United States firms began building resorts on Cayo Largo in 1957, only to be shut down by the Revolution. The island remained uninhabited until 1982, when the Hotel Isla del Sol was developed to pleasure visiting Russian dignitaries. Today it is one of Cuba's fashionable "ecotourism" destinations. Three thousand hotel rooms are being developed along its pristine white-sugar beaches: one Canadian coventurer is building golf courses in partnership with Scotland's sport-of-kings specialist Gleneagles.

The Hotel Pelícano, to which we are bused with military efficiency by epauletted officials from the Ministry of Tourism, is a "Spanish-moderne" low-rise, organized around a series of patios dotted with monumental Afro-Cuban sculptures and bare-breasted maidens rising from the waves. Its 324 rooms have air conditioning, mini-bars, and satellite T.V. (nothing on all 90 channels, just like home). Built in 1994, when INTUR, the state tourism monopoly, was dismantled and Cienfuegos took over as minister of tourism, the hotel still feels unfinished: the bathrooms have built-in hair dryers but no toilet seats. Rates for the spacious, comfortably if austerely furnished rooms run at $110 a night, beyond the reach of most Cubans. The other guests are primarily French, Italian, and sunburnt Teutons: one Cuban christened it "summer camp for Aryans."

Presumably, the state's hospitality does not include the pretty mulatto waitress who makes a point of informing Patrick, our pilot friend, that her dormitory arrangements have kept her apart from her husband for far too long. He flees to us for protection, which seems a shame: this is the only contact with Cubans we are likely to have on Cayo Largo, where even the Cuban service staff is segregated in their own dormitory north of the airport. Their families remain on the mainland and the bread earners are transported by the government ten days a month for visits.

"Tourism apartheid" has a long history in Cuba, where vacationers might bring in much-needed hard currency but at the cost of pointing out to the Cubans the difference between their quality of life and that of their foreign visitors. In 1980 an American intelligence source at the Mexican embassy in Havana reported that President Castro's brother, Raúl, a powerful figure in Cuban government, opposed courting large numbers of Western tourists on the grounds that they might contaminate the ideological purity of the Revolution. President Castro is said to have laughed and retorted that they could always build cages for the foreigners. Speaking more officially, Castro declared, in words now commonly applied to prostitution, that he was only encouraging tourism in response to an "economic need of the revolution."[3]

But unless someone finds oil or gold, Cuba is now stuck with tourism as it was once stuck with sugar. Its extreme dependence on this fickle and recession-prone business began in the early 1990s, when the former Soviet Union collapsed and cut off all foreign aid. For a period of three years, known grimly as the Special Period, the Cuban econ-

The supply of electricity in Havana's back streets and to a tourist restaurant: serious differences in the quality of life for Cubans and their foreign visitors.

The ideological purity of the Revolution: a five-story image of Che Guevara on the Ministry of the Interior.

omy flattened out like a house in a hurricane. Imports from Eastern Europe dried up, the oil pipeline evaporated, and the government was reduced to selling foodstuffs abroad for hard currency.

By 1992 trade with the former Soviet Union, also Cuba's primary export market, shrank to 7 percent of its former value while world prices for sugar and nickel, its two main products, caved in as well. By the end of 1994, half the country's factories had closed down, along with most of its public transport network. The total economy dropped between 34 percent (official estimates) and 60 percent (unofficial estimates). Inflation ran between 80 and 90 percent. The fuel shortages drastically curtailed air conditioning, fans, refrigeration, and lights: electricity is still scarce, even today. Harvests rotted in the fields, and people whose faith in their government rested on a federally subsidized daily food basket containing at least two high-protein, high-calorie meals a day were cut to iron rations. A hydra-headed black market began trading almost every commodity in short supply: black marketeers were even said to be melting down condoms and selling the rubber drizzles for pizza cheese.

During this Special Period, even Castro's tenure hung by a thread as his former Soviet allies were exiled or executed. In 1990 the desperate Cuban leader ordered that major resources be devoted to expand the tourist industry. Despite the financial crisis, as much as $500 million was invested in the tourism infrastructure over the next four years, including the new José Martí Airport, which, despite its elegance of design, was cavernously empty when we arrived in Havana. Perhaps the government should have spent the money on upgrading its air fleet.

The Cuban government also built a $130 million sports complex on the outskirts of Havana, more than a dozen luxury hotels, and fifty tourist-only restaurants across the island, as well as a $1 million discothèque in the posh suburb of Miramar, decorated with indoor waterfalls and teenaged girls for the elderly Spanish business clientele. Most of the investment capital came from foreign, particularly Spanish and Canadian, companies that were lured by Cuba's former fame as a tourist hot spot. Cuba put up the land and labor, which were both free as land belongs to the state, and citizens were called on to "donate" their spare time.

Although the government's efforts paid off quickly in record influxes of package tours from Canada, Western Europe, and Latin America, the lot of the average Cuban failed to improve. All dollars earned from tourism had to be turned in to pay off Cuba's foreign debt. Mothers who could not afford milk or bread or eggs for their children had to explain the food mountains at tourist restaurants and luxury hotels. To make their lives even harder, inflation soon followed.

In 1993, in order to corral the black-market economy, the government legalized the Yanqui dollar. Today, the visitor is confounded by a three-currency system: U.S. dollars (which are used for almost every tourist transaction as well as by Cubans to buy foreign goods in state-run "foreign-exchange recovery stores"), pesos convertibles (dollar-pegged pesos, which are essentially Monopoly money), and pesos, which are virtually worthless. According to one economist who worked in Russia when a similar three-currency system was introduced, this is a clear sign that the country is bankrupt.[4]

Although it is difficult to obtain reliable statistics, Cuba's foreign debt is reported to have risen from $2.8 billion in 1983 to $9 billion in 1995, much of it in high-interest short-term loans. According to Cuban Central Bank figures, Cuba's convertible currency debt at the end of 1997 totaled $10.14 billion. The main creditors were France, Argentina, Japan, Spain, and Britain.[5]

Starved of external financing and squeezed by yet another fall in commodity exports in 1998, Cuba is seeking to restore relations with the Paris Club, stalled since 1986, when Castro halted payment on most of its debt. The debt is now viewed as an obstacle to the island's efforts to gain access to development financing and attract more foreign investment. But Paris Club debt rescheduling agreements are usually linked with International Monetary Fund reform programs. Cuba, not itself an IMF member, has a long-standing enemy in the United States, which is a member, and which has the power to block any formal multilateral debt rescheduling deal. For this reason, Cuba has pursued bilateral debt rescheduling agreements with Japan and Italy. But these cover only a fraction of the more than $10 billion owed.

John Kavulich explained, "The Cuban government does a lot of robbing Peter to pay Paul. When they get dollars, they use them to pay off their short-term commercial debt. At the end of the day, all the dollars Cuba earns, the government puts into a common pot to import comestibles and combustibles."

The brief of Kavulich's council, a self-described nonpartisan service, is to improve business relations between the United States and Cuba. Its membership is not public, though the council publishes a Cuban business newsletter on the Internet. Kavulich says its users include Jesse Helms, the Cuban-American right, the U.S. government, and the Cuban government, which does not have access to trained statisticians. It also briefs journalists dealing with Cuba.

Kavulich admits that, if not bankrupt, the Cuban government is not doing a particularly good balancing act. "They're doing an extraordinary job given their limitations from above, i.e., Castro. They're coming to terms country by country, and with the Paris Club. But this begs the question, has the life of the average Cuban improved? The answer is no."

Carlos

In Havana, our Turistaxi driver is Carlos, a man in his mid-fifties with a meekness that belies his bristling moustache and a nose that has secreted a lot of rum. For the sum of fifty dollars, we hire him for half a day. We have been told that taxis "fix" their meters and everyone runs whatever scam is necessary in order to survive, but there is something about Carlos' mournful eyes that takes the relish out of bargaining.

Carlos is a good Party man, as one must be to get a job anywhere in tourism, now more sought-after than any of the "professions" because of its access to dollars. In a byzantine and sometimes extortionate system, foreign-owned companies must hand in their payrolls in hard currency to the state, which then doles out wages to the workers in pesos. Foreign-owned hotel companies, aware that they must provide some incentive for good service, also pay monthly dollar bonuses of between 5 and 30 percent. It is better to work for a foreign-owned company than for a state-owned company, as does Carlos, who must turn in all his tips to his "syndicate" (a curiously apt synonym for a cooperative), where the government deducts for a dizzying number of worthy causes before giving back about one-twentieth to Carlos.

Still, Carlos considers himself privileged. Because he is a good Communist, he has been given a house, built in 1854, which he is renovating in his spare time. Also in his spare time, he bicycles ten miles into the countryside every week to farm a small plot of land he cleared himself in order to grow the tubers and vegetables with which he and his family eke out their monthly food rations from the state. These consist of five pounds of rice, five pounds of beans, five pounds of potatoes, two pounds of meat, a small daily loaf of bread, four ounces of coffee (when available), and four ounces of lard (when available) per person. A pound of meat costs approximately twenty-five pesos, or one dollar, in the market (when available). Carlos' salary, like that of most Cubans, is between fifteen and twenty dollars a month.

To make sure that Carlos gets something for showing us points of Revolutionary interest on his day off, we invite him to lunch with us at the dollars-only restaurant of his choice. This is what Cubans covet more than the dollars themselves: access to the good food that only dollars, in the new Cuba, can buy. Rather than a hotel, he chooses a "paladare," a family-run restaurant owned and operated by friends, with money sent them by relatives in the United States. Originally organized illicitly to counteract the food shortages of the Special Period, these small eateries in private homes were legalized in 1994 and authorized to serve up to twelve persons at one seating. (Under Cuba's punitive new tax laws, the licensing fee for these restaurants has leaped from twenty to six hundred dollars as they have become successful.) Prices for our restaurant ran ten dollars for lunch, on a par with the good hotels, or slightly higher for lobster, which is banned. We ordered the lobster anyway, to make sure that Carlos would, but Big Brother was watching: Cubans still lack refrigeration because of the shortage of fuel oil, and at least one of us got sick.

Under the influence of rich food and a few cervezas, Carlos began to speak to me in rusty French, learned while he was studying diplomacy and agriculture at the university in Trinidad, in the days before the Revolution. Carlos has ruddy fair skin and Spanish features, and it is just conceivable that he was once an aristocrat. "Look at me," he says, with a sad smile caught in the corner of his yellowing moustache, "I was going to be a diplomat. I was going to be an agronomist. And now I am a chauffeur."

Carlos' wife, an engineer, has been unemployed since the subway project she was working on fell apart along with the Soviet Union. They have four children, the oldest aged thirty, the youngest sixteen. Carlos' hands start to shake when he talks about the son, "the handsomest of the three," who left on a boat for Florida without telling his papi. Unlike at least half of those who risk the ninety-mile crossing to Key West on rickety boats or rafts, he made it, and he is now living in Atlanta with a stewardess, who is trying to get him his green card. He calls from time to time, but Carlos has nothing to say to him. "He left," he shrugs, and that is all.

His youngest child, a girl, wants to go into restaurant management. "The young don't want to be doctors, or engineers, or agronomists, anymore," Carlos says. "Why should they? There are no jobs. We have 60,000 doctors in Cuba. That was all the universities turned out after the Revolution. You used to get respect for being a doctor. Now you get nothing."

"Are your surplus doctors encouraged to go into tourism?" I ask. This seems to enrage him. For the past three decades, Cubans have been brought up to think they were equal to, or better than, the ugly Americans who had turned their country into a brothel during the Batista years. It has long been considered a Revolutionary duty for workers like Carlos to lecture foreigners about the wonders of Marxism-Leninism. Now, suddenly, at age fifty-plus, Carlos' government is asking him to unlearn everything he knows and to pamper the tourist-customer, who is not a potential fellow-traveler and who is always right.

"Why should they be encouraged?" he snaps. "The state has given them the best education, at its own expense. They should be grateful to the state. When there is more money in the economy from tourism, everyone will get a raise."

At the end of the day, when I hand Carlos his fifty dollars plus *propina*, or tip, he places it with trembling hands inside an ancient wallet cracked from too much folding. Moments later, he returns. "I dropped the money in the street," he explains with a fearful smile. One of the *chicos*, the young men hanging around without visible means of support, says that a guy came by on a bicycle and picked up the money just like that.

Carlos looks at me apologetically, his heavy brows and moustache like a comic disguise for a Bolshevik. I don't know if this means I am supposed to pay him another fifty dollars. "What will happen to you if you show up without the money?" I ask. He shrugs. "It really doesn't matter," he says, and shakes my hand once more before he quickly gets into the car and drives away.

Myra

Fifty dollars is more than I'd casually throw away even in the United States, but if Carlos doesn't see any of it, what does it mean to him? Perhaps he has a deal with the chico: the chico "steals" the money and they split it and cover up the loss to headquarters. Perhaps, like many of the older Russians I met while traveling in the former Soviet Union in 1995, Carlos feels that the Revolution has betrayed him by introducing a new class-structured society where rank and privilege are determined not by ideological purity but by access to the despised Yanqui dollar. Perhaps he feels that whatever form the "new" Cuba takes, it will belong to the young and not to him.

Self-doubt, or doubt of any kind, does not afflict Myra, the thirty-year-old sales manager of the Havana Libre, aka the Havana Hilton. The scene of noisy protests and at least one tourist death in the early days of the Revolution, it was seized in June 1960 in the name of the workers by the Castro government, along with the Riviera and the Nacional, because the owners had failed to produce "sufficient tourist business."[6]

Myra is one of the YUMMIES (young, upwardly mobile Marxists) levitated into positions of power in the tourist business, to the intense resentment of many other Cubans. Most YUMMIES get their start in the military, and they do not make the most customer-friendly executives. "They try," said one foreign executive, who declined to be named.

Along with her ruffled Laura Ashley–print minidress and big hair, Myra has chutzpah. Bustling around the recent renovation, completed "moments" before Pope John Paul II arrived early this year, she quips that the pope is the best PR agent President Castro has ever had.

Built in the 1950s, the Havana Hilton was a home away from home for mobsters and high-rollers of every stripe until Castro made it his headquarters and rechristened it the Havana Libre. In 1989, when writer Maurice Halperin returned to Havana after an absence of more than twenty years, he found it infested with cockroaches; it had been allowed to decay like the rest of the Cuban metropolis, seemingly beyond repair. Today the restored rooms are not lavish by luxury-hotel standards, but they are fabulous by Cuban ones, with plush carpeting and drapes, bar-fridges, T.V.s, and gleaming tile baths. The rooms are many times larger than the subdivided chambers in which we have glimpsed the intimate lives of whole families through open doorways in Old Havana.

This discrepancy does not bother Myra. Nor does she feel that it is a recipe for social unrest. "I live in a very large house with three or four bedrooms," she says somewhat vaguely (space-hungry Cubans keep an even closer eye on the numbers of bedrooms per dwelling than New Yorkers). "I am very comfortable and lack for nothing. In ten years, I will be able to come and stay in this hotel with my little girl. This is a necessary period. Some bad things, like prostitution, come with it. But these are necessary for economic advancement."[7]

Myra's well-drilled ideology may have got her a cushy job, but its machine-gun bursts smack of a nascent pride of ownership. Above her in the emerging Cuban business hierarchy, this young, upwardly mobile Marxist sees people not much older than herself in senior ministry positions: Vice-President Carlos Lage, Cuba's answer to Clinton's respected secretary of the treasury Robert Rubin, is in his forties, as is the minister of culture, former UNEAC (Union of Cuban Writers and Artists) president Abel Prieto. Although they must answer to the prostáticos, they have some latitude to develop a market economy.

In 1991 the Cuban Communist Party Congress adopted a resolution establishing profit-maximizing state-owned corporations that were free of the central state apparatus in the sense that they could engage in multinational commerce with foreign investors. These companies are in charge of their own purchases, negotiations, and marketing, which, judging from the plethora of glossy brochures they put out, appears to be a big ticket item. They must establish and maintain their own profit margins, surrendering to the state any profits remaining after reinvesting and paying dividends to the shareholders. "They all have the same owner, but they compete viciously with each other, just like Procter and Gamble," Kavulich says. "Cuba is set up wonderfully for mass privatization."

A troupe of dancers in skimpy rehearsal clothes reminiscent of the Batista days are bumping and grinding away as Myra leads us through the restaurant in the penthouse nightclub, the highest point in all Havana, with stunning 360 degree views. A few floors down, staring directly into the radio transmitters for the whole city, is the office of Cable News Network, until recently the only American news organization allowed by Castro to maintain a permanent correspondent. The network earns its keep by producing the weather reports for the region. In November 1998, hungry for public relations, Castro restored the status of the Associated Press for the first time since its expulsion in 1969.

A young mother with killer instincts, Myra doesn't worry that Mr. Hilton might want his hotel back now that the Cubans have done his renovation for him. "If he comes down here, we'll cut him down like that," she says airily, making a machete motion with one brisk manicured hand. "Chop-chop."

In 1991, for the first time since the wave of nationalizations following Castro's coup in 1959, foreign companies were allowed to buy a 50 percent share of new hotels (the land underneath them still belongs to the state). "They put up 100 percent of the capital in exchange for 50 percent of the profits," one foreign observer who preferred to remain anonymous said.

In theory, to encourage investment, foreigners have been promised a ten-year total tax amnesty, along with the ability to repatriate all their profits. In theory, they are also exempt from paying customs duties on imports of construction materials, furniture, and food. However, practice has been less than perfect. A law against "excess profits" stills stands on the books, although it is normally used against Cuban natives: in October 1994, the government confiscated cars, trucks, cash, and other property from too-successful Cuban entrepreneurs. Sources in the restaurant business say that if a restaurant does too well, the government starts cutting back supplies: first prime sirloin, then coffee, then rice.

Some foreign coventurers have attempted to reform the cumbersome wage-payment system. Although this seems out of character for postcolonial capitalists who are out for the cheapest labor possible, the invisible hand of self-interest is at work, particularly in the tourist business. "You just can't teach people to serve when they don't have any incentive," said one personnel trainer who preferred to remain anonymous.

The incentives began in the form of "goody baskets" of soaps, toothpastes, and other luxury items. Now Cubans who work for a foreign company get monthly bonuses in dollars of between 5 and 30 percent of their peso wage. The Cuban government resists this practice; according to one foreign businessman (who also preferred to remain anonymous), the government has accused some of his colleagues of being foreign agents and kicked them out of the country. "They can't kick us all out, because they need us," he said, without much conviction.

In May 1995 the Cuban government suddenly decided to cancel all contracts with the pension fund of the Spanish utility Endesa, which had been managing several hotels in Cuba. Spanish directors were replaced by Cubans, and Endesa's bank accounts in Cuba were frozen. The Cuban government claimed that its aggressive move was a response to a Spanish government decision to freeze fund investment in Cuba. Endesa and its affiliates demanded $12 million in damages from the Cubans through the International Arbitration Tribunal in Paris, a dispute that is still unresolved.[8]

Reliable information on the 225-plus coventures is hard to find: one precondition of coventuring in Cuba, say foreign investors, is keeping one's mouth shut. Bad accounting is also a problem: one investment manager who specializes in Latin America says foreign co-investors in Cuba keep their books murky out of fear of U.S. retaliation because of the embargo. In 1994, on gross receipts of $800 million cash, the island economy made just $250 million, even though the number of visitors jumped 13 percent. The president of Cubanacan, a state-run tourism agency, lost his job because of "mismanagement."[9]

For the record, foreign investors in Cuba state that they have seen no evidence of corruption in their dealings with government officials. In private, they say that it's pandemic. They also complain about preferential treatment for the military, which has preempted executive positions despite a lack of business training.

Another source of complaint is the favoritism showed by the

Cuban government to Spanish investors like the Sol Melia group, which took over the luxury Cohiba Hotel in Havana. Sol Melia, one of two hotel companies controlled by the Majorca-based Escarrer family, has bookkeeping problems of its own and was recently suspended for two weeks from trading on the Bolsa.

"We have become a colony of Spain again," said one Cuban businessman.

Ismail

> "I was here for Batista and I was here for Grau and I was here for Prio and Machado and I'm here for Batista again. Politicians come and go like the wind," said the duena at the Casa des Virgenes, "but there will always be virgins."
>
> *John Sayles,* Los Gusanos *(1991)*

The YUMMIES are on parade at the sumptuously restored Beaux-Arts masterpiece the Teatro García Lorca, where they show off their finery in the magnificent marble galleries and gold-encrusted boxes. Culture is one of the best excuses for self-display, and there is a lot of it in Cuba, where the Ministries of Culture and Tourism work hand-in-shoulder-length-glove. Tonight the offering is a national institution: Alicia Alonso and the Ballet Nacional de Cuba as the centerpiece of an international dance festival sponsored by many of the hotels. The audience is vociferously appreciative and almost exclusively white. I count only one mixed couple, despite all I have read about Cuba's success as an integrated society. The blacks throng outside, begging for money to go in, or hawking flimsy white cornets full of sugarcane candy.

At the Hotel Inglaterra, the colonial relic where we are staying next door, the distinction is even more evident. There are no blacks on the hotel staff. Receptionists, waiters, managers, doormen all have the deceptively delicate, creamy features of the conquistadores, making them a Caribbean version of the Irish.

Graham Greene favored this hotel above all others and used it for the setting of his novel *Our Man in Havana*. Given Greene's fondness for whoring, it is easy to understand why. The nineteenth-century wedding cake, with its vaulted, Alhambra-esque interiors, is around the corner from the ironically named Calle des Virtudes (Street of Virtues), one of the most squalid in all Havana. From its dark, rubble-strewn doorways every night emerge some heartbreakingly beautiful girls, their piquant faces palimpsests of Chinese, Negro, Indian, and

European. They are tall and sinewy, Ibo or Yoruba, with long, delicate bones and graceful carriage, but one in four is too young to have breasts. In immaculate chignons and long gowns, they pick their way on stiletto heels through garbage and sleeping mutts to the blazing doorway of the Inglaterra, where the doormen decide with imperious waves who will work that night. Elegance (and extreme youth) are the keys to employment: too-obvious tarts are turned away. One scrawny waif who keeps plucking nervously at the hem of her dress, which barely covers her thighs, is shooed away by her sister.

As a female writer, I have often bemoaned the fact that I am excluded from that petri dish of human experience, the whorehouse. Not to worry. I am living in one. The Inglaterra, described in our tourist guidebook as "the unofficial meeting-point for younger, independent travelers in Havana," rents by the hour as well as catering to more established guests. In fact, I catch a strong whiff of sex from my bedspread, which makes me wonder what happens when I'm out. It is not the place to bring your family, particularly if you have teenaged daughters (take them to the Nacional instead).

The Street of Virtues.

Since my translator and I are unencumbered, we take a keen delight in monitoring the comings and goings, much to the discomfort of several American men in their late fifties who do not wish to be observed. It's infinitely more entertaining than the ballet, and almost as choreographed.

In the rooftop bar, La Terraza, small men with large cigars are dazed by their good fortune as they find themselves flanked by two fourteen-year-olds apiece. The girls are very polite. They amble up on Bambi legs and offer to sell us raffle tickets. (The hotel maids, accustomed to catering to all tastes, have clearly decided we are lesbians: they salute us each evening with a fresh sculpture designed from our bathroom towels to resemble two swans, kissing.) The girls work in pairs, supervised by a tall, chic "Negrita" who arranges meetings and prices. Some men need more encouragement than others. Aware that the two of us are having a good deal of rude fun, one fiftyish mark with the soft look of a boy gone to seed keeps glancing over as if begging to be rescued from his teenager, who swings one long sandaled leg and yawns in his face until the Negrita packs them off to bed.

Prurient curiosity is its own reward. As we sip *guayapo*, a delicious drink made from crushed sugarcane, in the small park in front of our hotel, a rangy young black man in haute gymwear couture introduces himself as a "professor of basketball." His name is Ismail, and he has made up his mind that two such charming *gringas* cannot be allowed to see Havana unescorted.

Ismail is tall, beautifully proportioned, with a bullet-smooth shaven head and bold actor's eyes that are never still. He has many admirers of both sexes and does not understand why we don't admire him, too. But Ismail is nothing if not adaptable. As soon as he realizes that our interests are journalistic, he offers to be interviewed.

Ismail has an ax to grind: he says that black people cannot get jobs in tourism. Two years ago, he says, he would be put in jail for even talking to two *turistas*. Now things have loosened up a bit, and in fact he is very bold, escorting us into the lobby of the Inglaterra under the scowl of the doorman. But his bravado dries up when he meets Marlene, our guide from the Ministry of Tourism.

"Be careful," he whispers when, after a hard look at him, she excuses herself to make a call to the ministry. "Now they will try to control all your time so that you cannot speak to me."

And in fact our schedule is exhaustively arranged. But the next afternoon we sneak away to meet Ismail and his friend Mauro, another "professor," this time of "English." In point of fact, Mauro's claim to English is tenuous at best. Very few people in Cuba speak viable English even in the tourist industry. Outside of the embargo, this is one of the most isolating features of Cuban society today: even a senior ministry official had to ask for my translator's help.

Mauro is a delicate twenty-four-year-old with creamy skin and a mop of Rasta curls. Perhaps because he is lighter-skinned, he is even more vehement on the subject of race than Ismail. "The advent of tourism brought racism to Cuba," he says.

Well, not quite. Early on in his career, President Castro is on record as saying, "We've got to kill that Negro," meaning Fulgencio Batista. (Batista was a mulatto with some Chinese ancestry.) Blacks and mulattos are historically underrepresented in Cuba's fourteen-member Politburo and, for that matter, in the leadership of the Cuban-American National Foundation, the right-wing federation of Cuban exiles in the United States.[10]

Race has always been an issue in Cuban politics but is more so now, three decades after the exodus of the white upper and professional classes turned nonwhites into a majority. The Castro regime has made common cause with black populations in other countries, for example, the black African nations and the United States. In 1959, ironically, Castro invited down-and-out former heavyweight champ Joe Louis to work as a booster for Cuban tourism among American blacks. Louis told reporters, "There is no place in the world except Cuba where a Negro can go in the wintertime with absolutely no discrimination."[11]

But demographics belie rhetoric. A little more than half the Cuban population in the late nineteenth century was black, and the white elite feared that Cuba might follow Haiti in becoming a country under black rule. Although the black population supported the Cuban elite in the struggle for independence from Spain in 1895, they felt cheated of the rewards for their participation. When the Cuban government banned a newly formed black political party in 1910 as a "racially based" organization, smoldering resentment ignited two years later in the Little War of the Blacks. Four thousand blacks died in the fighting, which was quickly suppressed by the U.S.-backed white government. Cuba became a predominantly white country until the second half of the twentieth century.

Ismail lives in Miramar, a neighborhood of magnificent homes once owned by the white elite and middle classes. In the early days of the Revolution, blacks from the countryside and the Havana slums moved into these precipitously vacated mansions.

Today the children of the original squatters are still there. Although many of them, like Ismail, are not Castro fans, as long as he remains in power, the original owners cannot confiscate what the residents now regard, and defend, as "their" property.

The mariachis at El Floridita, where Hemingway did his heavy drinking, do not like our conversation about caste and tourism. They are white. They surround us and raise their volume, and do not move away even when asked to do so. Ismail and Mauro raise their voices defiantly. "A black man can't get any job in tourism higher than a doorman or a cleaner," Mauro says scornfully. "You have to apply for any job through the Ministry for Tourism, and you can forget it if you don't have relatives who are connected."

"Only whites get hotel positions of any power," says Ismail. "They control who comes and goes, who works, who doesn't. They get their wives and girlfriends admitted as prostitutes."

The mariachis sit down behind us and glare at us. I decide it is time to pay the check.

Racism in Cuba. Too intimidated to enter this elegant tourist restaurant, a black man lingers outside to listen to the music he loves.

Mauro and Ismail are uncharacteristically subdued on the subject of prostitution. Of course, the government does not want prostitution, but the government does not shut it down, because of "economic necessity." Prostitution is not legal, therefore it is not taxed. This means that it is probably the backbone of the black-market economy, which is the only economy there is. Does that mean that prostitutes, unlike other workers, get to keep what they make? "The police are too corrupt!" complains Ismail, with considerable umbrage.

There has been a great shortage of Cuban males since the Revolution, one man to every seven women to be exact. Many Cuban men keep their excess wives, mistresses, and girlfriends fully employed as *jineteras*, or female hustlers. How do Mauro and Ismail, as Cuban men, feel about this? "We are Cubans," Ismail shrugs expressively. "We laugh, we dance. In spite of everything, we have a good time."

Mauro, who is younger, is silent and brooding. Moments later, he asks me a loaded question about what we have read of Castro's private wealth in the United States. "Nothing at all," I gulp, my mind on hidden mikes. For the first time since we met, Ismail's eyes grow still, and very hard. He smiles at me unpleasantly, and it occurs to me that I may be having coffee not only with a gigolo but with a police informant.

They want us to go to a "folklórico ballet" performance in the old city late that evening. "Folklórico" is a euphemism for the rituals of Santería, the Afro-Cuban religion which is widely practiced in Cuba today, perhaps even more so since the Revolution. Despite repeated government efforts in the 1960s to discourage any religious expression other than that of Marxist atheism, Afro-Cuban cultism mushroomed after the flight of Cuba's upper classes, spreading from black townships in Oriente to white neighborhoods in Havana. According to some estimates, there are as many as 4,000 *babalaos*, or Santería priests, in Cuba, compared to only 305 Roman Catholic priests.

Castro has always viewed Africa as the last great frontier of socialism, and since 1973 Cuba has sent teachers and doctors there as well as troops. During the 1970s and 1980s, the estimated half-million Cuban soldiers who fought to aid Marxist President Jose Edouardo Dos Santos in the war in Angola brought home a renewed interest in Afro-Cuban religions. Most soldiers were black. At home, as food rations became shorter and government speeches longer, many Cubans of both races began worshiping, just as the slaves did in colonial days when African religions were forbidden by the Spanish, the same figurine as Santa Barbara by day and Chango, the Afro-Cuban god of war, by night. Catholic priests like Monsignor Carlos Manuel de Céspedes, the vicar of Havana, consulted closely with the babalaos to avoid losing their flocks and also to fortify their own position against Castro.

In 1990, enraged by a letter from Cuba's Catholic bishops demanding, among other things, that he start the process of democratic reform and reconciliation with the despised *gusanos* (worms), or Cuban exiles, Castro launched a vigorous propaganda courtship of Santería followers as well as of the Palo Monte Bantu magic cult and the Abakua, a network of mutual-protection secret societies that practice African warrior rituals. The Central Committee ordered a media campaign that would portray all three cults in the rosiest light. Documentaries were pumped into prime-time television, and an album by folk singer Celina González featuring the ditty "Long Live Chango!" was distributed and heavily promoted by the regime. In 1991 the Party-faithful UNEAC published a "reference" guide to the Santería deities and their taste in sacrifices. A new museum, the House of Africa, opened in Old Havana with exhibits and lectures on Afro-Cuban cults. And in a Marxist rendition of sensitivity training, the Communist Party gave members time off from their jobs to take crash courses in Santería to "stay in touch with the people."

But "the people," who had been lifted to middle-class status by the Revolution and were consequently hit hardest by the rigors of the Special Period, were more interested in dollars than in cultural mollification. Growing numbers of Venezuelans and other Latin Americans, as well as Germans, had begun visiting Cuba to become initiated into Santería, paying an average of four thousand dollars each for the ceremony. This is a somewhat specialized taste, as it involves having one's naked torso rubbed with a recently decapitated chicken. The Castro regime, which controlled all tourist contacts, directed these tourists to the babalaos but kept most of the money, only permitting the babalaos to accept gifts like electric fans or televisions.

The babalaos, who had initially responded to Castro's courtship by elevating him to the position of *elegido*, chosen by the Orisha gods as their envoy to guide the Cuban people along the right path, turned against him. They were used to making small fortunes as well as to a certain amount of independence. Even the prospect of power-sharing with the Ministry of the Interior counterintelligence forces, who sought their collaboration eagerly in ferreting out personal information as well as any counterrevolutionary activities in their parishes, did not appeal. As the numbers of Santería-based tourism soared, the antagonism deepened. By late 1991, even those Santería priests who had collaborated with ministry recanted. Those who offer these services to tourists today are likely to be bogus or worse.[12]

It is easy to develop a strong dislike for one's fellow tourists while traveling in Cuba. So many of the "attractions" are rooted in the attraction of the decadent to the primitive, or of the corrupt to the innocent. There is nothing sadder than the look of infinite patience on the face of a twelve-year-old whore as she waits for her madam to strike a price with a fifty-year-old American man whose generosity fails to match his vanity. Even Ismail, as he visibly calculates which of his many talents the customer is most likely to buy, looks momentarily lost. These Cubans are trapped between two betrayals: that of the capitalist who knows that his purchasing power is unlimited in the land of the desperate, and that of the Communist who sells his own people for the Revolution. The deal degrades both buyer and seller. It is very depressing for an American woman to feel, as strongly as I did, that the Communist knows his market.

Leaving the Capitolio, a trio of tattooed German males envelop Ismail, touching his smooth chocolate skin and twittering like bats. He breaks free and insists on walking us back to our hotel, kissing me ostentatiously in front of the Inglaterra doorman. We turn down all invitations to the "folklórico" and stay close to the hotel. Much later that night, sipping *mojitos* on the terrace where, according to the tourist books, "young Havana likes to meet," we see the man Ismail has introduced as his brother working the Inglaterra as a pimp.

Roberto

Roberto's business card says, "Pintor, escultor, y ceramista." A distinguished-looking gentleman in his sixties, with a well-brushed white beard and navy blazer, he lives in a house-studio that occupies an entire block between Calle O'Reilly and Calle Obispo in the old city. It is filled with choice antiques and a collection of nineteenth- and twentieth-century Cuban art, including his own. Among other modern conveniences, it boasts its own electric kiln, in a city where most streets are still completely dark at night owing to the fuel shortages caused by the U.S. embargo. Asked if he thinks artists are a privileged class in Cuba, he replies, "Work hard, and you will be rewarded."

A good Party man, Roberto has traveled widely, with the permission of his government, to France, Italy, Czechoslovakia, Russia, the Baltics, Miami, and New York. He is a member of UNEAC, which he describes as a "nongovernment" syndicate of writers and artists.

According to historian Robert Quirk, UNEAC, an official union, was formed in 1961 in order to enforce Revolutionary discipline and mobilize support for the regime. Its membership was instructed by government spokespersons that financial reward depended on their militancy and their reliability, as well as on their ability to create wealth for the nation. *Viajar*—permission to travel—became the most coveted reward, in a country where the entire population is under house arrest. Between 1988 and 1991, UNEAC donated more than three hundred cars to its most prominent members, as well as hundreds of visas for trips abroad. Some Cuban artists, like Roberto, were also given visas for extended journeys. In a tacit understanding with the Ministry of Culture, they were granted extensions to their six-month visas in exchange for not criticizing the regime in public. The liberal-leaning minister of culture, Armando Hart, who authorized travel abroad for reform-minded artists and writers and often gave his blessing to artworks that exceeded Party limits, was replaced by UNEAC president Abel Prieto in 1995.[13]

Far from imprisoning his intellectuals, *El Gran Jefe* (The Big Chief, Castro's nickname) is now their best friend. He graced the sixth UNEAC congress, which took place while we were in Havana, and remarked approvingly on its conformity to Revolutionary standards. The congress concluded with a gala for the artists at the fabled Tropicana nightclub, kept intact since its gangster heyday for the entertainment of the Party elite.

In association with the Ministry of Culture and various "cultural representatives" (each hotel has its own), UNEAC decides which artists will be exhibited and promoted. The state provides gallery space, newspaper promotion, and catalogue aid to the favored few. Criteria include graduation from the six-year course at one of the state art academies, but most important is the artist's political standing. The majority of nongraduates are reduced, "out of economic necessity," Roberto says, to selling their wares on the street.

Roberto's cultivated tones change to a snarl when we inquire about the standing of some of the young artists whose work we have seen that afternoon at the studio-gallery of Frank Carlos Vasquez, an avant-garde dealer who specializes in the unestablished. "That muchacho is going to disappear," he promises. We wonder what, exactly, he means. It is a relief to hear him say, "His prices are totally out of touch with reality."

Actually, the prices charged at the Estudio-Galería Frank Carlos Vasquez are pretty close to the prices in Roberto's own galería, which leads us to suspect that the young dealer's real offense is to attempt pricing parity. The stakes are high. Through UNESCO the United Nations has championed the exemption of art objects from the U.S. embargo; but again, the exemption is only for the chosen few like Roberto, who now can sell his collection, and possibly even keep the proceeds, outside Cuba. Artists, like other entrepreneurs, are now taxed at between 10 and 50 percent.

Roberto looks forward to revisiting New York but not the former Soviet Union, which welcomed him in its glory days. "I prefer to travel without seeing so much suffering," he sighs.

Our ministry duenas are very keen that we experience the cultural glories of Havana, and so we dutifully make the rounds of the "museums" which have sprung up around the Plaza de Armas in the old city. It is a strange experience to go to a museum in a country that has amputated its non-Revolutionary history. There is nothing even resembling curatorship at the Museum of the City of Havana, which is filled with massive silver objects "collected" by the Banco Nacional after Castro took over. Although the objects are of vastly different styles and epochs, they are all dated "late nineteenth century."

The same airy disregard for facts applies to the Museo de Arabes, which is housed in another mansion, along with Havana's only mosque. The very pretty, very polite young female curator informs us that the house originally belonged to the family of José Martí, Cuba's apostolic martyr. Curiously, the house is dedicated to the memory of the Lebanese tailor who invented the *guayabera*, the traditional loose, embroidered shirt favored by Cuban men. The carpets on display, most of which are carelessly rolled against the wall, range from rare Persians to Turkish kilims to 1950s Navajo and shag. All are classified as "Arab."

The next day, we escape on a Cubanatur day trip to the nineteenth-century landscape-painter's paradise of Pinar del Río and Viñales, approximately 112 miles west of Havana. It is the heart of the tobacco-farming region, and we are taken to a "typical" farm as part of our tour. The strikingly pretty farmer's wife is the only woman we see wearing full makeup in the countryside. While her husband, a godlike specimen of a "paysan," as our guide describes him with breezy dogmatic incorrectness, plows stoically away, she shows us the television, fridge, and radio with which communism has blessed them. Her five children, each prettier than the last, have bicycles on which to go to school and watch Saturday morning cartoons while she tries to sell us cigars. Outside, a state-manned kiosk larger than the farmhouse hawks *refrescos* and T-shirts bearing Che's picture.

It is nightfall when we drive back to Havana, and the *autopista*, or highway, is innocent of electricity. Our shiny new bus has no windshield wipers, and the windscreen is quickly encrusted with dust and bugs. The men are called outside to donate their saliva to the state. One by one, they solemnly spit on the windscreen, which the driver then scrubs with his hanky. And so we get back to Havana in time to catch the UNEAC congress' closing gala at the Tropicana.

Out of all the tourist attractions on offer in Havana, the Tropicana is still the best value for money. Like the Staatsoper in what used to be East Berlin, it has been immaculately preserved through both the heyday of Soviet colonialism and the darkest days of the Special Period for the pleasure of the Party elite. Ironically, like the wave of tsarist nostalgia that has washed over Russia since the Iron Curtain rang down, what the Cubans seem to remember most fondly of their own history are the old Batista days, and that is what the Tropicana embodies, so to speak.

The UNEAC stalwarts parade onstage to receive some truly hideous paintings in recognition of their contributions to Revolutionary thought in such areas as culture and marketing. At 10 P.M. the show lumbers under way with

Pinar del Río and Viñales, a nineteenth-century landscape-painter's paradise now populated by hotels.

the famous "Dance of the Chandeliers," in which 150 girls undulate from the top of the outdoor amphitheater into the audience wearing bodystockings and large twinkling chandeliers on top of their heads. The wiring is ancient and some chandeliers twinkle less brightly than others, but the cumulative effect is still delightful, and there is nothing that you could not take a twelve-year-old to see, with real dancers and no self-stimulation on phallic poles. Demi Moore would not make the grade. "Only a socialist country could afford a show like this," remarks the nice little foreign gangster who gets us our table. "Where else could they afford to pay 150 girls?"

A "typical" farm in Pinar del Río and Viñales.

"It's a wonderful country." The view from the Malecón is still one of the world's most romantic vistas.

His card identifies him as an "Especialista en Servicios y Marketing," and his speciality is "gastronomie," which seems harmless enough. He says he owned a five-star hotel and several ski resorts in Canada before he got into trouble with the law over the ownership of his hotel. Fortuitously, he was invited by the Cuban ambassador to Canada to come to Cuba in 1993 to help develop the emerging restaurant industry. Now married to a Cuban doctor (his fifth wife), he has an infant daughter. His wife is a mulatta, and, he says, his own mother is more racist than the Cubans.

"It's a wonderful country," he hastens to add. "Before I came here, I needed things. Mansions, Mercedes, yachts. . . . Now I have just a little apartment with a wife and child that I love, and I am happy."

Then he asks me not to use his name in order to protect his family. As the UNEAC faithful join the leg line onstage, Cuba seems caught in a timewarp. Those who forget, or obliterate, history are condemned to repeat it, and it is difficult to see how Cuba will grow out of its position as a satellite, at least in Castro's lifetime. Right now the embargo, while it imposes serious hardships on the Cuban people, is also a con-

Just in case you think communism will be forgotten by Cuba's children.

venient scapegoat for the country's systemic dependencies. Even if the United States relaxes its restrictions, said one ministry official, Cuba's biggest fear is becoming a colony again.

This is not entirely the paranoia bred of long isolation. Although the island has natural wealth in sugar, nickel, some petroleum, tobacco, and coffee, along with other potential for high food-stuff production, it has failed to industrialize because of its years of reliance on the Soviet Union. The country is only beginning to computerize. Even in the technological field of medicine, where Castro has made another huge infrastructure investment in the Genetic Engineering and Technology Institute outside Havana and in "medical tourism" centers which offer bargain-basement plastic surgery as well as treatment for vitiligo, psoriasis, and retinitis pigmentosa, a failure to meet Western European licensing standards has limited the market to wealthy Central and South Americans as effectively as the U.S. embargo. And, although John Kavulich regards the permission recently given by both U.S. and Cuban authorities to Denver-based Genesis Medical Technologies to test its needle-free vaccine injector on six thousand Cuban volunteers and a Cuban anti-tetanus vaccine as the first substantial crack in the decades-long embargo, it is clear that what the Cuban government brings to the table is, once again, Cuban bodies to put at risk.

Other recent events, such as the legalization of Christmas, Castro's decision to allow Associated Press to reestablish a permanent bureau in Havana, and President Clinton's easement of restrictions on humanitarian aid and travel to Cuba, suggest that an end to the embargo may be in sight. But timing is everything, and it may be a little late in the business cycle for Cuba to take advantage of this opening up, even if the U.S. president should revoke the 1996 Helms-Burton law penalizing foreign companies that invest in Cuba. It is also possible that once Cuba is no longer forbidden fruit, it will lose some of its attraction as a tourist destination.

In 1999, according to a ministry official, Cuban tourism figures turned downward. At the same time, the Ministry of Tourism's five-year plan called for the investment of $1.36 billion in hotel rooms alone, based on projections made in a PriceWaterhouseCoopers report prepared in 1994 which does not account for the impact of global recession on tourist arrivals for the year 2000.

"We are very worried," said a ministry official at the time of my visit, and with good reason. Cuba depends on "low-demographic" package tourists, who are the first to stay home when money is tight. New construction for 1999 was cut back to 80 percent of projections because of recessionary fears generated by the Asian money crisis of 1998.

Recession is a double threat to this enormous infrastructure bet. Foreign investors rush to minimize risk in downturns, especially the large number of investors recently burned by Russia. If the global economy heads south, Cuba will look very risky indeed.

Castro, who is in his mid-seventies, shows no sign of relinquishing his grip. His response to any corruption of the Revolutionary ideal has been ever increasing government regulation and taxation. The threat of confiscation in bad times (or in good ones) is still substantial. And his press control appears to reach all the way to the United States. *Forbes* magazine, which published an article entitled "Kings, Queens,

and Dictators" in July 1998, naming President Castro as one of the world's wealthiest people because of his putative $100 million personal stake in the Cuban economy, was rebuked by the Cuban Special Interests Section in Washington. *Forbes* has no documentary evidence of Castro's personal wealth, although the Cuban-American right quotes the article as if it were itself the proof.

"What we meant was that President Castro *controls* the Cuban economy, that he can seize assets and has done so before," says reporter Kerry Dolan, who

The threat of government confiscation of private enterprise is still real.

wrote the piece. "We're not saying he *owns* anything there."[14]

John Kavulich retorts that, if Castro indeed owns the Cuban economy, the $100 million figure cited by *Forbes* is low. "Is this a guy who controls everything? Yes. Is he running out and buying Hermès ties? No. Most dictators put money aside for a rainy day, when they get their ass thrown out. Castro doesn't expect to leave Cuba alive."

While some conjecture that Cuban military chiefs, allied with new political forces like the Catholic church, might invite Castro to step down and accept an "honorary chairmanship," this seems an unlikely choice for a leader who has spent the past forty years giving the finger to the United States. Castro's crown prince is his sixty-seven-year-old brother, Raúl, the current defense minister, who is widely disliked and whose succession might lead to civil war. *Fidelismo* might also end with the bang of a military coup, a possibility that is viewed with some equanimity by the United States.

"The military will all put on civilian clothes, just like in other countries," Kavulich said. "They're running everything now, from hotels to airlines to producing honey."

That's the confident voice of superpower speaking. But we have already guessed wrong on the ability of Communist-built states to cross smoothly or peacefully into democracy through the free market. The

Free markets at work. Cubans stay alive on remittances from relatives in the United States. They may not have food, but they have rollerblades.

amount of "humanitarian aid" Clinton proposes to increase is currently estimated at between $500,000 and $800,000 and will not begin to compensate for the attrition of tourism should a stock-market downturn prompt a recession. It is also difficult to see how Cuba can pole-vault from tourism to information technology and related services given the paucity of its English-language base; and until it can decrease its dependency on tourism, the economy is probably stuck with prostitution as its number-one employer. Although the industry may be moved out of sight of the fancier hotels, to otherwise regulate it would be, sadly, economically self-defeating. If, prompted by the misery of its people, Cuba follows the example of its role model, the (former) Soviet Union, Tourism Minister Osmany Cienfuegos may have good reason to get his uniform out of mothballs. "If Cuba goes like Russia," says one foreign executive who has worked in Cuba for five years, "I'm out of here on the next plane with my wife and kids."

CHAPTER 6 **Ireland** The Laboratory

I have met them at close of day
Coming with vivid faces
From counter or desk among grey
Eighteenth-century houses.
I have passed with a nod of the head
Or polite meaningless words,
Or have lingered awhile and said
Polite meaningless words,
And thought before I had done
Of a mocking tale or a gibe
Around the fire at the club,
Being certain that they and I
But lived where motley is worn:
All is changed, changed utterly:
A terrible beauty is born.
                    W. B. Yeats, "Easter, 1916"

IT IS AUGUST 4, 1994, at the height of the tourist season. I am standing in the middle of a crowd on Kildare Street facing the National Gallery of Art in Dublin. We are gazing at an unexpected exhibition, a parade of Northern Irish Catholics from Belfast's inner city. The marchers have appeared as if by magic, about five thousand strong. Without a whisper of advance publicity, they have traveled by car and bus and lorry the hundred short miles between the rubble of West Belfast and the trim brick squares of Dublin to demonstrate their weariness with "the Troubles." They are strangely passive as they march. There are no triumphalist slogans, no shouts of solidarity, just a seemingly endless procession of pilgrims whose pasty, exhausted faces flicker enviously at the Mercedes and burberries around them. The well-dressed crowd is conspicuously silent.

It is a long way from my glasnost junket to Finland in 1990 and yet there is the same sense of stagecraft. The somber marchers are like

Birnam Wood coming to Dunsinane. I almost expect the watchers to pat their gloved hands together in polite if tepid applause. It is quite unheard-of for Dublin to sponsor such a demonstration, as the position of the South has traditionally been one of cautious apartheid, allowing the Republic to prosper while the Six Counties remain economically paralyzed by war. Even now, socioeconomic class separates the marchers from the watchers as much as politics. These are the have-nots, the people left behind by the Celtic Tiger's bound into the twenty-first century. A week later, the first "cease-fire" is announced.

Twenty years earlier, in the spring of my first year at Trinity College, I had cowered on almost the same spot, shielding my face as three hideous thuds rent the soft air. For the moment following them there was complete silence, and then the screaming began. The thuds were three car bombs, released in quick succession in the city center at the height of the afternoon rush hour by a loyalist splinter group angry at the progress of peace talks then under way at Stormont, the seat of the Northern Irish government. Afterward, we heard that fifty-three people had been killed inside of three minutes.

Dublin was a quiet town in the 1970s, something that made such violence even more shocking. But it was quiet largely because it was poor. Half a century of civil war added to three centuries of colonial rule had left it a peaceful wasteland. There were few restaurants—only one in City Centre would serve you a meal after ten o'clock at night—no nightclubs, and precious little in the way of consumer goods. About the only chef worthy of the name was my roommate, who cooked me a six-course French dinner on our two-ring gas burner after I cleaned up for her when a lover who was even more overcome by Guinness than he was by her charms threw up in our sofa pillows. The tourists were largely earnest Germans in search of a cheap walking holiday and students like me. In my digs at Trinity, the only way I could brave the dank chill of my sheets was to warm them with saucepans heated on the gas ring, which was also my only source of heat.

Dublin was, in its way, a far more democratic society than the one I had left behind me: you could talk to anyone in the pubs, from senators to actors to dockworkers. People drank to get warm, and people of all ages and professions were to be found draping the long, dark, smoky oaken counters, with their deep gleam of old beeswax. I think I learned how to talk in Dublin, as well as how to drink. The city was an adventure for me, a nice Jewish girl from Beverly Hills on the lam from the insularity of my hometown, but the young Irish fled it as soon as they were able, to escape the legacy of sodden despair that haunted the once-elegant squares. Merrion Square, the prettiest of all, was kept locked up and remained overgrown with weeds. Those who left (including, eventually, me) lamented the city's peculiar magic almost immediately, that intense sense of community beautifully captured by Luke Kelly in "The Town I Loved So Well," his modern-day ballad about his own home, Belfast.

> In my memory I will always see
> The town that I have loved so well
> Where our school played ball by the gasyard wall
> And we laughed at the smoke and smell.
> And when times got tough there was just about enough
> But we all saw it through without complaining
> For deep inside was a burning pride
> In the town I loved so well.

Now Ireland is what Cuba and all the countries like it aspire to be. In Dublin construction is the most explosive activity today. Merrion Square is once again a fashionable trysting spot, and construction cranes graze up and down the Liffey like a herd of giraffes. The historic panorama downriver from the Four Courts, where many of the bloodiest scenes of the Rising took place, is marked by a bottle-green glass carbuncle housing a world financial center. Every second shopfront on Grafton Street is a restaurant featuring Irish nouvelle cuisine designed at a hoity-toity culinary institute in County Cork. The streets are jammed with Mercedes. The pubs are full of the under-twenty-five set, most of whom are yakking on their cell phones instead of to each other. Poets are no longer to be found in the familiar liver-colored haunts of McDade's but are glimpsed from afar, striding grandly to readings, wispy gray hair moussed back into ponytails and beer bellies tucked into embroidered waistcoats. Nobody over thirty goes to the pub because, it appears, all the middle-aged people still residing in Ireland have gone through A.A. When *they* talk, it's about their twelve-step programs.

Dublin has been discovered, not least owing to an aggressive publicity campaign launched by the Irish government in support of the peace. The city is "changed, changed utterly" but not in the way its bard W. B. Yeats meant in his poems about the terrors and beauties of Easter 1916. It is changed into a small, shrill New York. Rather than falling to the British tanks and guns apostrophized later in Kelly's lament, today's Ireland may become the victim of its own prosperity. While its ancient clannishness is at least part of what enabled this spectacular transformation, it is now splitting rapidly into a society of haves and have-nots. That this separation is tremendously destructive in a small, tight-knit society, where everyone knows everyone else, can be seen in the suicide statistics, which have skyrocketed, particularly for the young, who are supposed to be the beneficiaries of the "new economy," Irish-style.

Dublin "is changed, changed utterly" into a small, shrill New York.

Much of the division is driven by real estate as entire neighborhoods are redeveloped for tourism and wealthy foreigners buy second, third, and fourth homes well beyond the reach of many Dubliners, who must work second jobs to support their first mortgages. The ancient Viking settlement at the heart of the city, the scene of large stretches of James Joyce's *Ulysses*, has been Soho-ized into an upscale ghetto of shops, cultural centers, pubs filled with American undergraduates, and tiny apartments which, as one critic put it, are architectural arguments for birth control.

The area, known as Temple Bar, began in the 1980s as artists squatted in derelict buildings slated for demolition by the CIE, the local transit authority. Anxious to defend their fiefdom, they made common cause with Dublin's growing conservationist movement. One of the movement's founders, David Norris, took over the lease of an old tea warehouse and established a gay community center, which, together with the Project Arts Centre, a nearby theater on the fringes of Temple Bar, initiated the area's "discovery" as the young and curious came searching for nightlife.

Perhaps more than any other Dubliner, David Norris embodies the changes which have taken place in the city since 1980. A stocky ex-rugby player with fiercely blue eyes, he was Dublin's leading James Joyce exegete before he became a fixture in politics, both as a conservationist and as the leader of the Irish gay-rights movement. David taught Joyce at Trinity when I was a graduate student there and kept a graphic plaster depiction of a garden gnome performing fellatio on a toadstool in his office in order to intimidate the undergraduates. He was a rigorous scholar, despite the fact that he never, to my knowledge, finished his M.Litt. dissertation, and he knew most of Joyce's works by heart. He was also a riotous raconteur who delighted in outraging the bourgeoisie.

On my birthday, which falls on Bloomsday (the day on which *Ulysses* is set and on which James Joyce met his wife and muse, Nora Barnacle), David would present himself at my door in a natty three-piece suit, a boater, and a green carnation, and we would set off on the walk taken by *Ulysses'* hero, Leopold Bloom. By the end of the day, we would have a long line of stragglers following us like the children who followed the Pied Piper of Hamelin, for David would recite large swatches of the famous Nighttown sequence in every pub we stopped at. His fabulous memory translated into an intimate knowledge of every Georgian facade in Dublin (Joyce is nothing if not place-specific).

Today David is known as Senator Norris, having parlayed his passion for conservation into a political career. As an independent senator in the Irish Parliament, he is not affiliated with a party. "I can say whatever I like," he says; but then, he always did, in a peppery rush of staccato sibilants. Today he is empowered to say it in Cuba, Iran, Russia, Tibet, and East Timor, among other countries, where he travels to speak out on human rights as a member of the Senate Foreign Affairs Committee. Although he is probably proudest of being part of Ireland's lobby to have human rights included in the foundation documents of the European Union, conservation issues continue to be a major preoccupation.

Interviewed on the telephone between Senate sessions, he excoriated the Irish government's role in coopting Temple Bar, "in a fairly hardnosed commercial operation," ten years after the bohemians did the real work. "We were written out of history," he said, adding almost off-handedly that the community center had been bombed, a crime that was never solved by the police. Today, Senator Norris says, he regards the changes in Temple Bar, though "forced" by the government, as "fairly positive." "The area is full of life, though at the cost of neglect of small, organically based local things. It's overly full of pubs and restaurants and some of the life isn't the best sort, hen and stag parties from England, lots of rowdy behavior, that sort of thing." Although I remember the uprooting and upending of a Henry Moore statue in the men's urinal of the Trinity law society as a yearly ritual, Senator Norris protested finding a pair of boxer shorts dangling from the trees in Parliament Street. But on the whole, he thinks that the work of the conservation movement has been made easier. "The official attitude of the 1960s and 1970s, always siding with the developers, despoiling beautiful Georgian facades to avenge the crimes of eighteenth-century aristocrats, you don't find that anymore," he says. "We should forget about the crimes of the eighteenth century and only remember its accomplishments."[1]

The new Dublin, Senator Norris maintains, is far more cosmopolitan, "and that's to be welcomed," although he grumbles at some of the trendy new Temple Bar pubs like Pravda that tacitly refuse service to those over fifty. Still, "That's fine with me," he says before rushing back into chambers to enact anti-smoking legislation. "These new places filled with noise and smoke aren't for me."

More than $150 million of public and private funds poured into the twenty-eight-acre site that is now Dublin's "downtown" because of the efforts of David Norris and others. Some of the country's leading architectural experts predict that its cramped, pricey housing, much of it jerry-built almost overnight with substantial tax relief money and now even more expensive than New York City, will become the slums of Dublin's future. Certainly, Temple Bar already feels like a "location" to many Dubliners, including honorary ones like me: a movie set for tourists that resembles the reconstructions of London's Covent Garden or Paris' Les Halles. The new growth, says Senator Norris, which is driven by the tourism of "books and bricks, our literary heritage of Joyce, O'Casey, and Synge, which has imprinted our image all over the world, and our extraordinary architecture, which we preserved by staying out of World War II," will be sustained "as long as it is of value to the people, as long as we preserve our distinctive Irishness."[2]

On any given night, an estimated one hundred bands play in Dublin's clubs, a tribute to one of Ireland's richest and cleverest investors, the rock musician Bono and his cronies from the band U2. Together the group owns the majority of Dublin's trendiest hotels, restaurants, and nightclubs as well as the country's premier movie studio, Ardmore. Many of the clubs, like Mr. Pussy's Café de Luxe or Lillie's Bordello, celebrate Ireland's new "cool" sexual liberalism and its attempts to distance itself from its conservative Catholic heritage.

Every October, Dublin Castle is given over to the Festival Club for a cultural bacchanalia patterned after the venerable Edinburgh Festival, featuring well over a hundred plays and musical events performed in the infinite variety of venues the city now miraculously affords. And as in Soho, where artists pioneer, tourists will follow. "Like Roman candles, some cities blaze brightly for a time, set afire by converging sparks of talent, drive and luck," wrote Stephen O'Shea in the July 1995 issue of *Harper's Bazaar*. "The streets of places long asleep suddenly teem with people who have unfinished novels in their desks, invitations to art openings in their pockets, demo tapes in their handbags, and absolutely no need for sleep. Pedro Almodóvar's Madrid, Kurt Cobain's Seattle, Vaclav Havel's Prague—the last 15 years have seen the rise and fall of several unlikely meccas for the unmilitantly hip. Dublin has become a city of the arts in ways that other, more lavishly funded European capitals can only dream of."

In fact, Dublin's metamorphosis from boondock to Bloomsbury has been highly orchestrated. Even at its nadir in the 1970s, the city never suffered from a shortage of talent. (The filmmakers Neil Jordan, Jim Sheridan, and Morgan O'Sullivan were all living there at the time, as were Stephen Rea, Gabriel Byrne, and a host of other highly accomplished actors.) Theater arts were not taught at Trinity College, but the school had its own semiprofessional theater, a four-hundred-year-old drama society called Players which produced fourteen shows a year in a small, dank black box with an antiquated light board that were reviewed by all the major drama critics at the Dublin newspapers. Now there is a drama program, with its own lavish new theater, included in the curriculum, and Players as I remember it is no more.

It took heavily funded government programs applied to the arts to facilitate such change. Before the 1990s, the Irish government was known chiefly for its indifference to the arts, if not for downright hostility as manifested in a draconian censor. For the hidebound rural conservatives who ran it at the time to turn into Irish Medicis took not only a sudden appreciation of culture but a sudden appreciation of culture's use as a stimulus to tourism, export commodities, and public relations outreach to younger, well-heeled expatriates who needed to be convinced that Ireland was a cool place to live.

Shrewd country folk who now understand the crosscurrents of Brussels politics as well as they once knew the weather, can tell you that the speed of the transformation is due to large infusions of money from the European Union going into infrastructure repair: virtually the entire roadway system has been repaved courtesy of German taxpayers. The reason farmers are so au courant with economist-speak is that their industry, too, has been heavily supported by GATT grants, which, as the currents of Euroland have shifted, have been absorbed by larger countries with more clout than Ireland—for example, France and Germany. Because the government in the 1990s did not have to use tax money for infrastructure work, it could afford, in addition to unprecedented generosity in arts subsidies, to create tax shelters and low-cost, flexible loans for favored industries. Chief among these were construction, entertainment, and tourism, which in 1999 overtook agriculture as Ireland's key industry. These three, intertwined, have replaced faith, hope, and charity in the Irish pantheon—or even, perhaps, formed a new trinal unity and a model for countries which hope to emulate Ireland's success.

In 1993 the Minister for Arts, Culture, and the Gaeltacht (the original Gaelic-speaking community), Michael D. Higgins, crafted a tax break known as Section 35, which made moviemaking a government priority as a means of bringing jobs and hard currency into an economy wounded by decades of civil war. A similar measure was drafted by the same lawyers for the construction business. Both these bills were part of a long-term strategy designed by the Multilateral Investment Guarantee Agency (MIGA), a World Bank affiliate which coordinates public- and private-sector investment. The agency has a special interest in tourism, which is perceived in development terms as a "springboard" to other, "value-added" industries.

Michael D., as the Arts Minister is intimately known in the cozy world of Irish politics, is a poet from the seacoast city of Galway with perhaps an even greater flair for politics (Republican) than for poetry. He is shrewdly aware of the PR value of film for a society that wishes to be perceived as "healing." He is also known for his fondness for the company of movie stars, and his critics call him an opportunist who has simply capitalized on structures that were already in place. Critics have also commented unfavorably on Higgins' political biases: his family is said to have a long history of IRA leanings. But certainly he is to be credited with the vision of positioning Ireland's legendary storytelling culture as a tangible export in the global market, as well as for his inspired and persistent lobbying, which, for a brief while, engendered the kind of frenzy in which even stodgy E.U. bureaucracies offered screenwriting courses as an alternative to welfare. (The European Union might be well advised to throw some money at a study of unemployment statistics among Hollywood screenwriters.)

Higgins' government faced the daunting prospect of providing continuing employment for the first generation of under-twenty-fives to stay home since the Potato Famine of the mid-nineteenth century. It was necessary to promote fast-growing industries that were also glamorous enough to appeal to the young. Film and tourism seem to feed each other's growth and "vertically integrate" neatly. Film serves as an advertisement for both scenery and culture; the more tourists visit for the scenery, the more they see the culture at work. Tourism was also seen as a means of stimulating other areas of the economy, such as agriculture, fisheries, forestry, and rural development. Such movies as *Michael Collins*, about the IRA leader, were believed to foster political discussion and historical awareness among Ireland's large (voting) diaspora population at a crucial time for the "peace"—all, of course, against a backdrop of lush scenery that became even more interesting to visit once it was given a historical context, which, in turn, encouraged full employment for historically educated tour guides, who would encourage their charges to purchase historical Irish trinkets in historic Irish shops.

Did the "peace" create the tourism boom in Ireland, or did the tourism boom create the peace? Even more than their geniality, the Irish are known for their clannishness, which formed the backbone of Tammany Hall politics across the Pond. Studies show a high representation of Irish backgrounds among American CEOs as well. Although documentary evidence would be hard to find, the scrum of Kennedys and O'Reillys in the corridors of power supports the latter school of thought, as does the coincidence of unusual trade alliances and delegations that presaged and supported the faltering peace. Many of them, like Anthony O'Reilly, former CEO of Heinz foods group, can be traced to the Golden Circle of leading businesspeople and cronies of former Prime Minister Charles Haughey. The circle is currently under investigation by the Irish government for tax evasion "on a massive scale."[3]

In the decade preceding 1986, Ireland hemorrhaged tourism share in all major markets, the United Kingdom, the United States, continental Europe, Canada, even its own. Reasons included a decayed infrastructure of roads and transport, bland to wretched food, uncomfortable hotels, high prices, competition from cheap package tours to mass sun holiday destinations (when I lived there, the Irish themselves preferred vacationing in Communist Bulgaria), and of course, the Troubles. When I was a graduate student, I even had trouble persuading my parents to visit me.

Ireland had one surprising asset for tourism, distinct from its pastoral charms. Thanks to its geographical position between continental Europe and the United States, the country played a key role in early commercial aviation as a refueling station, a role that has been parlayed into a flourishing aircraft-finance industry. Through the usual combination of attractive financial incentives, a friendly government, and the flexibility needed to adjust to the demands of the rapidly changing airline business, Ireland emerged in the mid-1980s as a major player in world aviation.

During the Cold War, Ireland took advantage of its neutral status outside NATO to nurture close contacts with Soviet aviation authorities, ties that not only sustained themselves into the 1990s but led to a New Age anticolonial network of trade relationships. Shannon Airport, on Ireland's west coast, was the docking station for the Russian state airline Aeroflot, which was forbidden to land elsewhere in Europe throughout the Cold War. For many years, Shannon obtained most of its jet fuel free from the former Soviet Union in exchange for these landing rights. When oil prices tanked in the 1990s this barter system disappeared, but Shannon remained the essential transit point for passengers flying from Russia and other former Soviet republics to the United States and beyond. In addition to a commercial training and consulting center for Russian air-traffic controllers run by Aer Rianta (the Irish Aviation Authority) at Shannon, the Irish set up the duty-free shopping franchise system for Russian airports: the first sign that greeted me on debarking in St. Petersburg was "Aer Rianta." (The Irish also dominate duty-free shopping in Lebanon.)

The Irish own a virtual monopoly on duty-free shopping, centered in the person of Charles F. Feeney, a reclusive Irish-American who founded the DFS Group, which sells goods to duty-free shops around the world. With his partner, Robert W. Miller, Feeney made millions of dollars from the privately owned company until it was sold to LVMH Moët Hennessy–Louis Vuitton S.A., a luxury goods company. Feeney gave away some $500 million through his private charitable foundation. He is said to be one of the largest, if not the largest, donor to Noraid, the IRA-friendly fundraising group which has siphoned weapons as well as other forms of aid into Northern Ireland. Feeney initiated the LVMH sale in 1994, when he needed a more reliable flow of dollars for his charitable foundation than the volatile tourism trade could provide: DFS's dividend payments, which had ballooned from $40 million in 1978 to $400 million a decade later, shriveled to $12 million in 1991 because of travel disruptions linked to the Gulf War.[4]

In 1987 a bottle-green glass office complex known as the International Financial Service Center, or IFSC, erupted in one of Joyce's Dublin stomping grounds on the River Liffey. Aircraft leasing companies were particularly attracted to the specially zoned office area, where they could enjoy a 10 percent corporate flat-tax rate that made very expensive airplanes much more affordable. A series of bilateral tax treaties between Ireland and thirty-six other countries also exempted them from paying withholding tax on aircraft transactions.[5]

Unfortunately, Ireland's liberal tax laws attracted a lot of funny money as well. Shares of Russian companies formerly owned by the Communist state which underwent radical asset-stripping as their owners sought to keep the government from bankrupting them after 1991 now trade regularly on the Dublin stock exchange, known for its "relaxed" accounting practices. Many of these are transport-related, such as Baikal Airlines, the Irkutsk regional service of Aeroflot, which began trading in Dublin in 1995 through a British investment fund, Central Asia Investment Corporation. The fund bought the holding at a privatization auction but did not disclose the price. Lukoil, the Russian oil giant involved in a money-laundering scheme through the Bank of New York in 1999, also trades on the Dublin stock exchange through a British fund.[6]

Building on this base in 1989, the year that the fall of the Soviet Union kicked off the "peace process," the Commission of the European Communities approved a plan to give Ireland 150 million ecus, or close to the maximum available in assistance, through the European Regional Development Fund and the European Social Fund. These funds were earmarked for an "integrated operational program for tourism" that combined agriculture, fisheries, forestry, and rural development with tourism. Completion of payment was set for December 1, 1993, or nine months before the first peace was signed. Expenditure incurred after that date could be funded only if the amended dates were "justified." Anticipation of the peace, particularly among emerging market investors, justified a certain amount of delay. In Belfast, the European Union added a reward for good behavior in the form of a "millennium peace dividend" of some $250 million.[7]

Around the time that the first peace was announced in 1994, talk of a historic alliance between British Airways and AMR Corporation's American Airlines began to tantalize the tourism industry. Among the prizes were joint purchasing and code-sharing agreements that would allow the two gigantic airlines to all but monopolize transatlantic flights. The price demanded by regulators was high: a new British-American "open skies" agreement that would force British Airways to surrender up to four hundred precious gate slots at London's Heathrow Airport, the entry point to Europe for most U.S. travelers. After much heated debate in the British Parliament and the E.U. headquarters in Brussels, and following a lawsuit filed by U.S. Airways against British Airways claiming that the proposed alliance violated a previous agreement, the deal finally foundered in 1997, about the same time the Irish peace talks were breaking down.

Whether the mooted alliance was originally a carrot meant to help Britain swallow the humiliation of negotiating with Sinn Fein will never be known, but the coincidence is worth noting. It occurred around the same time that the late U.S. secretary of commerce Ron Brown was promoting Northern Ireland (pop. 1.9 million) as the "most important emerging market in the world." Then in 1999, as talks between Ulster Unionists and Irish Republicans disintegrated amid a welter of recrimination, a trade delegation that included Dick James, president of Boeing Europe, urged the British government to introduce special tax treatment for Northern Ireland to help the region compete with the Irish Republic, where foreign manufacturing companies pay only the 10 percent business tax. James said that his company had a well-established link with Northern Ireland and was anticipating buying $14 billion worth of goods and services from Europe-based companies over the next twenty years. Boeing is said to account for 25 percent of the 425,000 aerospace jobs in Europe.[8]

Among the projects designed to package and promote the peace in Belfast was a brave new Festival Hall built at enormous expense on the waterfront bordering a neighborhood which had seen a lot of sectarian fighting. Originally designed after the famous festival hall in Sydney, Australia, with its daring sail-like buttresses, it was eventually whittled down to a stolid, uninspiring structure because the Belfast city fathers couldn't agree on a single aspect of it. The hall is virtually unusable as a performance space and is now being promoted as a convention center.

Another new project was the Belfast Arts Festival, which concentrated on dance in order to avoid doing anything which would rile either side. Citizens were encouraged to come out of their houses and get their dose of culture in the Golden Mile, an area of the city which corresponds to the renovated Times Square in New York and was a focus for redevelopment. A good deal of the "peace dividend" also went into landscaping the infamous "peace walls," which still separate Protestant from Catholic neighborhoods, and into tourist-friendly architecture for the "new city." These were car-free shopping areas with azalea-planted bollards. As well, a new car bomb–proof facade was built on the Hotel Europa, where journalists used to get bombed in more ways than one.

But little or no funding was earmarked at the time of the peace to address the problem that had kicked off the Troubles thirty years earlier, when a single Protestant woman was assigned a council house of her own even as many Catholic families remained on the waiting list. As late as 1996, a visitor could still see vast tracts of vacant land on the Protestant side of the peace walls where people have managed to move into the suburbs while retaining their claims to the land. The

Catholics, with their generally larger families, remain cramped into their considerably smaller inner-city quarters out of fear, except for those who moved into the Protestant suburbs and took their struggle with them. (Portadown, where the Orange Day marches effectively ended the peace, is one such suburb.)

Both tourism and foreign investment in Northern Ireland have been slow starters because of the uncertainty of the peace. Tourism arrivals, which peaked in 1995 in the initial burst of good feeling and curiosity inspired by the first cease-fire, declined measurably through 1998. Belfast was promised an incentive payment of 250 million ecus by the European Union if a peace agreement was signed by the year 2000. The agreement was duly signed in December 1999 but with a potentially explosive review due in February 2000.

It is early 1995, barely six months after the first cease-fire has been signed. As I thumb through the pages of *Variety*, the entertainment weekly, an item catches my eye: "25 Movies Plan Filming in Ireland." Twenty-five movies! That's roughly the equivalent of 20 percent of the gross domestic product of Hollywood, from a country whose total population (3.9 million) isn't even a quarter that of greater Los Angeles. When I lived in Ireland, it made headlines if three movies were filmed there in a year. Inside of two years, from 1993 to 1995, the Irish film industry surged from $2–$3 million to $150 million. By 1997, *Variety* reported as many as seventy movies in production or development, although the majority of these never found distributors. Perhaps God intended the Irish to be movie producers all along. Blarney and moviemaking were made for each other. "After all," said Nicholas O'Neill, a young producer who made his first film in St. Petersburg in 1991, "in 1991, a movie industry here was about as likely as a cease-fire."[9]

The wildfire development of the Irish film industry parallels the development of the Irish tourism industry. In fact, the Irish Tourism Board, known as Bord Failte, works closely with the Irish Film Board in structuring Irish moviemaking as a form of global branding to raise worldwide awareness of Ireland as a tourist destination. "Walk down a street in Santa Monica, and everybody knows something about Ireland because of its movies," enviously observed Gregg Anderson, North American head of the New Zealand tourism industry. "Ask them about New Zealand and what do you get? A blank stare." (New Zealand is now developing its own film industry to assist its tourism, in ways which follow closely upon the Irish model.)[10]

The Irish Tourist Board gives generous assistance to filmmakers who implant "universal" imagery of Eire, such as the now-ubiquitous slide-whistle (otherwise known as "rent-a-flute"), step-dancers, and the cliffs of Moher. This practice—similar to Hollywood's product placement—has resulted in some curious anomalies. Such "negative stereotypes" as uncouth but warmhearted inner-city families with too many children have become global brand icons. The Troubles, previously perceived as the single greatest impediment to tourism in Ireland, have become the main attraction. Alcoholism, the legacy of colonialism as people

Other countries hope to emulate Ireland's success: an Irish pub in Izmir, Turkey.

drank to escape the humiliation of their oppression, is one of the country's leading exports: several companies, with the sponsorship of Guinness, manufacture and distribute prefabricated Irish pub interiors worldwide, even to Muslim countries like Turkey.

For many years the Troubles were avoided as subject material for movies because they were perceived as negative imagery; but with the publicity generated (and sought) by the "peace process," the Troubles have become yet another form of global branding. Between 1993 and 1996, Irish producers, encouraged by the highly politicized grant system, mined their own history for story material. At least ten IRA-themed movies went into production, until critics began to grumble that the Irish, once famed for their storytelling prowess, had nothing else to say or were were being influenced by the grant process to produce propaganda. Among these were *Michael Collins*, a romantic portrait of the IRA leader credited with inventing the high-profile terrorism which has characterized the IRA throughout the twentieth century; *The General*, a similarly gauzy portrayal of an IRA gangster who was so obnoxious that the IRA assassinated him to save the organization embarrassment when peace broke out; *Some Mother's Son*, a highly sympathetic film about the convicted IRA terrorist and hunger-striker Bobby Sands; and *Nothing Personal*, an unsympathetic view of loyalist terrorists.

Alexander Walker, the respected film critic for the London *Evening Standard*, believes that the Dublin government, through its heavy film subsidy program, was using film as a "second front" to make political points that politicians could not. "I'm not a conspiracy theorist," said Walker, who himself hails from the loyalist stronghold of Portadown, "but the Irish film industry, after establishing itself very successfully over the past five years, has run short of story material and has turned back to its own history. Films made in the South can't help but be sympathetic to the IRA. It's very attractive subject matter for Irish-American audiences, who consider the IRA romantic. So in part it's an economic choice."[11]

Arts Minister Michael D. Higgins denied this contention heatedly at a talk given at the British Film Institute, where Walker pointed out Higgins' own Republican background. "Since I became minister, I have never sought to read, or to express an opinion on, any script submitted to Bord Scannan na hEireann [the Irish Film Board]." Higgins found Walker's implication that he was disseminating propaganda "offensive." However, it would be naive, in political terms, to assume otherwise. Since the IRA is the oldest and best-established of the twentieth-century revolutionary movements, it would be surprising if its "legitimization" did not include the flagship business enterprises of the peace.[12]

On the one hand, *Michael Collins* director Neil Jordan and star Liam Neeson described the film as a "creation legend" for modern, post-peace Ireland and a "launching pad" for teaching schoolchildren a neglected part of their history, analogous to Steven Spielberg's Holocaust movie *Schindler's List*. On the other, here is Sinn Fein (widely regarded as the political mouthpiece of the IRA) leader Gerry Adams, who has been compared to Michael Collins (particularly in the likelihood of his meeting the same sticky end), "educating" a press conference in 1995:

> Some of you may be aware of the history of the hunger strikes in Ireland in the early 1980s, when there was first a hunger strike [the subject of *Some Mother's Son*] and it ended, and the British first saw the ending of the hunger strike as a sign of weakness, and they underestimated the situation, and out of that grew the second hunger strike, and ten men died, and hundreds have died since—And there's a film being made at the moment which has received some international attention, about a man named Michael Collins. Michael Collins, in Irish history, would be rather a controversial figure because he signed a treaty with the British. Many Irish republicans would have mixed feelings or be hostile to him. But I happened in terms of just doing some reading, to read that the first overtures from the republicans in the 1920s, from Eamon de Valera and Michael Collins and all the leaders—the British saw them as a sign of weakness. And what did the British ask them to do? To surrender their weapons. And Collins said, "The negotiations then broke down, and the Black and Tan War intensified." So you have this

repeat of history, and the primary responsibility lies with the British government, and they were given an unprecedented opportunity to build and to consolidate, to make a new beginning, you know, to have a sort of beginning of the end to the hostilities. And I think now we're facing the prospect that this could be the end of the beginning of this new opportunity.[13]

In fact, the peace did break down in 1996. Release of *Michael Collins* the movie, which at an estimated $35–$40 million was the most expensive Irish film ever made and received 10–12 percent of its budget from the Irish Film Board, was delayed from June to December because of the deteriorating negotiations. Rob Friedman, president of advertising and publicity worldwide for Warner Brothers, the film's distributor, which reportedly exerted pressure on the director to reshoot the ending and divert attention to the love story as the talks broke down, explained, "We obviously have to be sensitive to what's going on in the real world. We are consulting with people more educated than we."[14]

The Irish film community looked on the revolutionary saga as a natural epic that would make back its heavy price tag in tickets. The film failed to appeal to a broad audience owing to the density of both its accents and its exposition. Although he expressed public enthusiasm for the subject and said that he had been trying to make the movie since 1982, Jordan, a strongly idiosyncratic moviemaker who filmed the highly successful *The Crying Game* on a shoestring in Ireland after bitter disappointments in Hollywood, seemed stifled by the propaganda and by Julia Roberts' toothy performance as Collins' lover (not to mention her excruciating rendition of the lovely folk tune "She Moved Through the Fair," in a scene which seemed included strictly to please the Irish Film Board). Many critics, not all of them British, protested that the film's pro-IRA tilt combined with its undiplomatic release in 1996 close to the always-tetchy "marching season" actually played a part in undoing the peace.

What Ireland has to recommend it to moviemakers is the same as its credentials for tourism: an embarrassment of rich scenery along with a talented and energetic English-speaking population. In addition, it claims a contemporary city, Dublin, in which moviemakers can re-create any number of period settings, and a small but well-accoutred studio, Ardmore. But until 1993 and the pre-peace climate, when investors sought the sunshine of munificent government subsidies for filmmaking, all this was to no avail. "I couldn't get arrested," said Morgan O'Sullivan, Ireland's premier movie broker and producer of the epic *Braveheart*.[15]

O'Sullivan, a wiry fifty-something redhead, typifies the Irish businessman of the 1990s. With one foot in Ireland and the other in America, he straddles the Big Pond with tremendous agility and charm. He amassed considerable experience as an American television executive in the 1970s and 1980s, producing programming for CBS and NBC before returning home to put his expertise to work for Ireland. He is an adept marketer with a particular flair for finding the "Irish" in mass-market projects. Among others, he is responsible for *Scarlett*, the television sequel to *Gone with the Wind*, in which Scarlett O'Hara returns to her Irish roots. He has a considerable appetite for risk, along with the energy needed to generate the hundred projects that ensure one success. But even O'Sullivan spent twenty years shuttling back and forth between Dublin and Hollywood without much to show for it until, as he puts it, "Section 35 not only allowed us to get to the table but to put something on it."

Section 35, crafted by Michael D. Higgins in 1993, has precedents in Britain, Canada, and Australia, but, Irish-style, it has generated some extraordinary numbers. A country with a population that doesn't equal half the size of Los Angeles suddenly producing the equivalent of 25 percent of Hollywood's yearly studio output? Like many glamour industries in the 1990s, it created a bubble which encouraged ordinary people to invest in a highly speculative business.

Section 35 permitted a corporate investor to take up to 1.05 million Irish punts, or approximately $1.7 million, in tax relief through a qualifying film company or film production over a three-year period. Individuals were allowed to invest up to $40,000 and often borrowed the money to finance films. These breaks were extremely attractive in a country where the standard rate of corporate tax is 40 percent and the maximum tax bracket for individuals kicks in at about $14,300 for singles and $28,300 for married couples. The incentives were packaged by mutual-fund managers and stockbrokers: producers say that, come the end of the tax year, they were besieged with calls from fund managers and stockbrokers desperately chasing film projects in which to shelter their clients' money. "We don't care whether a film is a big success or an enormous failure," said David Cullen, a broker for BCP, the fund which floated the investor packages for some significant non-starters. "If a picture is made in Ireland, it develops the Irish film industry, and that's what the government wants." The bulk of the action comes from individual investors.[16]

That the system worked effectively is obvious in the fact that $10 million was raised through Section 35 for the $53 million Mel Gibson epic *Braveheart*, giving O'Sullivan the money needed to hijack the project away from Scotland, where it had already been filming for a month. But Section 35's vulnerabilities are also apparent in the many stories of financial scandals involving movies that were heavily subsidized but never got made, or, if made, were never distributed.

As in all heavily subsidized businesses, the smell of free money brought out the predators. In the words of one eminent writer-producer-director, "Every fuckin' cowboy in the world was out there," rendering the entire structure extremely vulnerable to overproduction, fraud, and plain bad moviemaking. Industry leaders, while accepting the largess, expressed discomfort with its political underpinnings. "At the end of the day, it's all about votes," said Kevin Moriarty, CEO of Ardmore.[17]

Notwithstanding its undeniable successes, this form of global branding can turn into a politician's worst nightmare. In 1995 a high-profile project called *Divine Rapture*, taxpayer-financed and heavily promoted by Higgins' ministry, folded ignominiously after weeks of heated press coverage. Rumors of fiscal improprieties flapped darkly through the halls of government and finance. Higgins, who had been much photographed embracing the principals of this project, vehemently denied that any taxpayer money had gone missing, while voters in his conservative rural constituency, hoping that their hotels and restaurants would benefit, instead were left holding the bag containing thousands in unpaid bills.

The stars included Marlon Brando, who announced his intention to become an Irish citizen upon his arrival. The first-time producers had raised enough money to begin principal photography on the strength of the Irish tax break but failed to get the rest of their finance in place. Brando, having collected the first $1 million of his $4 million fee, decamped hastily with the rest of the company, leaving the citizens of Ballycotton (pop. 450; winner of the All-Ireland Tidy Town competition) to eat around 100,000 Irish punts' worth of phone, hotel, and other bills. Said Sean McGrath, a local realtor who led the Ballycotton creditors' revolt, the film's producers seemed to be "very nice people, but amateurs."[18]

Higgins maintained that no Section 35 investor money was lost because the government would never release the funds to a questionable film company. But, said writer Suzanne Kelly in an issue of *Irish Film*, "It is difficult for a department that is often p.r.-driven for political reasons to admit of cracks in a business that is largely perceived to be successful," for "political ventures in the wings may be quick to use such cracks to try to break the industry."

The continuance of Section 35 came under review by the minister for finance, Ruari Quin, and was eventually much reduced, to the point that the funds were no longer attractive to foreign investors. By 1997 foreign production companies were already taking their movies to the United Kingdom, where Britain introduced its own legislation to compete with Section 35. (*Notting Hill* is very much a product of the British "Section 35": its thin tale is an advertisement for tourism and real estate.) But Michael D. still regards debacles like *Divine Rapture* as "blips onscreen." "I think we'll get past this," he said. "We've controlled it. Proportionately, between Los Angeles and the Irish film community, I believe we have a lower percentage of dives."[19]

According to Karen Millett, general manager of MIGA, another World Bank affiliate, tourism is what really drove private-sector development in Ireland from the mid-1970s onward. In conjunction with the International Finance Corporation (IFC), MIGA encourages private-sector investment. Where the IFC provides equity and debt-financing for projects in developing countries, MIGA provides political-risk insurance for the private companies that invest in these projects, largely to encourage them to go to places they might not otherwise go. Millett's job is to deal with both the private and the public sectors in transition economies to help them develop and implement a strategy to attract more indirect investment. Tourism occupies a great deal of her time: many developing countries figure that a couple of natural resource–based sectors like oil and gas, tourism, or agribusiness and tourism offer the greatest opportunity for economic development because they involve building on natural advantages. Countries where MIGA has been involved include several developing nations in Africa, parts of Eastern Europe, and the former Soviet Union.

In Ireland, the basic strategy developed by MIGA was for the government to make low-cost loans available to people who wanted to develop hotels, guesthouses, or country vacation packages. Millett had a specific interest in making the project work: she's Irish. "It works very well in Ireland," she said. "I don't know how well it works in other countries, as it all depends on how flush the government is with money and on how that money is linked. In Ireland it has been very linked to to overall private-sector development. You can't just have a government plan for tourism investment because normally government doesn't do it very well. It has to be driven by the private sector with government funds as an incentive."[20]

While economic growth across the European Union averaged a disappointing 2.5 percent a year from 1997 to 1999, the Irish economy surged ahead at 9 percent a year along with Spain and Portugal, which both enjoyed similar subsidy support. Ireland's strong growth owed a great deal to the country's business-friendly investment culture, including government giveaways on corporate taxation for foreign companies and the easy availability of cheap loans. In the hotel business these were made particularly attractive by a three-tiered system which subsidized large hotels for foreign investors, medium-sized hotels for substantial local investors, and guesthouses for small local investors. Now, Millett says, low, harmonized interest rates available through Euroland make the Irish model unnecessary. "Anyone can go out and get a loan at 3.5 percent on the private market," Millett said. "You don't need the government for that. But Ireland is still a model for countries where interest rates are prohibitively high."

In practice, the seemingly bottomless supply of cheap money for loans fueled an uncontrollable building boom, to the point where it threatens to kill the goose that laid the golden egg—the gorgeous Irish landscape. (Cynics have been heard to remark that construction is the quickest way to get rich in war zones: what gets blown up must be rebuilt.) Although tourism is responsible for much of the growth, it is also responsible for much of the damage. Not only is the hotel business suffering from overbuilding, but the boom sustained since the late 1980s has littered the countryside with sprawling ranch guesthouses sporting such excrescences as wagon-wheel gates inspired by the American television series *Dallas*. Beauties like Spanish Point, a peninsula near the high-tech capital of Galway and its new web of bedroom suburbs, are now a vast parking lot. Germans and Scandinavians who visit every year for romantic, low-budget walking tours complain bitterly about the ruined scenery.

Hoping to safeguard their country's share of the fickle tourist market, Irish architects and environmentalists, encouraged by Brussels, belatedly tried to set aesthetic standards for new building in rural areas. But their pleas (and those of the Irish Tourist Board) have largely been ignored as infringements on personal freedom. Eager to show off their new affluence, the rural folk erect ever-larger *palazzi gombeeni* that rely heavily on images of the tile-roofed haciendas in violent shades of yellow and pink glimpsed on their holidays to the Costa del Sol. (A "gombeen man" is a country sharpie who gets ahead of his neighbors by wheeling and dealing with the local rack-rent landlords. Coined by the Irish architectural press to describe the new school of building, *palazzo gombeeni* is not a compliment. It is used interchangeably with *bungalow blitz*.)

Though the need for guidelines is glaringly evident, many Irish resent such directives, which evoke bitter memories of the long British rule in Ireland. "To have the foreign tourist trade dictate standards of authenticity for Irish building really reawakens old colonial issues," says Emer Hughes, editor of a Dublin-based planning magazine.[21]

These feelings are further fueled by the fact that tourism has eclipsed farming in these areas of the country, which have derived their culture from the eternal cycle of agriculture for untold generations. As E.U. policies in the 1980s drew GATT farming subsidies away from Ireland to the larger republics of France and Germany, political power also shifted away from its traditional rural base to the Labour Party in Dublin. Today some 80 percent of new rural housing is built for people with no functional connection to agriculture—vacation homeowners, those commuting to city jobs, or bed-and-breakfast proprietors catering to the booming tourist trade. In 1998 Ireland's tourism revenue soared to a record $4.37 billion as the industry overtook agriculture as the country's largest employer, a total revenue equivalent to around 5 percent of Ireland's gross domestic product.[22]

In the absence of local standards, a consulting company, Dublin-based Tourism Development International, has proposed guidelines of its own. It recommends that all new housing in rural areas be designed by "environmentally sensitive" architects employing one of four basic traditional styles, each topped with dark slate roofs and sheathed in nap plaster walls. The company also advises against trimming hedges and the "ad hoc" planting of flowerbeds because "these are not always beneficial to the character of town or landscape": presumably, marigolds and mums are considered too vulgar for the nouvelle Ireland.[23] It is not difficult to understand why the rural Irish would prefer their creature comforts to the pretentiousness of such caveats. I am reminded of a holiday village in Donegal where I stayed as a student. Built to the quaint specifications of the Irish Tourist Board, it was so cold that I had to warm the sheets with saucepans and woke up every morning with interesting bruises from the battery of hardware with which I'd spent the night.

In the late 1980s Frank McDonald, the environmental writer for the *Irish Times*, coined the term *bungalow blitz* to describe the rural invasion, a barb that borrowed from the title of a popular do-it-yourself book, *Bungalow Bliss*. McDonald blamed the book for leading to the "desecration of the landscape." His solution: stop building altogether. McDonald, the architectural profession, and tourism officials were all blasted as elites intent on enforcing their own agenda at the expense of the people's rights.[24]

Not all the concern is aesthetic. The new buildings, most of which are built without any architectural planning whatsoever, also consume significant amounts of arable land; lots are typically a half-acre each. Their septic tanks have begun to threaten the groundwater, and studies estimate that up to 70 percent of the water supply in rural areas is contaminated by bacteria. Given the reversal in emigration patterns added to the fact that more than half the population is now under twenty-five, it is estimated that about 300,000 new houses will need to be added to the country's stock by 2007. The Irish Tourist Board and other environmental interest groups predict that if growth continues at this rate, it will kill the tourism industry. Ironically, the only people interested in restoring the many fine old farmhouses, some dating back to the eighteenth century, are the French and Germans along with the occasional American in search of something older than the 1960s.[25]

The rural Irish have often been accused of being philistines, and not without cause. When I was visiting the village of Dingle in 1994, I found a page torn out of a book of records in the town library. The missing page noted the recommendation of a Dublin tourism consultancy against building a ring road around the peninsula. Certain of the county council members, coveting the busloads of Japanese and German tourists that a ring road similar to the one proposed had brought careening around the Ring of Killarney in the neighboring county of Kerry, had removed the offending page in the interests of pushing the road through.

The Dingle Peninsula is one of the most—if not the most—scenically and archaeologically rich places in all of Ireland. The westernmost point of Ireland, and indeed of all Europe, it is isolated from the rest of the country by a narrow neck and high mountains, including the Connor, the highest point in Ireland. *National Geographic Traveler* called it "the most beautiful place on earth." It is bounded on three sides by the North Atlantic, bisected by ancient mountains whose green-brown slopes have been rubbed to such a velvet finish by the elements that they resemble the flanks of some sleeping leviathan, which may rise up some fine day and shake off the bonds of low drystone walls and beehive huts, cultural centers and Texas-style ranch houses, that the impudent passersby of the centuries have erected on them. Its byways, paradise to walkers, are a litany of beautiful places: Gleann na nGealt (the valley of the mad); Faiche na Manach ("the green fields of the monks" who resisted the English invasion); the twisty coast road from Ventry to Slea Head, with its gorgeously desolate views of the Blasket Islands.

The Dingle Peninsula: Slea Head and a view through a ruined cottage on the Great Blasket Island.

These have been abandoned, with one exception. The former Taoiseach (pronounced "tee-shuck," more or less), or prime minister, Charles Haughey, now the central figure in a corruption scandal, bought one of the Blasket Islands for his summer home when the islanders were evacuated "for their own good," which meant that he got it at a very good price. A bit farther along the Slea Head Road, David Lean filmed *Ryan's Daughter* at Dunquin to take advantage of the spectacular coastal atmospherics: the filming took nine months because of the fierceness of the winter storms, which are one of the region's great beauties. Long ago the village of Dingle itself evolved into a haven of crafts shops and galleries because of the many artists, Irish and otherwise, who vacationed and remained there; they can still be found, picturesquely garbed in tweed pinafores and handknit sweaters, hanging around the doorways of their cottages to attract the walk-in trade. But the village remained in a Gloccamora-like state until the early 1990s, when peace and public-private investment in tourism hit at the same time.

I chanced upon Dingle in 1982. Bicycling over, and down, the Connor Pass without goggles, I burned the corneas of my eyes and arrived in the eerily well-preserved village at its base without being able to see it. This was truly like going back a hundred years—a crazy quilt of low, whitewashed cottages with small diamond panes that gave back the glint of the harbor beyond. There was barely a light on. The loudest sound came from the waves lapping the shore. I made my way to an address that a friend had given me, a small art gallery created by an errant Sussex man, and was promptly taken in by his partner, Dermot, who put me up until my eyes healed.

Dingle was just making the transition from a manual to an electronic telephone switchboard. Dermot, the son of the local postmaster, ran the post office and the love lives of the young telephone operators, who all used him as a confidant. In his forties, he had never been out of Dingle in his life. He lived in a warren of books and old cheese sandwiches above the shop. He was what the Irish call a spoiled priest, never married and monastic in his habits, with a long, unkempt reddish beard and a gloriously thick Kerry accent, which was even harder to understand because his shyness made him mumble. Aside from Guinness, his chief pleasure was a formidable store of local lore, which eventually made him the best-known amateur archaeologist on the peninsula. When the post office went electronic and was sold, he sought another outlet for his many talents. He was a logical partner for the Sassenach, who needed a fluent Gaelic speaker and scholar to help him with the local population.

The gallery became Dermot's life and, like Dingle itself, a runaway success when the peace dividend kicked in. The Taoiseach himself flew in on his private Hovercraft for their wine-and-cheeses. When I last saw him in 1995, Dermot still had the scraggly beard but carried a sheaf of credit cards that would choke a cow and lost no opportunity to flash them in one of Dingle's new four-star restaurants. He was always to be found at the gallery, day or night, poring over some artwork like a medieval monk; and he grumbled that his partner left him there to hold the fort while he gadded about the international circuit. Instead of going Euro, Dermot became the David Norris of Dingle, one of the conservationists who eventually defeated the ring road. "It used to be that the young ones couldn't wait to get away from here to see the world," he said. "Now they stay and the world comes here."

Today, the strongest influence in Dingle is not fishing or farming but tourism. Fishing, the legendary pursuit of the Blasket Islanders in their coracles (ancient shell-shaped boats, which survived until this century), has been discouraged because it provoked trade wars with Spain as modern Irish tuna boats ranged into Spanish waters. Local farmers have lost their GATT subsidies to France and Germany and have turned their acres into holiday guesthouses: the woman I stayed with in 1995 at the recommendation of the Irish Tourist Board resented the intrusion of strangers into her home as much as she wanted their money. Dingle's narrow streets are choked with traffic. The restaurant crowds spill into the streets, as does the amplified music from the pubs, and the once-friendly owners growl and audibly anticipate shutting down for the Christmas season, when they can get some rest. At the local watering hole, the publican asks me whether I know Tom Cruise, who drank there during the filming of *Far and Away*. When the answer is no, he turns to the next customer. "Tom drinks in here when he's in town," he sniffs.

The village has more than nine resident millionaires in information technology and other fields. But success has fostered division and discontent. Dermot and his partner quarreled over division of the spoils as the stakes got higher. Their small but successful gallery is no more: the Englishman took his lists and went back to Sussex. And Dermot, who lived in Dingle all his life, is not even listed with the telephone exchange he helped to build.

Ireland's postcolonial economy has a history of boom and bust. In the 1970s, similar conditions in the European Economic Community (EEC) created a bubble of affluence, which evaporated when the European funds changed course, leaving Dublin filled with the rusting cranes and half-demolished Georgian squares left by the bankruptcy of its largest construction company. Ireland's highest-flying aircraft-leasing company, GPA Group PLC, expanded too rapidly in the late 1980s and early 1990s and came close to collapse following a failed share offering. With housing and stock-market prices rising by nearly 40 percent in 1998, the asset market in general began to look dangerously euphoric. Consumer-price inflation was held down by low commodities prices and the falling cost of imports as long as global demand and inflation stayed low. With any shift in that scenario, the same E.U. policies which helped Ireland onto its feet looked likely to knock it off again.[26]

What's good for developing tourism is not necessarily good for the rest of the country. By signing up to the euro, which the tourism industry regards as a plus since it does away with awkward currency exchanges, Ireland accepted a single interest rate for conditions across the entire euro zone, where activity was 1 percent below the level consistent with stable inflation. Economic activity in Ireland in 1999 was already 3 percent above the level consistent with stable inflation, meaning that the country should have been raising interest rates to avoid inflationary overheating but by then lacked the autonomy to do so. This has inspired some controversy: the United Kingdom has essentially preempted Ireland's neutral position by staying out of the European Union. "We're all tied to the euro now," Senator Norris said, predicting that the United Kingdom, under pressure from other countries, would join the European Union within two or three years.

At the same time, the E.U. subsidies which supported Ireland's 10 percent preferential tax rate for corporations fell under serious criticism by neighboring E.U. countries, which accused the Irish of siphoning off valuable investment capital. In 1998 the European Commission outlawed all forms of exceptional tax treatment that affect competition and trade between member states. The Irish corporate tax was raised to 12.5 percent for all companies; although the commission agreed to allow newcomers and investors on a preferred "pipeline" list to continue to benefit from the 10 percent rate until 2010.

The true gauge of inflation in Ireland is housing, up 190 percent from 1989 to 1999. Irish property prices were driven beyond the means of the middle class by Wild Geese returning with their nest eggs tucked under their wings: a significant number of property investors are "roots tourists" who have elected to retire to their ancestral homeland. Since the Great Famine in the 1840s, Ireland has had a grim history of emigration. Yet today the country is a center for immigration, with 22,800 more people entering than leaving in 1998. Jobs in the fast-growing high-technology sector are a main attraction. The single greatest reason for the economic and sociocultural change during the 1990s has been reversals in emigration patterns, which caused jobs to be created at record rates and reduced unemployment, the single greatest contributing factor to the sectarian struggle. Or so the Irish government would have us believe.

Tourism-driven emerging markets are marked by the feverishness of their publicity; and Ireland probably originated the trend. However, despite the country's claims to a "miraculous" recovery, an E.U. Commission report in early 1999 concluded that without generous grants, Ireland's growth—as well as that of Greece, Portugal, and the more undeveloped parts of Spain—would have been 5–10 percent lower than it was in the 1990s. The report allowed considerable debate as to whether the grants had worked as they had been intended, pointing out that regional discrepancies had actually increased. Southern Spain, for example, which enjoyed the greatest amount of the grant monies (although proportionately Ireland received more in terms of population), is now stuck with an official jobless rate of 30 percent, three times the figure for the European Union overall.[27]

The favored zones of Dublin and Lisbon have also benefited far more than the rural hinterlands. Officials of the European Union now worry that regional authorities have become dangerously dependent on intensive aid, or rather, lazy. They are also concerned that national economic policies are skewed toward intensive aid programs: since grants require that the host country supply matching funds, they draw national resources to E.U.-backed projects. Regional development plans are the prerogative of national governments, but they are usually prepared with guidance from Brussels and geared to projects eligible for backing. This has resulted in "infrastructure" overkill and a screaming deficit in human resources. Opponents of the grant schemes say that they are anticompetitive; they ultimately make the labor market less flexible by inflating wage bargaining.[28]

A high proportion of EEC monies were used to rebuild Ireland's road system. Since the government essentially got away with expending nothing on infrastructure during this period, large quantities of tax money were freed up for subsidies to favored industries, notably film and construction. The preferred form of construction was hotel building, for which enormous sums of low-interest loan money were also made available under a program conceived and implemented by the International Monetary Fund and its private-sector corollary, the IFC. First call on much of this money went to members of the "Golden Circle," cronies of former prime minister Charles Haughey, who was indicted for arms smuggling for the IRA in the 1970s and whose name resurfaced twenty years later in connection to a series of campaign-finance bribes and tax improprieties.

In late 1999 the deputy prime minister, Mary Harney, called for a court inquiry into alleged tax irregularities dating back to the late 1980s. The subject of the investigation was the "Ansbacher deposits" made to the eponymous offshore bank in the Cayman Islands, where 120 members of the Golden Circle are alleged to have salted away several hundred million pounds. The roots of the scandal lie in a family feud and court case that ensued in the early 1990s after the heir to Ireland's biggest department-store chain was revealed as both a benefactor of Charles Haughey's and a tax evader through his Ansbacher account. Although Prime Minister Bertie Ahern argued that it was illegal to "name and shame" those guilty of tax misdemeanors, the *Irish Times* published a partial list.

Among those named were Peter Sutherland, former head of the World Trade Organization and now head of Goldman Sachs International, and Tony O'Reilly, former CEO of the H. J. Heinz food group and one of the most important figures in Irish-American politics. O'Reilly controls Independent News and Media, Ireland's largest media company, which publishes the *Irish Independent*, the main rival to the *Times* and until the 1990s the strongest voice of the Protestant ascendancy in Ireland. O'Reilly "categorically" denied any improprieties, pointing out that he has not been a resident of Ireland since the late 1960s. (He resides largely in the United States.) He also denied that he has ever held deposits with Ansbacher, either directly or indirectly.[29]

O'Reilly's denials notwithstanding, the scandal led to a number of indictments, as well as resignations. The first business leader to announce his resignation was Jim Culliton, former chairman of CRH, a building group. Eight of the fifteen directors of CRH were included in the court affidavit. The revelations threatened to unsettle both Ireland's political structure and its prolonged expansion as Harney, also leader of the right-of-center Progressive Democrats, unearthed allegedly serious breaches of company law, tax law, and exchange regulations. At the same time Nora Owen, deputy leader of an opposing political party, Fine Gael, whose sister, the European parliamentarian Mary Banotti, was named as an Ansbacher depositor, accused Harney of leaking the names—a development that should sound familiar to any follower of recent American politics.[30]

While the full events of the investigation may never be made public, the scandal is an argument against using tax money for favored industries like hotel construction (corruption is almost inevitable) and accelerates the dependency-inducing spiral. The basic problem in using tourism to jump-start economies which began as single-crop colonial economies is that it can become yet another single crop, sucking up resources that could be used elsewhere. From her vantage point at MIGA's Washington, D.C., headquarters, Karen Millett has adopted a worthwhile philosophy. "It's very nice to develop what you have in the way of natural resources, but if that's all you can do, you've done your country a disservice," she points out. Tourism should be used as a springboard to develop similar or related industries. "You need to look not only at where you have a comparative advantage but where you have a competitive advantage. You need to figure out where you could go with the value-added components of that kind of industry," for example, cultural products like film and theater, information technology, and light manufacturing like furniture or textiles. Again, the problem is that in order to compete, the developing country needs to keep its wages lower than they are in richer countries, which already have the competitive advantage, and this returns the two to a colonial relationship. "That would be a bad strategy in the long run," Millett said. "It has to be an interim strategy in some places."

Today the assumption in Irish government, and in E.U. circles in Brussels, is that the boost given to tourism and such value-added components as film and information technology has been sufficient to put the Irish economy on its feet. However, its competitive advantage is already being threatened by countries like India and Jamaica, which, ironically, derived their excellent educational systems from the British colonial network they belonged to, but which can offer even lower wages to foreign employers than Ireland. Ireland, with an entrenched union system, is now wracked by labor strife. Coupled with sensational allegations of corruption in high places as a result of the boom, the labor problems are potentially as politically destabilizing as the Troubles themselves.

Whether the peace sustains itself is another issue, although Senator Norris feels that this is less important as the southern economy gathers strength. "Dublin's growth is not dependent on the peace succeeding," he said, but adds that he takes the "optimistic" view. "A strong economy in the North with strong links to the South will eventually be another driver for the Irish economy."

The appetite for risk evidenced by Ireland's high-flying business elite will eventually be financed by Irish taxpayers. Duty free does not necessarily translate into risk free: encouraged by their successes, the Irish also took over Moscow's famous Gum department store only to have it confiscated by the Russians once they had turned its losses around. The few outstanding successes produced by the Irish film industry have yet to redeem its many flops. Giving away tax money to foreign corporations can continue only so long as money flows in from other sources, such as subsidies. The euro subsidies now under attack by competitors may dry up soon.

To Senator Norris, the E.U. subsidies are by now irrelevant. "We're becoming net contributors. The exchequer is awash with funds this year, and that will continue for at least ten years. After that—no economist would venture to predict what will happen. We're riding a pretty sustainable boom. We were a very poor country and now we've come up to the European standard. We'll probably exceed that in another two years."

To those on the lower end of the scale, the view looks different. "They tell us that a door has opened," said an Irish UNIFIL soldier in Lebanon, where he was exposing himself to unfriendly fire from both sides in order to pay his mortgage. "It feels more like a coffin instead."

The Middle East CHAPTER 7

"Whose idea was it to plant the fake bomb there?" Ernest asked.

"It's the ideal place," Obermann said. "As a protest against ham-
mot, against idolatry. Against religious tourism, you might say. And I'm
sure the structural dynamics were favorable. The question is, who found
it? The Temple builders and their underground?"

Before long, he thought, despite his best efforts, the underground would
succeed in destroying the mosques, in beginning the war that would remove
the Arabs. Out of it would come a different Israel. It would be less American. It
might just partake of the purity of purpose that had been lost. . . . Just as the
underground would one day destroy the Haram, Zimmer thought, one day
the Moslems would assemble a nuclear bomb in America. That particular stork
would come home to roost. And who knew what might follow? No doubt, in
the long run, the Moslems too might feel their sense of purpose flagging.

Before long it would not matter. He might go and live in Africa. A
man might acquire some Italian fascist's former villa in the Ethiopian high-
lands. Walk in the cool of the morning. Rest under thorn trees hidden
from the blaze of noon, watch the sunsets, listen for lions.

Robert Stone, Damascus Gate *(1998)*

TO FIND SOMEONE like Cord Hansen-Sturm working in tourism is a
bit like finding Captain Hook working in the post office. With a mane
of wavy blond-gray hair and an unwavering blue eye, he even looks like
a buccaneer stuffed into a business suit. At six foot two, he weighs in at
230 pounds and has a fatal weakness for key lime pie. All in all, he is
not a man to be taken lightly. His background includes a career in military intelligence served in the Soviet Union at the height of the Cold
War. After a long stint in the executive ranks of American Express,
Hansen-Sturm took over the now-defunct Pan Am's air routes to the
former Soviet republics. He gives a meaty chuckle when asked about
his previous aviation experience, which is nil. His world is realpolitik,
and he does a deftly mean-spirited imitation of Henry Kissinger, shak-
ing all over with appreciation of his own act.

In Hansen-Sturm the neocolonialism underlying tourism-as-peace-process is made flesh. He claims a part in brokering the Middle East peace accords first presented at the Madrid summit in 1991 and later turned into substance with the Israeli-Jordanian-Palestinian Oslo agreement in 1993. He is a pragmatist, not an Arabist: his quarterback's frame contains no room for mysticism. But it is difficult to broker anything in the Middle East without at least an understanding of the Armageddon glimpsed in Robert Stone's thought-provoking suspense novel *Damascus Gate*, in which terrorists plot to blow up the sacred sites of East Jerusalem in order to prevent the mystery of the Holy of Holies from being photographed by a lot of sweaty day-trippers.

Hansen-Sturm is a formidable Cold Warrior who needs a good fight, but since the breakup of the former Soviet Union he has been working in tourism. Occupying himself with the care and nurture of the young, he headed the travel program of the New School for Social Research before it was sold to New York University. Today he heads the Middle East and Mediterranean Travel and Tourism Association (MEMTA), a trade association which sprang into being around the time of the Madrid summit for reasons which many Arabs feel were politically motivated, designed to transform Israel's military clout into economic muscle. Hansen-Sturm brings the ideological blunt force of his former occupation to his new eminence.

"A lot of these countries are still breaking away from a strong, very authoritarian socialist agenda," he says. "They have to come to terms with the private sector abroad. We're designed to put tourism ministers in the back seat and replace them with industry professionals."[1]

It is not difficult to imagine how a minister would respond to the intimidating bulk of Hansen-Sturm and the promises of World Bank and other international assistance that he brings. But though on the one hand, the assistance is needed, even solicited, it is associated through MEMTA with Israel and the fears of colonialism that Israel's neighbors associate with Israel. The not-so-hidden agenda of MEMTA is to promote peace in the Middle East by creating a joint regional stake in tourism, with open borders stretching from Turkey to Egypt. In MEMTA's view, the lure of potential profits from Year 2000 pilgrimages to Jerusalem should overcome the blood feuds about possession of the Holy City. Many of the coventures it sponsored were underwritten by American Express.

As MEMTA's trajectory shows, economic incentives go only so far in resolving complex disputes, and may, in fact, add further complications in strongly nationalist regions like the Middle East. Before the first peace accords in 1993, the Middle East ranked in the bush leagues of destination regions, attracting less than 2 percent of tourist arrivals and tourism receipts. In 1994, not by coincidence, the region zoomed to the top of growth statistics for the industry. Until late 1996 it also benefited from strong oil prices, which boosted regional economics and consequently the market for inbound business travel. Against this ebullience, many of the world's major hotel companies undertook vigorous expansion in the region, encouraged both by the IFC and by good annual reports in hotel stock. Against this background, it is worth noting that tourism lobbyists were quick to capitalize on remarks made by President George Bush at the 1991 Madrid summit concerning tourism's potential to promote the peace process and that they leaked a copy of the speech to the world press.[2]

The Middle East and Mediterranean Travel and Tourism Association sprang full grown from the vision of former Israeli prime minister Shimon Peres, who stepped into Yitzhak Rabin's shoes when Rabin was assassinated in 1995. Peres, who served as Rabin's foreign minister, wanted to weave Israel into the Arab economy on the premise that economic superiority would ultimately prove to be a better form of peace insurance than more traditional systems of defense. As a 1994 report from Rabin's office puts it, "Steps between rapprochement between Israel and the Arab states create a process that turns economics into the moving force that shapes the regional relations instead of national interests that were dominant in the past." Trying to re-create the Middle East, Peres scoffed at the notion that good fences make the best neighbors, but earned contempt from his political enemies with the remark that hotels would be of greater importance than military checkpoints on Israel's borders, a comment that captures the foundation of MEMTA's philosophy.[3]

Peres originally suggested disbanding the Arab League and creating a Middle Eastern League that would include non-Arab countries—that is, Israel—but the Arabs rebuffed him. He then advocated regional organizations that would serve as competing influences and admit Israel as a member. Hence MEMTA, midwifed by the United States and comprising Cyprus, Egypt, Israel, Jordan, the Palestinian Authority, and Turkey. The purpose of the organization was to plan joint tourism projects, including development of the Sinai and Red Sea areas. The jewel in the crown, so to speak, was the reward promised by an anticipated surge in travel to all the Holy Lands of the Middle East by the mystical year 2000.

The bubble burst in 1997, when a lurching peace process, rising political tension between secular and religious Jews in Israel, and a savage attack on tourists in Egypt (the region's biggest destination) frightened off investors as well as tourists. When the credibility of the Clinton presidency was jeopardized by delays and prevarications, MEMTA defected to North Africa, building up tourism in Morocco and Tunisia which benefited greatly from Kosovo-driven cancellations in the eastern Mediterranean. Impoverished countries like Jordan were saddled with millions of dollars in debt for new hotels. "Where is MEMTA now?" asked Akel Biltaji, Jordan's minister of tourism.[4]

"We're back full bore," said Hansen-Sturm when Ehud Barak took power in May 1999, an action that promised an end to the hard line on the West Bank settlements with which Binjamin Netanyahu had scuppered the 1995 peace accord. But while Barak and President Clinton announced, or re-announced, their commitment to promote tourism in the region to advance the peace, MEMTA's future still hinged on politics: whether Egypt would recant its support of the Palestinians who wanted Barak to guarantee the handover of West Bank lands by Israel. Barak put the weary and politically insecure Yasser Arafat in an impossible position by offering more land than that initially agreed upon but fudging on the even more emotional issues of release of guerrilla prisoners and resettlement of Palestinian refugees. And, as long as Egypt held out, MEMTA could not incorporate as a public-private entity, a necessary step in order to be eligible for World Bank funding. This is particularly important for large infrastructure projects like those needed in Palestine, where basically everything has to be built.

Syria, the Palestinians' other strong ally in the region, is cash starved and anxious to expand the tourism potential of its Crusader castles and historically rich cities like Damascus and Aleppo. For this and other reasons, including the advancing years and declining health of its former president, Hafez Assad, Syria was surprisingly conciliatory toward Israel. Syria wanted Israel to return the Golan Heights, the fertile and strategically important plateau separating Israel from South Lebanon that was seized during the 1967 Six Day War. Israel wanted hard guarantees that the region would not be used to launch attacks against the Jewish state by Syrian-backed Hezbullah troops fighting in South Lebanon. These troops reduced their operations under Syrian instructions that went so far as to order Damascus-based splinter groups to lay down their arms and confine the fight with Israel to purely political means as negotiations began.

One of MEMTA's priorities was to make Israel the transit hub of the region, a move that would truly make it the dominant economic power there. Air-traffic entry constitutes the most prized resource of tourism: whoever controls air-traffic entry wields heavy economic and political clout both because travelers tend to stay longer and spend more at their point of entry and departure and because their access to other countries can be controlled through border agreements. Egypt, Cyprus, Turkey, and Lebanon all have the same ambition, not to mention Malta and the Palestinians, who, after much fighting, finally have an airport of their own. "We're still looking at a colonial network here," said Hansen-Sturm. "It's logical to have an airport in Gaza, even if it's just an extension of Greater Israel." However, the Palestinians themselves regard the new airport on the depressed Gaza Strip as the most concrete symbol of their fledgling sovereignty. "I am standing on Palestinian soil, and I have an airport, I have a flag, I have an airplane," said Ahmad Abdel Rachman, general secretary of the Palestinian cabinet, at the airport's opening ceremony on November 24, 1998. "This is our path to the independent Palestinian state." (The Israelis closed the new airport immediately after the peace accords broke down in September 2000.) The political importance of airports is underscored by the ongoing rivalry between Beirut and Tel Aviv to be the entry to the region: Beirut, which dominated air travel before the war began in 1975, has rebuilt its international airport into a stunning facility, but American carriers are still prohibited from flying there because, Lebanese officials claim, American transport officials are working for the powerful American-Israeli lobby.[5]

The ambitions of MEMTA undoubtedly fly in the face of notions of pan-Arabism and a Greater Syria, which have roiled the region since 1916, when the First World War broke up the Ottoman Empire. But the business of tourism is nothing if not nationalistic. In early 1999 Lebanon, Syria, and Jordan signed a "transborder" tourism agreement designed to eliminate visas between the three countries that actually re-creates the Syrian empire. "We're still trying to undo the Sykes-Picot agreement," one Arab observer said.[6]

Turkey

Turkey, because of its many races and former imperial status, considers itself apart from the Arab world, but of the matters that divide the Middle East today, both the Syrian claim to control Lebanon and the national Palestinian movement are grounded in the fact that in Ottoman times most of Lebanon, Palestine, and what is now Jordan were economically and administratively part of "natural" or "Greater" Syria, which was in its turn an Ottoman province. When the empire broke up, British forces took control of the area from the Mediterranean to Iran in a campaign which began with the Arab Revolt in 1916 and ended with the conquest of Aleppo in 1918. Their chief ally in the conquest of Syria was Prince Faysal of Arabia, who rode with the famous British agent T. E. Lawrence.

After the fall of Aleppo, the British divided Syria into sectors much like Berlin after World War II. The British ran a zone which later became Israel; the French, in the Sykes-Picot agreement that is still detested by Arabs, were given the coastal region between what are now Israel and Turkey including the coast of Lebanon; and Prince Faysal, who was the son of the Ottoman governor of Mecca, the Sharif al-Husayn, scooped up Transjordan as well as everything that didn't border on the sea in today's Lebanon and Syria.

The Sunni Arabs who had joined the British forces did so in the expectation that they would replace Turkish rule with a united pan-Arab state encompassing Greater Syria. When Britain, with an eye to the region's incalculably valuable oil interests, divided and conquered instead, the disappointment rankled for most of the century.

As late as 1987, the Syrian government laid claims to Alexandretta and Hatay in southwestern Turkey on the grounds that Turkey had stolen all the land south of the Taurus and Anti-Taurus Mountains, an area roughly the size of England. Thus Syria's harboring of the Kurdish terrorist leader Abdullah Ocalan is the latest outrage in a long history of testy relations: significantly, when the Syrian government gave him up, the Turkish government opened up the border near Alexandretta as a reward. But while Syria signed a "transborder" tourism agreement with Lebanon and Jordan in early 1999, Turkey, which likes to distance itself from its Arab neighbors, still allies itself with Israel.

Minister Tan Has the Sniffles

Minister Ahmet Tan has the sniffles. He is a handsome man in his early forties with large, soulful, puppy-dog eyes, and in his official capacity as Turkey's minister of tourism he has a penchant for evoking the protective instinct in journalists, particularly females. Like many tourism ministers in the Middle East, he does not come from the ranks of the business itself but appears to have been appointed for political reasons. "I am your colleague," he tells me while listening anxiously to television reports on the formation of Prime Minister Bulent Ecevit's new coalition in his office in Ankara. This translates to, "Please do not hit me."

Tan, who writes a weekly column for the German newspaper *Die*

Frankfurter Allgemeine Zeitung, is in trouble. Turkey's economy depends on tourism for almost 50 percent of its revenue owing in part to the aggressive reallocation of farm resources, and it suffered grievously in 1999 both because of the NATO bomb campaign in Kosovo and because of security fears attendant on the trial of Ocalan, imprisoned on Imrali Island near Istanbul. The catastrophic earthquake in August of that year was the last in a series of blows which almost finished the Turkish tourist industry and the economy along with it.

Ocalan, leader of the Kurdish Workers Party (PKK), was commander-in-chief during a fourteen-year war in which an estimated 29,000 people died. The war stemmed from what the Kurds regard as a promise by the modern Turkish state's revered founder, Kemal Ataturk, to grant them their own state. In the postmodernist world, the Kurds demand cultural and linguistic rights along with autonomy and self-determination. Not only does this subvert Ataturk's life's work to unify the shattered network of the Ottoman Empire, but southeastern Turkey, the Kurds' territory, contains the hydroelectric resources which are Turkey's most valuable strategic and economic asset for the twenty-first century. (Iraq, to name only one example, was brought under control during the Gulf War when Turkey threatened to shut off its water supply.)

Ocalan was captured after two warring Iraqi Kurdish parties united to drive the remnants of the PKK from areas under their control in northern Iraq, close to the Turkish border. Although they had granted safe havens to the PKK in the past, the Iraqi Kurds were worried that Ocalan was using his calls for pan-Kurdish independent statehood to proselytize in Iraqi Kurdistan, which limits demands for Kurdish autonomy to within the borders of Turkey, Iraq, and Syria. They were also worried that the Turkish army would suspend its leniency toward the flow of illicit, customs-free goods, which supply the backbone of their underground economy, to and from Turkey.

At the same time, the Turkish army launched hot-pursuit raids both by land and by air on PKK bases in Iraqi Kurdistan, encouraging the Iraqi Kurds to negotiate. Ocalan, who had been expelled from Syria the previous October when Turkey threatened military action against Damascus unless it ended its support for the PKK, was finally seized in Kenya and brought back to Turkey to stand trial for treason. Turkey rewarded Syria by opening up a section of the border near the southern city of Antalya to allow day-trips to Aleppo in Syria. Although Syria's economy improved in the 1990s because of moderate oil finds, it is still relatively cash poor and desperately needs the hard currency even such limited tourism affords.

Turkey's hotel resources are catnip to Syria, which has few of its own. With its more than 5,000 miles of coastline, rich archaeological treasure, mountains, rivers, and hot springs, Turkey is the biggest tourism draw in the region. The government, along with private business, made an enormous infrastructure bet in the 1980s. A vigorous leg up was provided by the World Bank, which financed the original development of Antalya in order to wean the country away from terrorism. Prime Minister Turgut Ozal, himself a Kurd from the university town of Malatya, in southeastern Turkey, used the World Bank program as a platform to launch Kurdish entitlement programs on the principle that if young hotheads who would otherwise join the PKK had jobs and savings, they would think twice about doing so. Under Ozal these programs were tightly controlled, but after his death, particularly under the stewardship of Tanzu Ciller, the controls slipped, and many of the government subsidies went to drug lords, some with political agendas which managed to fit the profile of the entitlement programs. Like drug lords the world over, they laundered their profits through legitimate businesses and soon became the rivals of the biggest conglomerates in Turkey.

Turkey is the biggest tourism draw in the region: views of the mountains above Antalya, the Turkish Riviera.

So Greece dominated regional tourism throughout the 1970s while Turkey was in shock from the oil crisis and wracked by terrorism from both left and right. In 1980, to the relief of many Turks—who tend to dislike their largely corrupt and ineffectual civilian governments—the military seized power, rewrote the constitution, and restored control. One measure enacted to spur investment was the 1982 Tourism Encouragement Law No. 2634, brainchild of none other than Turgut Ozal, at that time an economist and head of the center-right Anatavan (Motherland) Party.

Ozal saw tourism as a means of providing employment to the disenfranchised, who of course included a large percentage of Kurds. The generous tax subsidies and land grants still enjoyed by Turkish tourism were created by Ozal, who served as prime minister from 1983 to 1989 (when the army again lost favor) and was then elected for a seven-year term as president. He died in 1993; many believe he was assassinated by the military, who resented his popularity. Among his controversial friends was Greek leader Andreas Papandreou, with whom he worked toward a rapprochement between their two countries, facilitating exchanges between business people and entertainers and abolishing visa requirements in the hope that Greek tourists would flock to Istanbul.

Under the stimulus of Ozal's subsidy system, Turkey's tourism capacity exploded from 56,000 hotel beds in 1980 to more than one million. The numbers of foreign visitors rose from 1.2 million in 1980 to 9.8 million in 1998. Foreign-exchange revenues from tourism were $300 million in 1980; in 1998 they were $8.3 billion, ranking Turkey among the top twelve countries in world tourism—ahead of Greece, which earned $7 billion in 1998. Tourism now represents more than 30 percent of Turkey's overall exports, according to government figures. According to unofficial estimates within the business, it represents 42 percent.[7]

Because of the subsidy system, which gave away land for free, capacity became overcapacity in the nineties, and areas like Antalya, once justly celebrated for its pristine beauty, became seaside hotel strip malls, lurid with neon and jammed with unruly foreign drunks. Today, Kusadasi, "the island of the birds," resembles nothing so much as Fort Lauderdale during spring break. The proliferation of hotels is a puzzlement until one recalls the cardinal rule of subsidies: it is more profitable to build than not to build.

And indeed the construction business is as rampant in Turkey as it is in countries like Ireland. The wildfire and often shoddy construction boom was blamed for the appalling extent of the destruction during the 7.8 magnitude earthquake, which leveled several towns east of Istanbul in 1999 and threatened the foundations of Prime Minister Ecevit's new government.

Desiring membership in the European Union and conscious of the need to improve its poor public image, the Turkish government entered the expansionist era in tourism at the same time that it introduced a series of E.U.-friendly market reforms, like abolishing protec-tionism and privatizing state airline and other resources. When mass tourism was introduced, it quickly became one of the twin pillars, along with textiles, on which the economy rested. But the mood in Greece turned sour over the continued division of Cyprus and the proposal by President and Prime Minister Ozal to supply water and electricity to the eastern Greek islands, which was increasingly seen as a move to undermine Greek sovereignty. The distrust continued until 1999, when the two NATO allies clashed over Turkey's threat to prevent the deployment of Russian missiles by the Greek Cypriots in southern Cyprus. Although the deployment was eventually called off, the inci-dent did much to increase tensions between Greece and Turkey.

Ocalan's capture virtually paralyzed Turkish tourism as tour oper-ators rushed to cancel their block bookings following a wave of bomb-ings in Istanbul. While government officials minimized claims of their losses at 20 percent, industry leaders estimated them as high as 42 per-cent, making the military triumph an economic disaster on the scale of the Islamic fundamentalist massacre at Luxor which killed fifty-eight tourists and four Egyptians in 1997. Egypt's tourism industry suffered a 40 percent drop and still has not recovered. Turks, who originated the term "byzantine," hypothesized that the Syrians may even have sent Ocalan forth as a kind of Trojan Horse, knowing that his capture would immobilize their neighbor, which is not only Syria's rival in size and power but enjoys relatively friendly relations with Israel. In fact, Turkey's strongest diplomatic relations in tourism are with Egypt and Israel, but these were also damaged by the Luxor incident as well as by the stalemate in the 1998 Wye accords.

The catastrophic attrition in tourists was largely among Germans. Before Ocalan's capture, Turkish travel agents had been forecasting a 15 percent rise in German visitors, who are their most important source of business, for 1999. Germany, which harbors a large population of Kur-dish laborers, or *gastarbeiten*, was the first to pull the plug on its block bookings when Ocalan was captured, for fear of terrorist reprisals at home. Oger Holding, Turkey's biggest tour operator for German tourists (headquartered in Germany), complained that 70 percent of its March and April bookings were canceled because of the crisis.[8]

The Turks blame the German hysteria on negative world press generated by the PKK war machine and on the PKK's ability to dove-tail its agenda with that of the European powers; Danielle Mitterrand, widow of the French prime minister, is a self-appointed Kurdish spokeswoman. "Germany and France want a weak Turkey," said one businessman who preferred to remain anonymous, who believes that E.U. politics feature most importantly in Turkey's poor PR. "They want us to need them. They want us to make an end to the Cyprus war." The United States, an important ally, also brought pressure to bear out of concern that the perennial tension between Turkey and Greece could weaken NATO's southeastern flank and hinder any rapprochement between Turkey and the European Union, of which Greece is a member.

In fact, many Turks believe that Greece harbored Ocalan in order to destroy the tourism season of their closest rival and longtime enemy. This is the same constituency that believes in the Ocalan Trojan Horse theory or that Greek interests in the United States pay a major television network at the start of every tourist season to run the movie *Midnight Express*, which paints a horrifying picture of the life of a hapless young American tourist imprisoned in a Turkish jail for drug smuggling in the 1970s. In fact, it is worth noting that in 1998, just before Ocalan was captured, Turkey overtook Greece in world tourism rankings for the first time. Ocalan was living under the protection of Greek diplomats in Kenya when he was seized by Turkish commandos in February 1999. An official at the Turkish Office of Tourism in New York said that all tourism investment in Turkey may be frozen for the next few years while the issue of Ocalan's execution is decided.

No wonder Minister Tan has the sniffles. His job is made even tougher because Kurdish businessmen control some of Turkey's choicest assets in tourism. Turkey has what amounts to the type of set-aside programs enjoyed by key minorities in the United States: if a tourism employer has 20 percent Kurdish employees on his payroll, he receives considerable tax breaks from the government. In addition, the government has granted free land to a number of Kurdish entrepreneurs to build hotels and other tourist facilities, notably in the prime coastal region of Antalya, the Turkish Riviera, originally developed under the aegis of Prime Minister Ozal. Conservationists and others complain that he gave away state parklands to his relatives. This created enormous political problems and magnified anti-Kurd resentment among the most established members of the Turkish business community, who feel that their own government is undercutting them.

Caylan Holdings, the Kurdish conglomerate that owns the Intercontinental franchise in Antalya, is suffering along with everyone else, but there is undoubtedly a potential for enormous redistribution of wealth at work. Caylan, which started from zero in the 1980s, now eclipses Nurol, formerly Turkey's largest holding company. The Kurds, say their competitors, have the deep pockets to wait out the recession because of monies from the PKK war chest and from the Turkish government. According to some Turks, Ocalan himself claimed that Caylan supported him, although the company publicly denied it. The PKK is known for its ability to marry a political agenda to destabilize the state to organized crime, in the form of drugs and arms, as well as for its tendency to let profiteering drive strategy as much as politics. The hotel business has become increasingly popular in organized crime circles as a means of laundering money because it is difficult for regulatory agencies to keep track of precisely how many guests are on hand. Thus a manager can go to the bank with big cash receipts from either real or imaginary guests, convert them into another currency, and transfer them to another country. In a quickly hushed-up scandal, a high-ranking official in former prime minister Ciller's government was discovered shot to death in a car along with large quantities of cash, a local police official, and a prostitute. The scandal was said to involve laundering money through tourism.[9]

"It is hard to explain to our Western friends," says Tan, who in his fervor to embrace the uses of tourism as a peace weapon is a little indiscreet about its uses as a political pacifier. "We have no Kurdish problem. Kurdish businessmen own a five-star hotel complex [the Antalya Intercontinental]. One-fifth of their employees are Kurdish. We have no trouble in Antalya—only one bomb in fifteen years. There are no security forces in Antalya. If they allow terrorist activity, they foul their own nest."[10]

Tan is Candide-like in his convictions. "Tourism plays an important part in the unifying role of Turkey in the international arena," he asserted as the government quaked and swayed around him. He pointed proudly to the fact that Turkey is the only country in Europe and Asia that has seven neighbors, even though they are not the most desirable ones: Iraq, Syria, Georgia, Armenia, Bulgaria, Greece, and Iran. All, with the possible exception of Bulgaria, are hostile and politically unstable. Tan gushed, "In fact, tourism is such a powerful unifying force that we see all these countries and their citizens as our friends and partners."

Today, says Tan, "sustainable development" which will preserve the environment is the top priority of his ministry. But "sustainable tourism" includes a roundup of the usual suspects. The winter holiday business in eastern Turkey, planned to diversify the industry away from the choked and polluted Mediterranean coast, is being developed with huge government subsidies in the way of free land, tax incentives, and low-interest loans to Caylan Holdings. Erzerum, which has a largely

Kurdish population, is also the location for a huge hydroelectric project with a high strategic value. "The Kurdish people will protect their base in Erzerum," promises Tan. He also thinks that the majority of Turks, who hate the Kurds, will flock to a Kurdish ski resort for their winter fun. "Turks love to ski," says Tan. "Almost 4 million go outside of Turkey every year. But in this area the snow lasts much longer than in Europe. It has gorgeous scenery, yellow pine forests, and no civilization to distract the attention. It is another opportunity for the locals, to give them a good reason not to leave the land. We did the same thing in Antalya. We paid the locals to greenhouse their farms and grow flowers instead of food. It's a great tourist attraction and of course has an aesthetic [value] which gives them greater prestige than heavy-duty farming."

Going back in time in a Turkish mountain village.

Minister Tan lost his portfolio when Ecevit organized his new coalition, even though he belonged to the prime minister's political party. He was replaced by Erkan Mumcu, an aggressive candidate from the same party. The disastrous earthquake which hit Turkey on August 17, 1999, coincided with an equally seismic change in Turkish politics. The PKK announced a unilateral cease-fire, signaling that they wanted "cultural rights" rather than the transformation of Turkey into a state in which Kurds would enjoy a separate political status and threaten the constitutional integrity of Ataturk's republic. The Kurdish conflict has been a primary cause and excuse for Turkey's abuse of human rights and for its repressive stance on journalistic expression, the country's chief obstacle to E.U. membership.

On the positive side, the earthquake appeared to break the logjam both with Greece and with the European Union. The scale of the disaster, in which more than 15,000 people died, led Greece to drop its objection to sending hundreds of millions of dollars in E.U. grants and loans to Turkey as well as its veto of Turkey's E.U. membership application. A team of rescue workers from Emak, the Greek state-run disaster-prevention agency, was among the first dispatched to the stricken town of Izmit. Only weeks later, Emak's Turkish counterpart, Akut, helped search for survivors when Athens was struck by another, lesser quake.

Considerations of tourism accelerated at least some of the miraculous thaw in diplomatic relations. As it became clear that the turbulence in the Balkans which chilled the 1999 tourist season in the Mediterranean would continue well beyond the "peace," Greek companies evidenced a desire to get into the Turkish market and improve tourism in the eastern Aegean by better transport links between Turkey and Greece, which depends even more than Turkey on tourism for its gross receipts. But, having been down this road before, officials were cautious. Here follows a representative sampling of issues which remain to be resolved.[11]

Gaye

Gaye Carmikli is the secular answer to Turkey's famous headscarf debate. (For those who did not read an international newspaper between the months of March and May 1999, Turkey's schism between secularism and fundamentalism crystallized in a violent debate over the right of parliamentary candidate Merve Kavakci to wear her Islamic headcovering in the House. Kavakci, a U.S.-educated software engineer, was discredited when it was discovered that she is an American citizen, but not before student riots erupted in the university stronghold of Malatya, which political observers said were an offshoot of the Kurdish question.)

Carmikli, a fiercely attractive Las (native of the Black Sea coast) and heir-apparent to one of the largest business empires in Turkey, heads the tourism division of Nurol Holdings, which is owned by her father. She is thirty, thin, intense, with a Golda Meir streak of white in her long, jetty curls. If her brother were more interested in running the family business, she would still be in England pursuing her Ph.D. in English literature. She asks me longingly whether I have seen David Hare's *Via Dolorosa* in New York. Judging from the photographs that line her small, cozily appointed office, she is the apple of her daddy's eye. But she is also bright and passionate and probably, one day, will be a candidate for Minister Tan's job.

According to Carmikli, on February 14, 1999, the day after Ocalan was captured, tourist reservations dropped from 24 million to 3 million, and Britain and Germany canceled all charter flights to Antalya, where Nurol has major hotel interests. "All the leaders of the tourism business had a meeting with the prime minister (Bulent Ecevit). We were almost crying. He said, 'Relax, don't make such a fuss. Just wait.' Wait for what? Apu (Ocalan) managed to destroy Turkish tourism, and the government won't do anything about it. They are paralyzed. They change their appointments every six months. What do they care? But our two main industries are textiles and tourism. If tourism goes, what will keep the economy afloat?"[12]

Business's often testy relationship with government in Turkey reflects the country's peculiar schizophrenia toward its Islamic roots. Poised between Asia and Europe, Turkey has always looked down upon its less Western neighbors, but the past few governments have made many compromises with Islamic fundamentalists backed by Iran. When Muslim conservatives complained that the glamorous casinos from which Nurol and other hotel owners derived a handsome income violated Sharia, their Quran-backed legal code, the government of Bulent Ecevit closed the offending institutions down, giving the competitive advantage to Turkey's hostile neighbor, Cyprus.

Carmikli, not without a streak of self-serving, feels it was wrong for the government to close down the casinos. "Closing the casinos killed weekend tourism. Now people are going to Cyprus to gamble. It's so cheap, they don't even charge for the hotels, just for the gambling. Our casino owners are all known as mafia leaders. The government should find another way to check them. They should close down all the casinos . . . except those in Antalya."

Carmikli complained that if Turkish tourism was still stagnant in the year 2000 she would have to sell her division. Although she is too diplomatic or perhaps too competitive to say so; much of her family's business dilemma arises from the heavy subsidies granted by the Turkish government to Nurol's Kurdish competitors. Before the 1990s, Nurol was Turkey's largest holding company. Now Caylan, which was "nowhere" in the early 1990s according to one competitor, has eclipsed it. "They make a different product than we do. It's a highly competitive business. As long as they do it well, why should we complain?" she said. But the Intercontinental near Antalya competes with Nurol's Sheraton; and Nurol can't compete with investment for the huge new government-subsidized winter resort development at Erzerum, also being developed by Caylan. "The Kurds are the only ones who can get investors to go into southeastern Turkey," she said. "How would we protect our investors?"

Carmikli charged that the PKK "aims" at tourists. Several years ago, the guerrilla army exploded a bomb on a crowded beach at Kusadasi, killing two Dutch tourists. All Dutch tours were canceled. "The Kurds want more money," said Carmikli. Two years ago sixteen German and Italian tourists were kidnapped from her Antalya holiday complex by PKK guerrillas who wanted them to deliver a political message to their governments. (The tourists were later released unharmed.) "When they have a risk to their jobs, they do something."

Like most people in the tourism business, Carmikli insists that the media magnify the danger of terrorism and castigates the government for not muzzling them—though such an action would only reinforce Turkey's negative image abroad. Inside Turkey, in fact, the government still imprisons journalists for criticizing its track record on human rights. Outside Turkey, there isn't much it can do. German television showed footage of Panzer tanks patrolling the streets of Antalya after Ocalan was captured. British expatriate residents of Antalya insist that the footage was nothing but propaganda. However, the same residents boast of the advantages of living where the police presence is so high that, when one woman was walking her dog late one night, the (machine gun–toting) gendarmes were patrolling the beach looking for her.

The European powers, in Carmikli's view, are deliberately choking off tourism as an economic weapon against Turkey until the country conforms to the wishes of the European Union. "This is so political. In Germany, England, and Italy there are so many Kurds. They have real political influence, much more than Turkish people. They 'explain' that there is no such thing as human rights in Turkey and people listen. The government thinks that the longer it postpones the sentencing of Ocalan, it will get better. The opposite is true. It will drag on and on, and we will lose half our economy. The collapse of tourism may be the catalyst to tip the whole country over."

Carmikli closed down the company's nearby holiday complex at Kusadasi because of the volume of Ocalan-related cancellations. She said that she saw civil unrest brewing in Antalya, formerly one of the country's most prosperous areas. The tourism development boom of the 1980s has exacted a high, if hidden price. Absent the jobs provided by tourism, "What are they going to do with Antalya? Rebuild it into a port again? Antalya used to be a fruit bowl. The farmers sold their land for hotels. What will they do? Now they're all unemployed . . . unless they're Kurdish."

Mahmet

If the collapse of the middle class in Turkey had a poster boy, it would be Mahmet. A U.S.-educated technocrat in his late thirties who moved back to the country on the promise of the economic reforms initiated by Turgut Ozal, he has watched his life career from the pinnacle of success to near ruin in the past two years.

An investment manager whose portfolio includes construction, tourism, and personnel carriers, Mahmet is small, fierce, and elegant. He speaks excellent English acquired from eleven years of working in Chicago. He inhabits a large new duplex apartment built by his company in a posh bedroom development in Istanbul with his eleven-year-old daughter, Lisa, and his twenty-year-old nephew, Ali. The sophisticated complex, home largely to business executives like Mahmet, has a fancy new mosque for a neighbor, built by one of the many mysteriously funded construction entities in the country. It is the neighborhood alarm clock. Every night, just before dawn, the muezzin blares the call to prayers over a loudspeaker system that would be the envy of any rock-concert promoter.

Mahmet is caught between Asia and America in more ways than one. His first wife, an American lawyer, would not abandon her career to move to Turkey, so they divorced. His second marriage, to a traditional Turkish woman, failed. His daughter, who has been living with him for a year to become acquainted with her Turkish roots, is his "sweetie," but he will soon be losing her as Lisa returns to her home in the United States.

Mahmet hates to be alone. Over the past year or so, he has begun drinking heavily to dull the pain of losing both his second wife and the value of his personal investments, halved by the decline of the Turkish stock market. The pressures of his job do not help. At 11 P.M. it is not unusual for him to rush out to drink with clients. He does not want to go. He is from a small village and innately conservative. On the one hand, he is happy that Allah has come to Chicago when I tell him about the big new mosque that has gone up on since his departure. On the other, he is not at all happy about his noisy neighbor. "My mother covered her head all her life, and she doesn't make a big deal about it," he said. "Nor does she care what I do."

Much of Mahmet's drinking is motivated by fury at how hard he has to work while the "land mafia"—the rurals who have flocked to the city because of terrorism in their villages and the lure of manufacturing over agricultural jobs—virtually appropriate land from the government, which needs their votes. Owing to the rural influx, the population of Istanbul has risen from 3 million to 12 million over the past thirty years. On the way from his home to the airport, Mahmet points out squatters' complexes with washing dangling from their balconies next to fancy mosques. These have been built with money raised through "charities" similar to the Iranian bonyads: Mahmet and others think at least some of the money may actually come from Iran.

"Part of the reason that the government supports tourism is to prevent the absolute collapse of the rural economy," Mahmet explains. Historically, Turkey, like Ireland, has been agriculturally self-sufficient. "If they have to import, inflation, which is already high, will skyrocket."

The Carpet Sellers of the Grand Bazaar

The incredibly persistent carpet sellers in the Grand Bazaar and the Arkasi in Istabul are predominantly Kurdish: they are the only travelers

The Kiplingesque world of the Grand Bazaar.

allowed by the army to pass through the mountains that separate southeastern Turkey from Iran, where they buy their most beautiful Bakhtiari carpets. They haunt the tourist mecca of Sultanamet, the heart of Old Istanbul, which houses the Topkapi Palace, the Blue Mosque, the ancient basilica of Hagia Sophia, now crudely converted into another mosque, and the Roman Hippodrome. Stepping into one of their shops is like stepping into the pages of Rudyard Kipling's *Kim* or through the looking-glass into the world of intrigue that was Istanbul after World War II. Men in dark glasses and natty blazers, flipping worry-beads in an insinuating cadence, pad up to you in soft expensive loafers and press you to take tea. Once you accept, the doors are closed, and a barrage of questions is directed at you; the carpet merchants peddle information as much as carpets.

Omar is one of these, appearing from nowhere inside the Arkasi, the row of carpet shops behind the Blue Mosque whose rents all support the mosque itself.

A tall, gracefully shaped man, gigolo-handsome, with sharp fine features and dark brows so eloquent they appear plucked, he affects a Ralph Lauren faded-jeans-and-loafers look. When he cannot get me into his shop to buy carpets, he asks for my help. (The carpet-sellers are adept psychologists and have figured out that female tourists who are otherwise annoyed by their persistence will not refuse them help with English.)

Omar is a Kurd from Malatya. He wants me to write a request for him to transfer funds into an account given him by one of his customers. The request seems odd because his spoken English is actually exquisite, but he claims that he can't write. Later I am told that the carpet merchants, who all work with satellite phones, have been victims of a Russian fraud gang, which has imported the technology to intercept their telephone and Internet commerce. It is also possible that the carpet shops are handy vehicles for laundering PKK cash.

Omar is political, and sees a tourist as a walking Western Union for sending messages to the larger world. He wishes to disassociate himself (and, clearly, his tourism-based business) from the upcoming Ocalan trial, which will disrupt the entire tourist season, perhaps for years to come. The trial is a sham. Ocalan will be allowed to languish in prison until his people forget him, another ten years. "We are already through with him," Omar declares, casting a long-lashed conspiratorial glance at the closed door, where two burly men with briefcases stand motionless, apparently with nothing better to do. "He lost the war. A very stupid man, Ocalan. He is not like Hitler. Hitler did not do very good things, but he was a leader. He did not let them catch him. He shot himself instead."

Omar has traveled widely for a small-town boy from the boondocks of southeastern Turkey. Following his three-year compulsory military service, he bummed his way through Los Angeles, New York, Malaysia, Australia, and India, scratching a living by selling fruit, he says. But he has been exposed to far more than the life of an itinerant fruit-peddler. "Ocalan was stupid because he fought from Syria, not Europe. He used guns instead of weapons to bargain for his country. He could have used our borders, which are important ones since southeastern Turkey is next to Syria and Iran. Trade there has been allowed to flourish even while the army has occupied the territory. We are the breadbasket of Turkey as well as the traditional center of the carpet trade. We have the Nemrut Mountains, more beautiful and interesting than any other place in Turkey. Tourism should boom once the PKK quiets down. But the Turkish people are stupid," he says with a twist of his fine lips. "We have got used to not working. We wait for someone to hand us something, the Fazilet Partii (the religious political party), the government, the E.U."

Soon, Omar says, the country will blow. Maybe in two years, maybe less. Even if Ocalan is irrelevant, if the government tries to shut down the religious Partii, the country will split and revert to military rule: already there have been student riots over the famous headscarf incident, which Omar sees as a way to keep the PKK ferment bubbling. Corruption is everywhere. The middle class resents the sleazy officialdom to the point where many actually welcome the notion of a coup. "Our last honest president was Ozal, and the army managed to assassinate him," Omar says, again with a glance at the two men patrolling his shopfront. "He wanted everything to open up. Now the government preaches control, but everyone in it lies and cheats and steals, from the top down. So everyone in Turkey lies and cheats and steals because according to the top guys it's O.K. Everyone is just trying to grab as much as he can and get it out of the country before things fall apart."

Omar will never leave Turkey, even if it does fall apart. For all his travels, he is still a good peasant. "I will go home to Malatya," he smiles sadly. "I will build my house with a high wall around it and some land maybe. No one will touch me. In this world, you have to kill to live."

"In this world," says Dai Krokodil, "you live by keeping one ear and one eye shut." Dai Krokodil, or Uncle Crocodile, is another carpet merchant, a cheerful thirty-year-old with an endearing snaggle-toothed grin and a permanent three-day growth maintained for the sake of the Taliban, in whose country he is a frequent visitor. I am introduced to him by his tout and cousin, Ali, who has walked me all over the Divan Yolu, the main street of the old city, as well as the Egyptian spice bazaar, and has showered me with roses and a silver ring in a vain attempt to persuade me to buy his carpets. "You deal with her," says poor Ali as he parks me on the sofa and goes out in search of fresh prey. "She's impossible."

Dai Krokodil rolls out ten carpets for me to admire and orders Turkish pizza, a delicious soft tortilla wrapped around salad, onions, and chunks of fresh tomato. He plies me with several glasses of Yakut, the excellent local wine which is like a good California cabernet. I am very curious about how he acquired his beautiful Bakhtiaris, the unique geometric berry-dyed abstracts which come from the mountains bordering western Iran whence the Turkish army launches its blitzkrieg attacks on fugitive Kurds. Dai Krokodil says with typical insouciance that he goes through these mountains all the time. What about the military? "The military is nice," he grins.

"Bullshit talks, cash walks," is Dai Krokodil's motto. As we talk, he juggles two phones on each shoulder. A deal for two tons of Beluga caviar at $60 a pound? "Too cheap," he growls into one phone, then, "but 20 percent profit is better than no profit at all." He likes to say he will do anything for cash. "That's the best bad smell in the world."

At the same time, he is deeply troubled by what he has seen on the Silk Road. Some of his best carpets, those most favored by tourists, are made in Afghanistan and Pakistan, where the carpet makers buy little girls from the villages to knot the carpets because their fingers are so thin. At age nineteen or twenty (twelve to fourteen, according to U.N. sources),[13] they sell the girls to Bombay's infamous brothels. "The rooms are just cages," Dai Krokodil says from firsthand experience. "They unlock the door to let men in, they lock it again when they go out. That's all the girls ever see. They are not even allowed to talk to each other. If they talked to each other, they could rebel. How can a man do that and still call himself a man? I saw the same thing in Cuba. I stay in this Hotel Intercontinental, and ten minutes after I go to bed there's a knock at the door and there's a prostitute. The hotel desk sent her. I say no, I'm not interested. Ten minutes later there's another knock and another prostitute, much younger. I say no thank you, that's not my thing. Ten minutes later there's another knock. They send me a guy this time. No thank you. The next morning they tell me I can't stay at this hotel, that's how they make their money. And you know the government is behind it. The government is the biggest mafia of all."

Dai Krokodil also buys carpets made in camps in Pakistan, which has been taking in refugees from the Taliban in neighboring Afghanistan. "It's slave labor," he says. "The little girls get ten dollars for six months' work. The refugees get nothing at all. Just a bare bed in a tent and enough rice from the United Nations to live. The guards give them nothing. They keep all the food for themselves. What is the United Nations going to do about it? The United States isn't about to take in 200,000 Afghani refugees."

Dai Krokodil squints at our glasses. Mine is full. His is empty. "I love wine almost as much as I love cash," he says. "When I drink, I talk too much."

Another Kurdish country cousin wanders in. The carpet bazaar is an Underground Railroad of sorts. This one has been run out of his village of Mardin on the Syrian border by the PKK because he refused to join them. Dai Krokodil is teaching him to sell shoes over the Internet. "Too honest," says Dai Krokodil like a genial Turkish Fagin. "He hasn't been with me long enough."

Dai Krokodil looks at his watch. I have spent more than two hours with him and he hasn't made a dime. He throws open the window and bellows at Ali. "I can't do anything with her! Go catch me another!" Then he laughs and salutes me on both cheeks. Dai Krokodil actually enjoys it when someone gets the better of him.

Neke, Julia, Dorbus, Emin, and Bertan

On the ferry from Istanbul to Izmir, a nineteen-hour journey on the comfortable state-owned Turkish Maritime Lines car ferry, men and women are jumbled together in the crowded sleeping compartments. They don't think twice about this, beyond wondering who can grab the best seat. Some are sacked out as early as 6 P.M., or use their small children as placeholders while they enjoy the portly, vivacious torch singer in the fore cabin. By 1 A.M. the place is packed like a sardine tin with unshod feet hanging into the aisles and is decidedly close. I escape to the deck and spend the night watching the jewels of the eastern Mediterranean slip by: Troy on one side, Gallipoli on the other, then Lesbos, Chios, and Samos. I meet a quartet of Turkish career women traveling south for their thirtieth high school reunion. Neke, Julia, and Dorbus are journalists, Emin a teaching doctor who runs a rehab clinic in Istanbul. They invite me to the cabaret to drink Scotch—lots of it— and look at pictures of them in their pleated high school uniforms. All, with the exception of Dorbus, are divorced. Divorce is now common in Turkey. "Jealousy," says Emin, meaning career jealousy.

In the morning, one of the pairs of stockinged feet turns out to belong to Bertan Tolkun, "big daddy" of the Turkish textile industry. Bertan has taught textile design for twenty-five years and his alumnae form the backbone of the Turkish textile industry today. He has a low opinion of the government set-aside programs for Kurds. "Twenty percent government subsidy for employing minority [workers] leads to 20 percent lousy work," he says in the low amused rumble well known to his students all over the country.[14]

Sheep are Turkey's main livestock, and Turkey is the biggest producer of wool in Europe. Co-owner of one of the largest textile factories in the country, a twelve-acre plant in Konya, Bertan spends most of his time shuttling between Paris, Milan, Düsseldorf, and Bombay to hunt down new, innovative design ideas. Worldly and attractively world-weary, he lives in one of the charming late-Ottoman wooden houses that line the Bosphorus and are now, given the inflation of Turkish real estate, conservatively valued at one million dollars.

Known as Iconium in Roman times, Konya, due south of the seat of government at Ankara, is one of the oldest continually occupied cities in the world. The capital of the Seljuks, who conquered Byzantium after gobbling up Persia in the eleventh century, it is home to a sect of whirling dervishes established by the mystic poet Mevlana Rumi and is one of the more religiously conservative areas of the country. Textiles and tourism are interrelated, and the same set-aside programs are applied to both, belying the image of the Kurds abroad as a chronically impoverished and discriminated-against people. Bertan, like most successful business people, has learned to walk both sides of the street, although he may enjoy complaining to a Western visitor.

While much has been made of the dangers for women traveling alone in Turkey, I feel quite safe accepting a lift from Bertan and barreling at top speed in his Cherokee "Brute ute" through the lush mountain passes between Kusadasi and Izmir with the plaintive Parisian strains of Charles Aznavour and Edith Piaf pouring from his tape player into the Turkish countryside. The innate conservatism of Muslim life makes Muslim males, on the whole, rather more protective of women than their Western counterparts. As long as one dresses and behaves with reasonable modesty, men are courteous and helpful, even on the coach buses that are generally exclusively Turkish and segregate the sexes. Up to a point. The young attendant who serves us tea and washes our hands every hour with fresh-smelling lemon soap according to Quranic custom asks me to help him with his English. On a raggedy slip of paper he has written phonetic phrases which gradually become more intimate until the last one reads, "Pliz, ken I kom slip wit yu et yur otel?"

I pity the pool attendant at the Sheraton Antalya who has been trained to turn studiously aside when young women wearing the sketchiest of thongs parade in front of him. Obviously, in the hotels which cater to the European trade, tourists can flaunt themselves with impunity. On the beaches, even the private ones, it is quite a different matter. I am sunning myself in a modest one-piece bathing suit on the beach front of a condominium holiday complex outside Kusadasi when a family of patrolling fundamentalists invades the boundaries. The heavily veiled women hiss rude things at me in Turkish, probably, "Cover up, you slut!" My male companion, also Turkish, hisses back at them. They retreat to a safe distance but stay put to safeguard our morals, sweating and itching under the fierce sun. It is a battle of social class as much as religion: my companion's family was one of the first to buy into the compound thirty years ago on a tip from a friend in government. The patrollers are waiting for their connections to buy them in; meanwhile, they are watching over their investment.

Kurt

"I can't even buy the right produce for the hotel," complained Kurt Johnson, executive chef for the Antalya Sheraton as we climb the 12,000-foot mountains behind the coastal tourist strip in his fire-engine-red 1967 Volkswagen Bug.[15] Kurt is a face from home, or more exactly, from Chicago, a former Army Intelligence cryptographer who just happens to love to cook. He is a clean-cut thirty-eight with the eyes of a sharpshooter, in love with adventure and with his Turkish wife, Selma, whom he met on a ferry ride on the Bosphorus in Istanbul and who followed him to Moscow, where he was a chef for Swissotel before the bottom fell out of the Russian economy in 1997. Next, Kurt and Selma gambled on Antalya, which doesn't seem to be paying off either. The best, or rather, the only clientele he's had all summer is the U.S. Navy patrolling the eastern Mediterranean end of Kosovo, coming in for a little R & R.

Turkey, like Ireland though several times its size, has been completely self-sustaining in agriculture; in fact, it is a net exporter of food. Crops are varied and abundant, including wheat, cotton, sugar beets, sunflowers, hazelnuts, tobacco, and, because of the country's range of climates, virtually any other fruit or vegetable a tourist could demand. But now, Kurt says, "I ask for Dutch peppers. One day they have them. The next day, they don't. It's the same with artichokes, aubergines, you name it. I can't get pineapples. I can't get grapefruit or melons or anything out of the ordinary. All they grow now is apples and oranges. And bananas. I can get lots of bananas. The locals all got rich years ago, selling off their farms to build hotels. Their lives haven't changed very much. They just bought bigger houses and Mercedes. Now there's a population of 200,000 here and very little left to farm."

Where agriculture once ranked as Turkey's chief industry, manufacturing and services now dominate the economy as Turkey builds motor vehicles, makes appliances and consumer goods, and exports them throughout the region. This has occasioned an enormous and potentially dangerous shift in demographics as millions of farmworkers have moved off the land and into the cities in search of jobs, collecting in pockets of poverty which provide fertile breeding grounds for political agitrop. The government, keenly alive to the possibilities of ward-heel politics, has sought to buy off potential anarchy with the large grants of free land and housing, angering Mahmet and the rest of the middle class who are bearing the full impact of sky-high inflation. The government has also, in a desperate attempt to get farmers to stay on the land, promoted certain arcane forms of agrotourism as a "high-prestige" alternative to the sweatier forms of farming: in Antalya, plowmen have been encouraged to grow flowers instead of food.

But the terrain we are chugging through looks the way Antalya did a hundred years ago. It is like the Swiss Alps in spring. Tiny chalets pop like timber mushrooms out of snow meadows, and goatherds with hunting rifles slung casually over their shoulders urge their flocks up vertical meadows, accompanied by huge, unfriendly dogs, which chase our car and threaten to jump in the windows. It is difficult to imagine them happy in the cities: the population of Istanbul alone has ballooned from 3 million to 12 million over the past ten years.

I buy Kurt a tank of gas at a decrepit station because I suspect they are not paying him at the Sheraton. Kurt would like to come home but the great adventure hasn't paid off the way he expected. It takes bucks to open a restaurant Stateside, and the hopes of a tourist boom in the Middle East are fading fast. Kurt's romantic gamble has suspended him between two worlds. He has lived in Turkey for five years and speaks the language fluently. Learning a new language and marrying into another culture have changed him so subtly and in so many ways that he can't go home again. "Cheffing is a burn-out profession," he says, his light-green eyes fixed on the narrow road ahead of us. "By forty-five or fifty you have to cash out."

Back at the Sheraton Antalya, a Mayan-influenced structure like those which dot the Côte d'Azur, you could fire a cannon through the luxurious lobby, with its tinkling waterfall of sculptured metal. Manager H. Reza Elibol pooh-poohs any suggestion that the Ocalan trial has killed his millennium trade. "The millennium comes in Ramadan in Turkey," he says. "No one makes any special arrangements." (A mantra repeated in Lebanon, Jordan, and Israel as the peace negotiations dragged on.) Elibol is confident that things will return to normal soon. But things haven't been "normal" since the government, swayed by the religious Partii, banned gambling in Turkey in 1998; Antalya, like other resort areas in Turkey, lost a large part of its Israeli trade to its archenemy, Cyprus. Elibol said that the government's decision to close the casinos had "little impact"; he supported the decision because "innocent Turkish people were getting hooked and losing their families."[16]

Elibol cannot afford to be supportive of his government for much longer. By late summer 1999, tourism officials were saying that government support of tourism might be frozen for several years, or as long as it takes to resolve Ocalan's case. The Sheraton's main source of business is wintertime conferences and seminars, which have also experienced a significant drop-off because of fears of exposing top management to the dangers attendant on the trial.

"Last year there was little money," confirmed Nancy Thomas-Ward, a British expatriate and longtime resident of Antalya. "This year there is no money. People will be starving here again this winter. Next year there will be more unrest." The British expats, who with retired Germans form a large part of the year-round population, say they will never leave Antalya. But Panzers or no, Thomas-Ward said, "We're glad the army is here. Having a benevolent dictatorship is a plus. If the army were not here, I would go."[17]

Welcome, Welcome to Lebanon

> Balqees. . . . Oh princess,
> You burn, caught between tribal wars,
> What will I write about the departure of my queen?
> Indeed, words are my scandal.
> Here we look through piles of victims
> For a star that fell, for a body strewn like the fragments of a mirror.
> > *Lament of the Lebanese poet Qabbani for the death of his wife,*
> > *Balqees, in the bombing of the Iraqi embassy in Beirut, 1981,*
> > *trans. Lisa Buttenheim*

> Our contemporary modernity is a mirage.
> > *Al-Shi'riyya al-Arabiyya (Arabic poetics),*
> > *by the Beirut poet Adonis, trans. Fouad Ajami*

Landing at midnight at Beirut International Airport is exciting for many reasons. American carriers still will not land at the stunning new facility built in 1995 to replace its bombed-out predecessor. Reasons range from the bargaining power of the American-Israeli lobbying groups to the fact that the airport was constructed with its runways facing directly onto the tenements of Barj-al-Barajimat, the Hezbullah stronghold of West Beirut. Glued to the window during final descent, I wonder whether the young bloods are partying tonight, and whether they've checked their rocket-launchers at the door.

I am flying Middle East Airlines, the state carrier of Lebanon, infamous for its ragtag fleet, bloated budgets, and inverse efficiency. Owing to still-volatile political relations, Middle East cannot fly directly from the United States, and I embarked in Istanbul. The airline now flies state-of-the-art planes leased from French Airbus, but flying with them is rather like driving with an adolescent who has taken his father's Mercedes out for a spin: the pilots, accustomed to flying trash cans, haven't quite got used to the powerful new planes.

When Beirut International Airport originally opened in 1954, Beirut was the financial and recreational hub of the Middle East, and most major international carriers used the city as an overnight stop between Europe and East Asia. During fifteen years of war, the airport was frequently shelled, shot up, or shut down. It was a preferred destination for hijackers, including the Palestinian Liberation Organization, who commandeered a TWA jet and dumped the body of an American passenger onto the runway in 1985, eliciting a presidential ban of the airport from Ronald Reagan.

When peace broke out in 1990, Lebanon had a half-built, rocket-scarred terminal begun eight years earlier, a bankrupt national airline, and no cash. Under the whip of former prime minister Rafic Hariri, a construction tycoon determined to restore Lebanon to its former glory as a tourism and business center, reconstruction commenced in 1994. The estimated budget of $500 million was financed in part by selling off franchises to build and manage duty-free shops and by grace and favors from Minister of Tourism Walid Jumblatt. Jumblatt, warlord of the mysterious Druse sect, which inhabits the fortresslike Shuf Mountains a few miles east of Beirut, offered a unique package to build a new marine runway. He "sold" the aviation authority a mountain he owned (which stood in the way) and cement from one of his own factories. As part of the exchange, his urban Druse constituency received new, free housing on the other side of the runway from the Hezbullah. Their enclave is aptly named Shou-e Fed or "Little Entry": it is guarded by sullen young men in black Mercedes and small boys who chase the cars of visitors waving their arms and shouting "Allah akbar!"

Today, the immaculate white Arrivals Hall boasts state-of-the-art metal detectors and security doors at the gates that require both a key code and the swipe of a security card to open. Built by a joint venture between a local company named CCC and the German construction giant Hochtief, it looks like a set for a Peter Sellars opera dotted with the black-clad figures of females from the Emirates taking their traditional break from the summer heat of the Gulf. One particularly striking young woman, tall and lithe, is veiled in diaphanous layers of black chiffon, buttoned up the leg with tiny black buttons and framing her beautiful face. I'm tempted to ask her if her burka (the head-to-toe black veil worn by strict Saudi women) is by Chanel, but at that moment a young soldier with a machine gun slung casually over his shoulder takes my American passport. He looks me up and down with Crusader-blue eyes set in an Arab face. "Welcome, welcome to Lebanon," he says, and hands my papers back to me.

"Make sure you're kidnapped by the right people," quipped a friend in the State Department shortly before I left New York for Beirut. The Syrian desk manager at my hotel in the Christian quarter of Achrafieh seems to have exactly that in mind as he escorts me to a room with no inside lock. I am too tired to mind and roll straight into the large, blissfully clean-sheeted bed.

Much to the resentment of the Lebanese, their country is now a protectorate of Syria. When Syrian troops swept into a ravaged Beirut in October 1990, ostensibly to end the sixteen-year-old war, the exhausted Lebanese welcomed them. Even the Israeli and U.S. governments, in need of Syria's help against Iraq, tacitly approved. However, Syria failed to honor its inter-Arab agreement to withdraw from Beirut in 1993 and today remains tightly entrenched. The army that came to make peace has stayed to make money in construction and tourism, and to reclaim not so much the barren Golan Heights but the much richer prize of Lebanon itself, carved out from Syrian territory by French colonialists after World War I.

The Syrians know that I am a nice Jewish girl from Beverly Hills. Out of all the consulates I visited in the United States, theirs was the only one to demand that I specify my religion on my visa application. "I'm Jewish," I told the Syrian cultural attaché, on the principle that it was best he find out from me rather than from someone else. "Is that going to be a problem?" "Oh no, no, no," he assured me. "My best friends are Jewish." But then there was a consultation in the back room, and a few minutes later I was told that they couldn't give me my visa because I'm a "journalist."

Not surprisingly, my reputation has preceded me to the Ministry of Tourism in Beirut, where I present myself bright and early the morning after my arrival. "I have your file," says Nasser M. Safieddine, otherwise known as "Mr. Tourism," who has left a string of telephone messages at my hotel to reassure me. It is the week of the Israeli elections and tensions are high. Safieddine is a career minister of tourism and has survived a number of administrations. A refined, quietly intense and elegant man, he has also survived being seajacked by the

Israelis. His second-in-command is Mme. Boushra Haffar, a tall, chic woman in her early fifties with a penchant for short slit skirts, which she wears as stylishly as she wears trousers. Like many Middle Eastern women, she has the bold look of a 1940s American film star. She and Safieddine are the organizational guts of the Ministry of Tourism. Balancing a phone on each broad shoulder, she ratchets from the dulcet tones of Middle Eastern womanhood to a drill-sergeant's screech in the flutter of a false eyelash.

Minister Nazarian

Mme. Haffar is like a proud stage mother with Arthur Nazarian, the new minister of tourism, prompting him when he flags in English. Hers is surprisingly better than his. Like many tourism ministers in the Middle East, Nazarian's provenance is not tourism but private finance. He is also an Armenian, which makes him an outsider in the tribal world of Lebanese politics. This is almost an advantage in a world that is so deeply divided between Muslims, Christians, and the Druses who are first one, then the other as it suits them; between Sunnis and Shiites; between Lebanese, Syrians, and Palestinians. Critics in the service end of the business, angry at the ministry's unwillingness to promote tourism as long as the peace remains unstable, grumble that Nazarian's chief qualification for his job is the fact that he is a neighbor of the new president, Emile Lahoud.

Lebanon was once known as the Middle Eastern Switzerland, which the north of the country indeed resembles: a land of mountains, numbered bank accounts, and many cultures living in apparent harmony. Whether this was ever entirely true is open to question; the roots of the Lebanese civil war can be traced back to the foundation of the post–World War I modern republic and a merger between the country's two dominant majorities, the Sunni Muslims and the Maronite Christians. The Sunnis of Lebanon were the second-largest religious community after the Maronites and tended to be the wealthiest, most urbanized, and best-educated group in the country. The Maronites were also members of the ruling class. Adherents of an Eastern Christian Church founded in Syria in the fifth century, they managed to survive for centuries by entrenching themselves in the fastnesses of Mount Lebanon north and east of Beirut, and by forging alliances with Western Christians from the Crusaders to the modern French.

As part of the Sykes-Picot agreement, the Maronite leadership prevailed upon its ally France to set up a Lebanese state that would be dominated by the Maronites and smaller Christian sects allied to them. In order to make that state economically viable, the Maronites also appealed to France to include not only their Mount Lebanon eyrie but the predominantly Sunni port cities of Beirut, Tripoli, Sidon, and Tyre, as well as the breadbasket of South Lebanon, the Akkar Mountains and the Bekaa Valley, which were predominantly Shiite.

The Sunnis and the Shiites thus "unified" were not consulted and deeply resented the deal because they would have preferred to be part of Arab Syria; but, though they resented the Maronites, they did not get along particularly well with each other either. This factionalism mirrors a long-standing divide in the Muslim world between the Sunnis, who generally represent the upper classes, and the Shiites, who are the underdogs. In addition, the new Lebanese state contained a third Muslim element, the Druse, a splinter sect of Islam whose exact religious practices are a communal secret. Lebanese say that they are Christian or Muslim depending on who is in power: the Druse occupy a powerful political position because they constitute the swing vote in Parliament.

In the 1932 census, the Maronites and other Christian sects of Greater Lebanon made up only 51 percent of the population. They were able to govern by eventually reaching an understanding with the Muslims in 1943 that enabled the Lebanese republic to cut its ties with France. In this unwritten agreement, known as the National Pact, the Maronites guaranteed that Lebanon would be an "Arab" country, though its president would always be a Maronite and the Parliament would always have a 6:5 ratio of Christians to Muslims to ensure Christian predominance. The Muslims, for their part, abandoned their demands for unity with Syria in exchange for a Sunni prime minister and a Shiite speaker of the house. This power-sharing agreement held up as long as the country's demographics remained stable. But by the 1970s, the slender Christian majority had shrunk to one-third of the population while the Muslim population grew to two-thirds, with the Shiites by far the majority. As traditional Christian-Muslim tensions heated up, the Palestinian population displaced in the Six Day War relocated in Lebanon, made common cause with the Shiites, and tilted the scales toward full-scale conflict.

Today, Minister Nazarian's job is made difficult by the same factionalism that made the war so long and so virulent. The ministry's limited budget must be divided among all the contentious minorities listed above. Unlike the situation in other Middle Eastern countries, Nazarian says there are no government subsidies for tourism aimed at specific minorities; instead, infrastructure projects begun under the aegis of former prime minister Hariri have been designed to upgrade the quality of roads, telecommunications, and housing nationwide. "All people will benefit," promises Nazarian. "We are making it easier for everyone to move around." But not too much. Nazarian's ministry is also promoting agricultural tourism in order to encourage farmers to stay on their land and not crowd into the overburdened cities.[18]

Lebanon has received World Bank assistance through the World Monuments Fund to develop cultural sites. Such aid often amounts to the same thing as a set-aside program. "Monuments" like the splendid ruins of Baalbek are often located in the poorest and least developed areas of the country, in this case, Shiite areas. "Of course, when you have these service industries, hotels, etc., you need people and so new jobs are created," says Nazarian. "But we as government can only facilitate. It is up to the private sector to implement."

One reason why the new government does not promote tourism more aggressively could be that, unlike Turkey, the industry represents only 4–5 percent of gross national product. "Back in 1977 tourism represented 20 percent of the entire economy," said Safieddine, who is Nazarian's chief consul and shadow. "But we had no competition in the area. Turkey, Cyprus, and Egypt didn't exist as destinations in the 1970s. We didn't have to put in a lot of effort. It was natural that Gulf Arabs would come to spend the entire summer. Now they go to Syria, Jordan, and Egypt." Safieddine hastens to deny that Syria, Lebanon's military overlord, is a competitor in tourism, and he points to the new transborder tourism agreement signed by Lebanon, Syria, and Jordan. "These three destinations are very complementary," says Safieddine. "Syria is a plus for us, really. It's a two-hour bus trip to Damascus from Beirut and another four hours to Jordan. The name of the game is where the tour starts. It would be of enormous benefit to us if Beirut were to become the hub of the whole area."[19]

The much-vaunted private sector has assiduously dropped the tourism ball tossed by the Lebanese government. "No one wants to invest until they see how things are going to go," one hotelier explained. Others resent and fear the Syrians, who are muscling into the profitable hotel business and driving down wages by employing their own people at less than half the salaries earned by Lebanese.[20]

The Lebanese economy is curiously buoyant: no one quite knows what is keeping it afloat. One reason may be that, even during the sixteen-year war, Lebanon retained its popularity as an offshore banking center because of its strict secrecy laws and lack of currency restrictions. Owing to a gentlemen's agreement among the combatants, the Central Bank was left untouched. Conversely, those who made money—many of whom made lots of it—are loath to leave it at home.

A notable exception is Rafic Hariri, the construction magnate who served as prime minister from 1992 to 1998. His privately owned company, Solidère, is carrying out the world's largest single building project, the reconstruction of downtown Beirut, which covers an area measuring 445 square acres, including 150 square acres reclaimed from the sea. One of the reasons Nazarian's ministry is unpopular among industry leaders is that Lahoud's government halted Solidère's work during an investigation of financial improprieties, abruptly cutting off the flow of public monies and canceling its own leases on several new administrative buildings which were to be located within the prestigious new complex. Solidère is seeking legal reparation for damages because of the cancellation, but meanwhile the company is proceeding with a high-rise development that is not compromised by the government's deal. The project includes a Four Seasons hotel combined with a luxury residential and tourist complex. Hariri's admirers, who include Mme. Haffar, say that despite the former prime minister's problems with handling money, he does get the trains to run on time. Other sources say that the new government is asking Hariri to give back half the fortune he allegedly looted from the treasury, some $1.5 billion, which may include funds from the World Bank.

Minister Nazarian strenuously denies that the government's system of low-interest loans for hotel building and the duty exemption for all hotel-related imports which encouraged Hariri and others like him is responsible for the country's glut of overcapacity. "Tourism all over the world is seasonal," he insists. "During New Year and the three summer months, we have full capacity. Eighty percent of our hotels were destroyed during the war. There is a lot of rebuilding to do."

At the same time, Nazarian's ministry is reluctant to sink budget monies into promoting these hotels as long as the peace remains fragile. Lebanon is still too often a front-page story in ways that are not helpful to the tourist trade—for example, the Israeli bombing of Beirut suburbs that occurred two weeks after I left the country. "We try to rely on people like yourself to come here and tell everyone that the picture of Lebanon has been distorted," said Nazarian. "Beirut is one of the safest cities in the world. The Syrians are here, the Lebanese army as well. New York has more problems than we do."

Maybe so, but nobody in New York ever told me not to go into the East Village for fear of being kidnapped. Nazarian assures me that West Beirut will be fully integrated into Lebanon's tourism economy. "There is no East Beirut or West Beirut anymore," he said. "We are all part of the same country. We have to create new jobs in the service industry for these places."

Not so for Shatila, the still impoverished, still violent Palestinian community where I saw a man stabbed to death in a midday brawl on the sidewalk when my taxi stalled in traffic. Shatila has no such advocate as Nabih Berri, the powerful Hezbullah speaker of the house. "They can go back to Palestine if they want," said Nazarian. "They are not Lebanese nationals. This is a worldwide problem, not just a Lebanese one. We would like to see the world community take responsibility for these people."

Shatila: the Palestinian quarter of Beirut.

Nazarian would like to see tourism boom with peace but not at the cost of forgetting the past. "We know the meaning of suffering," he said. "We know how to survive. We lived for years without electricity or water and we are still here. We will always be here. We are looking for the day when peace will come. But we want justice before peace."

Two depressed-looking, clean-shaven men with the greenish skin that comes from spending a lot of time in rooms with no windows are waiting to interview me when I finish speaking with the minister. They claim to be journalists but do not ask the kinds of questions that journalists ask, and I wonder whether they are members of the Syrian secret police. One of them laughs and says, "That's a good one," when I tell him my book is about tourism as a foreign-policy tool. They want to know what my politics are and what I think will happen now that Ehud Barak is prime minister of Israel. "I don't know," I say, and take both their hands in mine. "I hope it turns out well for you." They stare at their hands as if they've been burned. Mme. Haffar smiles calmly. I am good for business and am allowed to pass.

A Syrian lookout point along the *ligne de démarcation*, the road from Beirut to Damascus.

Ali

My driver, Ali, works for a cab company recommended by the ministry. He speaks good French, and we have a lengthy discussion on the subject of *le chaumage* (unemployment) on the way back out to the airport to interview Faysal Mikdashi, director-general of civil aviation. Having arrived at night, I have missed seeing the full impact of the damage done to the city in sixteen years of nightly bombardments, during which there was no electricity and no water. To see Beirut today, almost ten years after the war officially ended in 1990, is to weep for a dead beauty. The glamorous city that was once known as the pearl of the Middle East is no more. Each building built before 1991 bears its rocket scars; some structures are so badly pancaked by the bombardments that their concrete walls hang in folds like a dead woman's gown, revealing rather than concealing the marks of abuse. I spent time in Belfast during the height of the Troubles in

Left: The shell of the Hilton Hotel, pulled down to make way for new development the week after I left Beirut.

Below: Beirutis just want to have fun.

1974, but the extent of the damage there does not even begin to compare. Even if a rush of new investment follows the signing of a new peace accord, it will take twenty years for the city to rebuild itself—and that is assuming twenty years without any new conflict. "You should have seen it right after the war," Ali assures me. "This is good."

"Our modern modernity is a mirage": mannequins in a Beirut shop window look out on bombed buildings.

The frenzy of construction is confined to the Solidère reconstruction project downtown. The swathe of destruction known as the *ligne de démarcation* separating East from West Beirut (which is also, significantly, the road to Damascus) remains untouched save for the occasional ironic billboard advertising cheap chic for young Beirutis starved for the pleasures they have missed in the long years of war. There is little affordable housing for the middle classes, who are being squeezed by skyrocketing inflation. Even in the shells of bombed buildings, with grass growing out of the cracks in the walls, laundry flutters like brave flags from the windows and

A rocket-scarred shell of one of Beirut's grand old buildings is open for business.

the few balconies that remain, while the expensive new housing designed for wealthy transients from the Gulf remains empty.

Despite universal government assurances that there have been no security problems since peace broke out in 1990, Mikdashi's office is still heavily guarded by men with machine guns. Refreshingly, he is an engineer rather than a politician and greets me in his shirtsleeves after the fashion of a Western CEO. His large, airy office is almost too tidy: like the airport which houses it, it gives the impression of a set waiting for the play to begin.[21]

"We are looking very much to a final peace agreement which will open the whole tourist route to Jerusalem," Mikdashi says. "People will fly here to Beirut and then take the bus to Jerusalem. Many things depend on this peace being signed. All Arab countries look forward to it. We can take all the money we now spend on defense and put it into the state."

The peace was signed on September 4, 1999, a good thing for Mikdashi's airport because, although the new structure was floated on the strength of leasing its 20,000 feet of duty-free shopping, the sole lessee, an Irish franchise, will not take over until June 2000. In the meantime, Lebanese officials have no way of judging how much money the project, which ran $100 million over its estimated budget, would cost or raise, or even who would run it. Mikdashi's civil-aviation authority is nominally in charge but so weakened by the factionalism which divides all of Lebanon that it needed cabinet approval to hire some temporary janitors.

Mikdashi has many problems to solve. Fare prices on the bloated state airline, Middle East, are almost twice as high as those of neighboring airlines. "Middle East has a financial problem due to a side effect of the war," Mikdashi says diplomatically. "It is a small fleet (eight carriers), and they are overstaffed." Middle East's main problem in cutting its payroll is political: it has to keep an even balance of Muslims and Christians to avoid possible mayhem as warlords like Jumblatt and Berri convert their energies to getting jobs for their constituents.

Looking to maximize its bottom line, Middle East has cut flights to and from two of the world's largest Lebanese communities, in Sydney and São Paulo, which send their children every summer to Beirut, in order to increase its more profitable flights to Paris and London. To get the best deal on leasing its Airbus fleet the airline signed an alliance with Air France, which carries its North American traffic through Paris. The high air fares limit travel to Lebanon to business people and wealthy Lebanese-Americans. This in turn keeps other tourism costs in Lebanon inflated. "Our tourism is almost exclusively high-end," says Mikdashi. "Our hotels and restaurants are very expensive. Either they are very costly, or very bad. We need to put our effort into middle-class, inclusive tours with middle-class hotels, restaurants, and resorts."

Even though he needs the business, Mikdashi shrugs when asked whether he wants American carriers to come back. "It's a free market," he says philosophically. "If they have interest to come, O.K. Right now, all the traffic that comes here goes through Europe. If the Americans don't take their share of the market, the Europeans will."

Although most European carriers have returned to Beirut, American carriers will not fly there for reasons which are unclear, to say the least.

The State Department travel warning cited continuing security problems as the reason for the ban, which was enacted by President Ronald Reagan in 1985 after the hijacking of TWA Flight 847. Ministry officials insist that the airport complies with the standards set by the International Civil Aviation Organization (ICAO), a high-level United Nations organization based in Montreal which is responsible for international agreement on relevant issues, such as liability for loss of life.

The ICAO officials say they have no way to determine whether international airport safety standards have been met as it is not part of their mandate to inspect. "The implementation of standards is up to the individual countries," said ICAO public information officer Denis Chagnon. "If the state issues a statement that it is in compliance and that turns out to be untrue, that country's credibility would be put to an extreme disadvantage."[22]

A delegation of Federal Aviation Authority officials did inspect the airport in 1999 but refused to comment on their findings. "It's a government-to-government matter," an FAA representative said. The White House Press Office announced that President Bill Clinton had rescinded the ban in 1998. But officials from the Department of Transport, which along with the FAA is responsible for safety conditions for U.S. air travelers, explained that U.S. carriers are still banned from flying into Lebanon with their own aircraft; what was lifted was the ban on U.S. carriers selling tickets for travel to Lebanon through an "interline carrier" such as Air France, the most popular airline to that destination. Officials of the ICAO say that the president would not be empowered to lift the ban if security concerns still existed. Mikdashi feels that the reason for the United States' coyness is political, having to do with pressure from America's powerful Israeli lobby to have its own way with the peace.[23]

Mikdashi is probably right. The reasons for this almost comical roundelay became clear around the time that Madeleine Albright sat down with Middle Eastern leaders to finalize agreement on the Wye accords. "We have been working with Middle East Airlines and the Lebanese airport authority," said Margaret Schmidt, deputy director for the State Department's Near Eastern Affairs Press Office. "The Lebanese have made excellent progress with their airport." Although she mentioned "continuing and serious concerns about the ability of the Lebanese government to fulfill its obligations under international agreements on airport security" and denied that decisions about where U.S. carriers are allowed to fly are based on bilateral relations, she offered as her personal opinion, "If the peace process between Israel and Syria leads to an agreement, and there are no more daily battles in South Lebanon, then obviously the whole scene will change greatly." As to the siting of the airport's runways so that they look into West Beirut, Schmidt said enigmatically that the FAA had worked with the Lebanese government on the original airport design, and the Lebanese government "seems to have solved the problem."[24]

After the interview with Mikdashi, Ali invites me home to meet his family. He comes from a small village high in the mountains above Byblos, a resort town to the north of Beirut, and he still has a villager's sense of hospitality. "Where do you live?" I ask him. "Right next to the airport," he says.

Ali's home is in Barj-al-Barajimat, in the heart of West Beirut, the source of the airport runway controversy, and what ministry officials laughingly refer to as the "suburbs" of Hezbullah-land. The State Department travel warning flashes before my eyes. "Do Not Go into West Beirut," it says in boldface letters. But I am trapped by etiquette, always a prime concern in the Middle East. I look straight into Ali's eyes. Even though from his geography he is undoubtedly Hezbullah and, at forty-four, of an age to have been a combatant, I do not have the sense that he wants to do me harm today. He does not flinch, or insist, and is so whole-hearted in his enthusiasm that I cannot bring myself to wound him by refusing.

I take a deep breath as we turn off the broad new highway that has been built to whisk people past the troubled areas and into the hotel strip where they can spend their money. We are in a neighborhood of veiled women with a huge new mosque. Formerly a warren of wartime refugees' illegal tenements, it is now quiet and peaceful, with freshly painted houses and well-kept yards. Plump, laughing children tumble in the streets. Most of the houses, like Ali's, are new. He parks his Mercedes cab, the vehicle of choice. The streets are full of them, some battered, some new. Bright cloths shade the windows from the white-hot sun: already, in May, the air is breathless. Ali has built a grape arbor on his terrace with vines from his native village.

Inside, the ceilings are high, the walls white, and the pebble-lino floor immaculately clean. The rooms are spacious and filled with comfortable plush-upholstered sofas and chairs. Ali likes to entertain. He built the house himself, he tells me, with others in the complex using materials brought from their village and land "donated" by the government. I gather he was a squatter; before the war, the Shiites were the poorest of the poor. After the war many of them, like Ali, benefited from the political bargaining of Nabih Berri. This is the Lebanese government's solution to the runway problem: although the controversial siting has not changed, today the runways face into brand-new homes whose proud owners presumably do not want them damaged again.

The apartment is good solid construction. Ali has some unexpected skills, whatever it takes not only to survive but to prosper in the chaos that is Lebanon. Great fortunes are made in wartime, and little ones too: he owns three Mercedes cabs and brags of his plans to buy a whole fleet.

His wife, who is heavily veiled, comes out from the kitchen to shyly shake my hand. She pops back in to rattle pots. Ali excuses himself. Suddenly, I am frightened. I can no longer hear the sounds of energetic pounding and mixing in the kitchen. I am alone, a stray from Beverly Hills 90210 in the middle of West Beirut. I stare at the open door, wondering what's going to come through it next.

Lunch comes through it next. I am served a six-course meal which I fear is their dinner. Ali returns with his reading glasses and shows me pictures of his children: his pretty daughter, dressed first in camouflage and then in an elaborate apricot wedding gown with butterflies in her curls; his village; his dead parents (his father wears a burnoose); his journalist friend "Madame Kim" from the *Times* of London. Ali is a daredevil who misses the war days, when he would drive foreign journalists in between rocket attacks in the south. "Nobody who ever drove with me was ever hurt," he assures me. The exact nature of his connections gives me some second thoughts, but because I have trusted him, I am his to protect. His eighteen-year-old son, who is studying the computer at a polytechnic high school, comes in to greet me in English.

"Welcome, welcome to Lebanon," his father says, and sternly instructs me to eat.

Madame Haffar

Mr. Safieddine is quietly unimpressed when Mme. Haffar, who is otherwise known as head of production, tells him of my exploits the next morning. "It is governments that want to do things like kidnap people, not the people themselves," he said. "The government here no longer wants that. You know, when I was seajacked by the Israelis, they took us to Haifa, and they held us there without even letting us notify the Red Cross so that our families would know we were safe." I get the message, and hold my tongue.

Madame Haffar is delighted that I trusted Ali enough to put my life in his hands. It is very good for business. She shares with him a hard and glittering joie de vivre that I have come to associate with Beirutis, who have made comedy instead of tragedy from their intolerable situation. She has the calm, still center of a performer: her temper is strictly for show. It gets results. I tell her she ought to give Ali a job conducting tours of West Beirut, and she chuckles. It occurs to me that she may have already done so and that perhaps I was his first customer from Beverly Hills High School.

Madame Haffar takes me home to lunch to meet her husband and granddaughter. Monsieur Haffar is an electrical engineer, now retired. During the war he was posted to Syria by the German company he worked for because, being Muslim, he could not cross the ligne de démarcation separating Christian East Beirut from Muslim West Beirut to go to work. Madame Haffar, who married him when she was eighteen, was left in Beirut to raise their four children alone during the darkest days of the war, which may account for the dangerous glitter in her eyes. Her husband, considerably older, spends his days tending to the ongoing renovation of their condo apartment, which took four direct rocket hits during the war. What they both like to do more than anything else is to walk and swim on the broad white beach close to their home, a pleasure which has been long denied them.

Today the Haffars' apartment presents a whole and serene facade: elaborate molded ceilings, the ornate chandeliers favored by the Lebanese, heavy, carved wooden furniture upholstered in Oriental brocades. The colors of California or of Tuscany accent the room in persimmon, ocher, coral, and cream. A glass-fronted cabinet holds precious glasses, bric-à-brac like dainty silver reproductions of Persian slippers, and heavy silver-framed photographs of the wedding of their son, who works for Chase Manhattan Bank in New York. Madame Haffar swears that it survived the war untouched. We chatter about real estate, as compelling a subject in Beirut as it is on the Upper West Side.

But mysterious cracks keep appearing in the smooth plaster from damage to the apartment's foundations, very like the conversation about Israel we have at lunch. I have been warned by Lebanese friends in America not to talk politics—particularly Israeli politics—because people are still too "volatile." But it is mid-May, the time of the Israeli elections, and the subject of Israel is like an elephant in the living room, too big to be avoided. "The past is past," says Mme. Haffar and reiterates official optimism about Ehud Barak's pledges to pull his troops out of South Lebanon. "The war is over." But every time the Haffars look around at their own walls, another bitter memory erupts, another Jewish act of betrayal. Then they remember that they are talking to a Jew. "Of course," says Mme. Haffar, bringing her decibel level down to its normal purr. "American Jews are different. They are not Israelis."[25]

Tripoli and Mount Lebanon

The next day Ali, with whom I have struck a deal to be my driver while I am in Lebanon, takes me up the coast to Tripoli, Bsharre, and the Cedars of Lebanon. More than half the world away, I feel as if I am home in California. The long curving embrace of mountains rising steeply from dark-blue waters, the pink granite buildings with red tile roofs, the white highway lined with bougainvillea and oleander—it even smells the same, a heady compound of eucalyptus and hot dust. Byblos and Junieh, where the Casino de Libane, made famous in the 1950s, is located, are Malibu, full of money and "super nightclubs," where pretty young girls line up for jobs that will expose them to the gaze of rich (Arab) players. "If a woman is not pretty there is no future for her here in Lebanon," Ali says. He is only half joking.

There has been a general loosening of morality since the war. Even a good Shiite like Ali has had his eyes and ears opened up quite a bit. It's a long drive, and he fills it with gossip about his VIP clients, "rich guys in government," who use his services exclusively to rendezvous with "Natashas" (local slang for the gorgeous young Russian hookers who have descended on the Middle East along with the tourist trade). His tone is a mix of fascination, disgust, self-disgust, and bitter envy.

Ali completed his baccalaureat and rose to be the director of a supermarket before the war began. He had sixteen years knocked out of his development at the same time that he made the capital to buy his fleet of cabs. His envy of his wealthy clientele is sharpened by his own upward mobility. Like many "modern" or "Western" Muslims, he regards supernumary females as part of the trappings of success. After all, under Muslim law he is allowed to have four wives. Having taken me home to meet his family, he proceeds to tell me with no discernible shame and a certain amount of pride that he himself has a "special friend." Prostitutes are not for him. "I can't go with just any woman," he says. "It must come from the heart."

I am careful to change the subject to *le chaumage*, or unemployment. I have become accustomed in my travels to the quaint notion that an American woman is expected to spread democracy in a very particular way. But Ali, like many Arab gallants, is more interested in flirting. When it becomes clear that there's nothing doing, he offers to

The Crusaders' castle, medieval Tripoli.

enrich my touristic experience in Lebanon by introducing me to his Hezbullah contacts.

Tripoli is a lively ferment of the Middle Ages and Miami. The waterfront, all new-built since the war, is a wave of glittering high-rises, including a twenty-first-century convention center that was hosting a congress of French surgeons when I visited. (Lebanon, like Northern Ireland, is in the vanguard of certain types of surgery because of the vast number of interesting experimental cases provided by the war.) Behind the glamorous new facade is the old city of Mina, a warren of narrow back streets faced with ancient stone walls and filled with homes whose only opening is the front door. They wind their leisurely and aromatic way up toward the superb Crusader castle built in the thirteenth century by the Frankish commander Raymond de St. Gilles which towers over one of the most colorful souks in the Middle East, an accretion of khans (courtyard inns), caravanserais (medieval hotels built for the merchants traveling along the Silk Road), hammams (public baths), mosques, and madrasseh (schools of religious study) from all eras of the city's history.

Settled by the Phoenicians, who named it Arados, Tripoli entertained a succession of Roman, Persian, and Byzantine invaders. Under Arab occupation from the seventh century onward, it became an important trading center until it fell in the twelfth to the Crusaders, who ruled it with the rest of what was then coastal Syria while the inland region of the country remained under Islam. Toward the end of the thirteenth century, the Mamluk sultans of Egypt (descendants of Turkish slave officers) expelled the Crusaders from their last coastal outposts and redivided the Syrian territories, including Tripoli, into six provinces called *mamlakas*. They left their architectural stamp on Tripoli in a distinctive black-and-white marble striping which adorns almost every significant mosque and madrassah including the Taynal Mosque (1396), with its magnificent inner portal, and the Al-Quar-tawiya Madrassah (1316–26).

When the Ottomans, who were also Turkish, conquered Syria in 1516, they maintained the mamlakas of Tripoli and Aleppo as separate provinces, which they called *vilayets*. Tripoli has always maintained a strong identification with Syria; to this day a greater proportion of Syrians may be found in Tripoli than in the rest of Lebanon. In the thirteenth century, the high northern ridges of the Anti-Lebanon overlooking the coast between Tripoli and the town of Jubayl, or modern Byblos, was called Jabal Lubnan by Arab geographers, who located it in the territory of the Syrian city of Homs; and Mount Lebanon by Crusader historians, who spoke of it as the homeland of the Maronite Christians, their sole welcoming committee on biblical turf. At the same time, the relationship between the Maronites and the Crusaders was always a vexed one owing to the brigand Maronite clans who inhabited the mountain fastnesses and were given to selling their services as mercenaries to the highest bidder, Crusader or infidel.

The Maronites arrived in Mount Lebanon around A.D. 900. A sect of Syrian Christians, their warrior-kings descended on the local Muslims and established control as far as the Bekaa Valley. The Muslims regained their land four centuries later only when the Maronites were riven apart by the heresies which flourished within Christianity at the time. To this day, the Lebanese have not forgotten the Crusades: when I asked a well-known television producer why they did not exploit their rich history in film in the same way that the Scots exploited theirs in *Braveheart*, he laughed sadly and replied, "With all the factions that exist in our country today, no one would survive the making of that movie." With the Muslims again in the majority, the small Maronite chapel pictured here is hidden away above the souk at Tripoli as if it were a brothel.[26]

During the Reformation, the Maronites became strategically important to the Vatican as the bulwark of Roman Catholicism in the Middle East. A Jesuit named Father Girolamo Dandini was dispatched to the Qadisha Valley to

A small Maronite chapel is hidden away as though it were a brothel.

Lodgings for war widows.

They're selling Quranically correct Viagra.

convene the first synod to reorganize the Maronite church along modern lines, a work that was completed in 1736. During this period, the Maronites gained a strong political presence in Syria, where Christians are still favored today. Their economic power in the region grew through their dominance of the silk and spice trades: many of their old caravanserai can still be seen in Tripoli but have been turned into lodgings for the widows of war martyrs.

Meanwhile, the French had emerged as the leading Roman Catholic power in Europe, and through the intermediary of a powerful Maronite family, the Khazins, they became the Maronites' special ally. This relationship continued until it was incorporated in the Sykes-Picot agreement. In the unwritten National Pact of 1943, Tripoli, along with other French holdings, became part of the new Lebanese state.

We pick up our guide, Mahmut, at the ministry office in Tripoli. He is a lovely, shy, local scholar, hell-bent on delivering good value, who talks in a nonstop spate of Franglais. He is relieved when I suggest we switch to French and starts speaking even faster. We duck into the souk, a patchwork of cool black shadow and hot white light, where a pair of Arab "pharmacists" sell us a local herbal variation of Viagra called *sharsh-al-shalouah*.

At the old caravanserai I meet the widows of the war martyrs. They are heavily veiled, like most women in the souk, which is plastered with posters of dead imams. Yet they are friendly, speak good French, and are delighted to see guests; I receive more coffee invitations than I can accept. Although the courtyard is relatively clean (at the cost of what labor!), they lack any visible sanitary facilities. Flies hover over the cobblestones, which stink faintly of urine. A beautiful little boy tumbles among them. His mother, sweet, gentle, and running to fat, invites me into their room. It is nothing more than a medieval closet built into thick stone walls on which all their clothing, and presumably some of the outfits they sell, hangs on wooden pegs. The door is the only opening, the bed, also heaped with clothes, the only furniture. I ask her whether she is comfortable. "Yes, yes, it suits me very well," is the smiling response.

Mahmut accepts an invitation to lunch with both dignity and alacrity. Determined to sing for his supper, he guides us into the Qadisha Valley. Surely the Song of Songs which is Solomon's must have been envisioned here in this gorge of terraced vineyards and fruit orchards filled with wild roses, snapdragons, sage, verbena, and a flowering tree with waxy white blooms called zanziphoon, which impregnates the balmy air with a dizzying scent that hovers between honey and vanilla.

Surely the Song of Songs which is Solomon's was written here: the entrance to the Valley of Qadisha.

Aside from lovers, the inaccessible gorge has through the centuries attracted monks and hermits to the many ruined monasteries originally cut by the Crusaders into its beetling cliffs. During the fourteenth century a deposed Mamluk sultan who had escaped from prison in Syria enjoyed the hospitality of one of the Maronite monks and, upon regaining his throne in Cairo, made rich endowments to reconstruct all the monasteries of the Qadisha. After this intervention the district appertaining to the Qadisha, known as Bsharre,

Crusade-era monastery cut into the cliffs.

Bsharre, birthplace of poet Kahlil Gibran and the Mameluke seat of government.

The mountain fastnesses of the Druse.

A Maronite chapel.

enjoyed immunity from direct Egyptian interference in its affairs, and its Orthodox Catholic *muquddams*, or chiefs, held the Mamluk title of kashif. They were granted immunity from taxation and did not have to file reports on their affairs.

In return, the muquddams gave their allegiance to the sultan, Barquq, himself a political interloper supported by the Venetians, who maintained trading outposts in Syria and Tripoli and who had a vested interest in keeping a stable and friendly Mamluk government in Egypt. But, drawn by the new prosperity of the district, heretics from Syria took refuge there in increasing numbers and attacked the unity of the Maronite faith. The conflict had immediate political repercussions as the local Muslims, quick to seize on any weakness, threatened to attack if the Maronites did not return to their original, isolating orthodoxy. Thus, in one of the numberless paradoxes of the Middle East, did Islam support Christianity.

Through the centuries, the fastnesses of Mount Lebanon have given it a reputation as a haven for the persecuted of Syria. Greek and Armenian Catholics sought relief from their fellow Christians, the Orthodox. Successive waves of Wahhabi raids beginning in the early nineteenth century drove the Orthodox there as well. (Wahhabi is an ultra-religious Islamic sect from the Arabian Peninsula. The Saudi ruling family are Wahhabis.) Certainly there is a sense of delicious freedom in the air: Ali takes the hairpin turns 10,000 feet above the valley floor with gay abandon, barking at dogs and miaowing at cats that happen to dart out into the road. "Do you feel safe with me?" he asks as I cower in the back seat. I must confess to being a total physical coward, but I manage to rise to the occasion and reply, "Yes, yes, of course I do." After that, whenever he takes a particularly hair-raising curve, he stops the car by the roadside, and he and Mahmut get out and pick branches of zanziphoon to toss in the back with me until I am near swooning with their heady perfume and quite deliriously happy as well.

In the village of Bsharre proper, birthplace of the poet Kahlil Gibran, lunch has been laid out at the Alpine-style Hotel Chbat courtesy of the ministry. Wahith Chbat, the proprietor, is a tall, barrel-chested Lebanese with a deep, burry voice and a passing resemblance to Sean Connery. He speaks English, French, Russian, and German, and is president of the regional tourism association. Chbat is boiling at the indifference shown by the ministry to the development of tourism and claims that it is due to the corruption of the Hariri government, which put all available monies into the favored business of construction, leaving the rest of the tourism infrastructure—electricity, telecommunications, and the like—in laissez-faire limbo. Like many Lebanese, he feels that Hariri's company, Solidère, has soaked up more than its fair share of the pot. "Beirut is Solidère," he says.[27]

Chbat is also angry that the Syrians are exerting what price control there is in Lebanon, muscling into the business and raising prices at the same time that they are forcing wages down by hiring Syrians at one-third the wages acceptable to the Lebanese. "Now we have *le chaumage* in Lebanon," he says. "We never had that before. Now it stands at 30 percent." Chbat thinks that the clock is running out and that domestic social unrest will begin again soon. The brand-new apartments which mushroomed after the war stand empty because there is no middle class left to buy them. Meanwhile, the Syrians are moving in their poor, like those in the wretched settlement we glimpsed on the road to Bsharre, ringed about with soldiers to keep the locals from doing harm.

Sidon and the Shuf

The next morning we leave for Sidon, which the ministry assures me is safe. "We have no problem anywhere in Lebanon," says Mme. Haffar. There is a car-bomb assassination the morning I arrive, a Palestinian politico knocked off by a rival. "It's the equivalent of gang warfare," a Lebanese-American who travels frequently to visit his homeland tells me. "They're more interested in killing each other than they are in killing Americans at this point."

Sidon, or Saida, is a small port city set among citrus and banana groves 28 miles south of Beirut. Dating back four thousand years, it is one of the oldest settlements in the region and has been invaded by everyone worth mentioning. Destroyed twice by wars and once by earthquake, few traces of the ancient city remain. Mohamed El-Sarji, a Lebanese-American documentary filmmaker from Los Angeles, has put in four years on a lost-city-of-Atlantis project involving the sunken portion of the ancient city which the ministry hopes will become a major tourist draw. He has no archaeological credentials, no carbon-dating equipment, and no funding to clean even a small section of the mossy stone hummocks he discovered—nothing except the "interest" of Mme. Bahia Hariri, sister of Rafic and member of Parliament for Sidon. El-Sarji proudly shows me pictures of "artifacts" which look like torpedo casings. "I'm a frigging dreamer," he says. "Everyone thinks I'm a spy." Thinking of those torpedo casings, I can only hope he's not working for us.[28]

We have lunch at Moussa's Castle, a Druse Disneyland deep in the Shuf, the rugged mountains east of Beirut. The Druse warlord Walid Jumblatt runs a tight shop, and the Shuf is filled with good new housing and well-fed people. Jumblatt is not a man to be taken lightly. Up until 1998, he commandeered the presidential summer palace at Beiteddine for his personal use on the grounds that it had once belonged to his father, Kemal, a chieftain who achieved international prominence as a diplomat during the creation of the Lebanese state in the 1940s. The new government's insistence that Jumblatt give the palace back occasioned a considerable rift.

The presidential summer palace at Beiteddine.

Moussa is one of Jumblatt's protégés. He built his castle from scratch and local stone, a fortresslike edifice with eighteen-inch walls. It is a family enterprise: his wife and muse is also his ticket taker. Moussa himself greets me at the door and asks whether I would like to buy a

It is unwise not to offer praise.

The grounds at Beiteddine.

copy of his lavish, red-leather-bound autobiography. It is unwise not to: even a polite demurral is met with icy silence from Moussa and twenty large men, who surround me and glower until I accept.

Baalbek

The next day I go to Baalbek and the Bekaa Valley on a guided tour with several other Americans, mostly State Department retirees. Ali has evidenced considerable curiosity about my childbearing status. I have told him that I am married but, in his view, that doesn't count: if I haven't borne children then I don't belong to anyone; and if I don't belong to anyone then I should belong to him. I am flattered but don't trust myself to navigate that particular cultural minefield, especially at high speeds on mountain roads. I find safety in numbers and plead my minuscule book advance to his face. He kisses me goodbye Arab-style, three times on alternate sides of the face. "Some day I will see you back in Lebanon," he says. "Inshallah," I reply, meaning, "God willing." For an instant I see a small red flicker of rage deep in his brown eyes. Then it is gone. "Yes," he says, overlooking my blasphemy. "Inshallah."

Baalbek, or Heliopolis to the ancients, rivals Ephesus in size and is even more breathtaking in grandeur. Named after the Phoenician god Baal, the city was renamed by the Greeks after their sun god Helios, and the Romans made it a site of worship for Jupiter. Its acropolis, which con-

Baalbek rivals Ephesus in size and is even more breathtaking in grandeur.

tains fortifications added by the Crusaders, stretches for almost a thousand feet. The columns of the Temple of Jupiter are twenty-two meters high, which gives some idea of the scope of the original building. Only six remain.

Baalbek was used as a resistance fortress during the war, to the outrage of the world archaeology community. Some of the ancient columns were destroyed by rocket fire, though the local guide denies this vehemently. Pointing to a pair of obviously new machine-milled granite columns, he tells me that their sheen is the "patina of centuries." When we hear the bass-drum thump-thump of a nearby rocket bombardment, the same guide says, "It's bird song."

From Tripoli to Baalbek and down along the ranges of the Anti-Lebanon run lines of com-

Left: Imams visit Baalbek.

Right: A Shiite, poorest of the poor, guards Baalbek.

munication from the interior to
the coast, whose strategic importance no Islamic rule in Syria
could historically afford to ignore.
In the seventh century, the
Umayyad caliph Muawiya brought
newly Islamicized Persian clans
from Iran and settled them in the
hill country between Tripoli and
Baalbek to guard the frontiers of
the Islamic state. In the eighth
century, their governors collected
taxes for all of Mount Lebanon.
Today, the fertile soil of the Bekaa

"The patina of centuries."

is the breadbasket for the entire country and for Syria as well: its mountains also contain hotly contested water sources. Muslims remain vastly
in the majority and are still under Iranian control, as witnessed by the
ubiquitous posters of local imams. Some of the most vicious fighting of
the war took place here; and Israeli planes still launch frequent raids
over the low-lying ranges of the Anti-Lebanon. Right next door, the
Jezzine still harbors the Israeli troops who are part of Barak's campaign
promises.

Of all the places I visited in Lebanon, this is the only one where I
feel the clammy armpits and adrenaline pulse that I got in the early
eighties wandering down the wrong street in the East Village in New
York. "Get out," my pulse advises me. Our guide drops us off in the
resistance museum organized by the local Hezbullah in the catacombs
under Baalbek that ten years ago served them as bunkers—and may
still do so on occasion. It is thronged with very young people in combat fatigues and other uniforms who don't like the look of us at all.
Their hostility is silent but implacable. When you look around the
museum, it is not difficult to understand why. The exhibits are bits of
equipment and scraps of uniforms worn by the dead men who were
their fathers and brothers. Photographs of mutilated children and
youths crushed under bombardments, rough models of guerrilla battles in dried-out wadis, and a crudely drawn poster of a skull with its
jaws dripping blood and its cranium branded with a broken Star of
David make up the rest of the exhibits.

This is too hideous to be mere propaganda. I cannot tear my gaze
away. If one is to be a tourist in Lebanon, this is more valuable than
any hoked-up cultural twaddle. In the words of the poet Robert Burns,

"Ah, what a gift the gods would gie us, To see ourselves as others see us." Which leads ineluctably to the arbiter dictum of the French film director Jean Renoir, who made two of the great war films of this century (*Grand Illusion* and *Rules of the Game*): "Everyone has his reasons."

"Of course it's safe," Mme. Haffar reiterates when I raise the possibility of another Luxor massacre occurring at Baalbek. "There are no problems anywhere in Lebanon."

Unfortunately for the party line, I fall in with a gang of UNIFIL (U.N. peace-keeping troops) soldiers in the immigration line at my next stop, Amman International Airport in Jordan. They have been stationed in the Jezzine, about 20 miles from Anjarre, where I sat on a broken Greek column and imagined the Israeli planes flying over. When I tell them where I was, they whistle and inform me that I was lucky to get out alive. (The day after we leave Jordan, two of their detail are killed by Israeli fire in a predawn attack, caught in the crosshairs between the Hezbullah and the Israeli-backed South Lebanon militia, whose actions they have been sent to monitor.) I remember Mme. Haffar's shell-shocked apartment, and Mr. Safieddine's unplanned vacation in Haifa. Everybody has his reasons, and how can they forget?

Lebanon today is like that. The plaster is smooth and pleasing, and highly decorated. But cracks appear in an instant, as profound as earthquake faults, as they did my last night in Beirut. I went to dinner with the charming and urbane man who started Lebanese television in the 1950s. He introduced me to the Beirut chapter of the Rotary Club, a collection of equally charming and urbane men, some now in their nineties, who donned navy-blue suits and starched white shirts to sneak out and meet at the Carlton Hotel every week throughout the war. Although he is Muslim, he reminded me of his Jewish counterparts in Hollywood in the 1970s in his tolerance and affection for the bygone business of making universal programming. Except for one point, late in the evening when we'd all had some red wine and talked about the elephant in the living room, Israel. He suddenly leaned across the table and, staring straight into my eyes, said, "You know, I've always wanted to make a movie about a singer who lived here once upon a time. She had beautiful green eyes just like yours, and she died going over a cliff alone in a car because she was a spy."

When Mme. Haffar drops me off at the airport to catch my flight out of Lebanon, she kisses me goodbye with a mixture of anger and affection. "We have been dying here for twenty years," her eyes say to me. "Why do I have to make such a fuss over *you?*" The affection is perverse: it comes from my having trusted *them* enough to come at all. Well, as they say back in Beverly Hills, that's what makes a horse race.

The UNIFIL Boys at Petra

> Near the west end of Wady Mousa are the remains of a stately edifice, of which part of the wall is still standing; the inhabitants call it Kazr Bent Faraoun, or the palace of the Pharaoh's daughter. In my way I had entered several sepulchers, to the surprise of my guide, but when he saw me turn out of the footpath toward the Kazr, he exclaimed, "I see now clearly you are an infidel, who have some particular business among the ruins of the city of your forefathers, but depend on it that we shall not suffer you to take out a single part of all the treasures hidden therein, for they are in our territory, and belong to us."
>
> *Johann Ludwig Burckhardt, the Swiss discoverer of Petra,*
> Travels in Syria and the Holy Land *(1822)*

The UNIFIL boys, Miles, Michael, Simon, Bernie, and Peter (known as "Tiny" to his bivouac-mates because he weighs 224 pounds) are in Jordan to play the King Abdullah Rugby Cup with a team of Lebanese that was got up by a Beirut entrepreneur. They grumble good-naturedly at being used as scrum-bricks for the privileged young men who make up the rest of the team. But they are delighted at the red-carpet treatment they are getting: free airfare plus four nights at the deluxe Royal Sheraton in Amman with all the food and liquor they can consume. "Sure beats sleeping in a tent," grunts Tiny as he hoists me and my bags onto their bus. "After sleeping in a bed with sheets four nights, I don't know if I'll be going back."

Sports is big business in Jordan as the government tries to cover the huge bets it placed on tourism when the Oslo peace accords were signed in 1993. The UNIFIL boys are playing their match at the new King Hussein Sports City, which stretches for acres like a white and sparkling modern necropolis, half-finished and almost wholly empty. After my visit, the stadium was filled to capacity for a victory game by the Palestinians.

Jordan has had little in the way of a viable economy since the Six Day War, in which Israel took

Scrum-bricks.

as spoils the tourist treasures of Nazareth, Jericho, and the Old City of Jerusalem. At that time, King Hussein was able to compensate for the loss of the West Bank by greater Western military support and sharply increased financial aid from the wealthy Arab states. But he also had to contend with intensified militancy in the Palestinian population, fueled by the occupation. The Palestinian Liberation Organization flexed its muscles inside Jordan until, in 1970–71, King Hussein's troops drove the Palestinian guerrillas out of Jordan and into Lebanon, thus igniting the Lebanese war.

With no oil and precious little in the way of other resources, Jordan must depend on trade. Up to the time of the Gulf War in 1990–91, Iraq was its main market, accounting for almost 25 percent of Jordan's exports. One U.N. assessment put the total cost to Jordan of the Gulf crisis at more than $8 billion. All trade screeched to a halt during this period, and Jordan was forced to ration gasoline and to seek alternative and more costly sources of oil in Yemen and Syria.[29]

Jordan weathered the storm by virtue of an economic boomlet stimulated by Jordanians and Palestinians returning from work in the Gulf in 1992. (Nine hundred thousand of Jordan's 5 million citizens are registered as refugees with the United Nations Relief and Works Agency on the East Bank.) The money they brought home with them unleashed growth by an unprecedented 11 percent. A flood of money washed in from Kuwait as well, as wealthy Kuwaitis seeking (relative) stability built magnificent houses in Abdoun, the Amman suburb where the British Embassy is located and where the UNIFIL boys blow off steam after their game. Iraqi oil once more flowed into the country in the form of debt repayment, and the government promoted tourism by investing in hotel construction: most of the twenty-four hotels found in Petra alone were built at this time.[30]

But in spite of an International Monetary Fund reform plan intended to boost investor confidence, today for the first time in many years there is poverty in Jordan. In signing the 1993 peace agreement, King Hussein placed a strategic bet that regional peace would lead to open borders for trade, within which Jordan, Israel, and the Palestinians would form a dynamic triangle. Success was within reach in November 1995, when Jordan hosted a U.S.-backed regional economic summit that attracted three thousand would-be investors, only to be dashed with the assassination of Yitzhak Rabin, Israel's prime minister and Hussein's friend and ally. By May 1996 the irredentist Binjamin Netanyahu was in power in Israel, and hopes for an enduring peace evaporated. By August there were anti-IMF riots in Jordan after the government raised the price of bread. "People cannot afford to buy shoes for their children," said one Greek Cypriot businessman working in Amman. "This is truly the end of the line."[31]

The vacuum at the center of the Jordanian economy has much to do with Israeli coventures, many in tourism and related areas of the service economy, that failed to materialize after the peace agreements foundered in 1996. Most of these were brokered by American-based MEMTA, which many Arabs feel used the much-needed peace dividend as a political bargaining chip for Israel. "We were very disillusioned," said Akel Biltaji, Jordan's minister of tourism. "MEMTA was another dividend of peace which was not realized. They all disappeared. We were told we had $10 million to start a tourism school and then—nothing. Just all these crazy letters about what we had to do before we got the money. All we heard was talk."

Although Biltaji and other ministry officials are careful not to risk offending the Israelis, with whom they have carefully observed the role of diplomatic broker to the Arab region, the prevalent fear is that Israel will use its superior clout to replace military imperialism with the economic variety. Under the leadership of the diplomatic Hussein, who ascended the throne in 1953 and reigned through fifty-six successive governments until his death in 1999, Jordan moved from the blazing anti-Western, anti-Israel hostilities of the Suez crisis and the Six Day War to a position as the most finely tuned listening post and conciliator of the region.

Although ministry officials today are loath to openly discuss their disappointment with the merry-go-round of peace negotiations from 1995 until a final plan was signed in 1999, their unvarnished view is that Israel and America used the peace to "integrate" Israel into the tight-knit clanship of business relationships that forms the economic backbone of Mediterrabia, or the unofficial federation of Arab states, by giving it the lion's share of pilot projects. These included an Amman satellite of the aptly named Jerusalem Mall, designed to attract Arab tourists to what bills itself as the largest mall in the Middle East; joint tourism projects in the Red Sea and Sinai areas; and a network of regional tour-operator agreements originated by Arkia Israeli Airlines. "They've all been abandoned," Biltaji said. "American Express was pumping money into them and then everybody got cold feet. The stagnation of the peace process was the cause of the delay. All of a sudden we had a mistrust with Israel."

At least part of that distrust arose from the nature of the coventures proposed by Israel but most particularly of those by American-

Israeli investors. For some reason, Biltaji says, although these were elaborate, multimillion dollar projects with hotels, water parks, and other amenities commonly associated with Las Vegas, they all centered on gaming, which is as strictly forbidden by Islamic law as it is by Orthodox Jewish law. "Why aren't there casinos in Israel?" Biltaji asks. "That's a question I always ask. After all, they made the Palestinians do one. With everything that's available here, with 50 percent of our tourism family tourism from the Gulf states [which are heavily religious], why would I focus on that? If Petra, with all its culture, isn't attractive enough, why should casinos be?"

That's a question that is hard to answer. Petra, which furnished the

Petra

set for the apocalyptic denouement of Steven Spielberg's *Indiana Jones and the Last Crusade*, is quite simply the most dramatically beautiful place I have ever seen. Petra is the ruined capital of the Nabataeans, Arabs who dominated the Transjordan area in pre-Roman times. They carved this staggering collection of palaces, temples, tombs, and stables out of solid, rose-pink rock cliffs in the third century B.C. From here they commanded the trade route from Damascus to Arabia, and here the great silk, spice, and slave caravans passed through a mile and a half defile known as the *siq*, which is the only approach. When the entrance was obscured by silt or quake, Petra was forgotten for a thousand years. It was rediscovered in 1812 by Jonathan Ludwig Burckhardt, a European disguised as a Muslim pilgrim who later became the first non-Muslim to visit Mecca openly and in safety. Archaeological excavations commenced in 1929, and the central city was uncovered in 1958.

To walk through the gorge in the cool of the evening with the swallows who nest in the ruined temples darting overhead is a religious experience even for the irreligious, as the UNIFIL boys and I discover. Gleefully, they plot how they're going to describe the towering carved facade of the Khazneh to Bernie, who opted to stay at the hotel and wait for a girl by the pool.

"You can't explain it to him, no matter how hard you try," says Miles, their captain, a wiry redheaded equestrian from Cork.

"Sure, he'll just say, 'Dude, I stayed by the pool and that's what I did,'" says Tiny, whose head is still wrapped in gauze from the kick he took in the match the day before. We shake our heads at Bernie's ignorance and our own enlightenment. Then we all fall silent, content to kick up the rose-colored dust, inhale its dry scent, and gaze in wonder at the 8,000-seat amphitheater, the Temple of the Winged Lions, and the Royal Tombs.

As we toil up the long, rock-cut stairs that lead to the monastery on the far side of the site, we hear what we take to be a recording of Bach's "Sheep May Safely Graze." As we stagger into the cool, dark vault, by now slightly dizzy from the heat and dust, the music turns out to be real and coming from a German church group of millennial pilgrims who are walking around singing as they must have done on countless Sundays together, flawlessly, from memory.

The Irish soldiers, as rough-looking as they appear, are more moved by this experience than any New York culturati. They seat themselves on the low stone ledge lining the room as big as the interior of a church that has been hollowed out of the solid rock and sigh as if letting down a heavy burden. Their faces soften and become almost childlike. Michael snaps a picture, but it is a reflex action. Tiny plucks at his bandage, already brown with old blood.

They are here because they are poor and have not benefited from the Irish boom. Inflation, particularly in housing prices run sky high by foreigners, has made it hard to make ends meet at home. The boys all work second jobs on their furloughs and are bitter about the Irish defense minister, Eamonn Smith, for doing away with career hiring in favor of a five-year evaluation plan. "It's just like 1972," Michael says, "and look what happened"—meaning that by 1974, Ireland had slid from the brink of signing a historic peace agreement to the brink of civil war.

Perhaps that is why they play so ferociously, as if their futures depended on the rugby match, which has been set up by a consortium of foreign business interests to keep their expatriate employees in the Gulf states happy. (It's a telling comment on life in the emirates that

Amman is considered a resort!) Their Lebanese sports impresario had promised them a life of considerably more ease if they won. They put up a good fight, but in the end their Lebanese teammates, who are younger, lighter, and have less depending on it, are no match for the opposing team, a cadre of very large Fijians, also UNIFIL troops. Tiny, who has taken a vicious kick to the head but plays to the end of the game, falls to his haunches and sinks his head in his hands.

There is something infinitely sad in these soldiers, who know that their lives are expendable, seeking a way out through a game. At the party laid on for them at the British Embassy (which must add insult to injury), they drink until they feel good enough to dance. I am a respectable woman from home to them, and at the stroke of twelve they send me back to my hotel in a cab. I know they need to get even drunker, chase wild young nurses, and throw up, not necessarily in that order. So, like a middle-aged Cinderella, I tactfully withdraw.

The day after I left Jordan, I read that two Irish UNIFIL soldiers were killed in a dawn attack on their post near the village of Braachit in South Lebanon by Israeli-allied militiamen. Amid the triumphalism of Barak's ascension, which includes his promise to end the twenty-one-year Israeli occupation of South Lebanon, I dispatch letters to a UNIFIL post-office box to make sure my friends are safe. I can't stop thinking of Tiny and Michael and Miles and Simon, on whose broad backs this peace is made. They are not combatants. They were shot at for doing their job and keeping an accounting of atrocities committed by both sides. I think of Tiny having to work a second job on his infrequent furloughs to pay the exorbitant mortgage on his modest house in Dublin. I think of Michael trying to save enough money to marry his girlfriend and of Simon's scarred legs and forbearing love for a Lebanese girl half his age. I think of their delight in sleeping in beds with clean sheets. "Don't know when I'll see this again," Tiny said. My letters go unanswered.

"Next Year in Jerusalem"

From his office in New York, Arie Sommer, consul tourism commissioner for Israel in North America, looked on the new peace with a jubilant eye. "There is great interest now in going to Israel," he said. "Nineteen ninety-five [after the first peace was signed] was the greatest year ever for the state of Israel. The year 2000 will be even greater than that."[32]

Peace issues are integrally entwined with tourism issues in Israel: MEMTA, as Israel's broker to the surrounding Arab states, has been holding out the promise of capacity bookings for Year 2000 travel as a reward for good behavior. Among the "final status" talks convened between Israelis and Palestinians and aimed at a lasting peace settlement within twelve months were divisive points which threatened to turn tourism itself into another theater of war.

These included the disposition of Jerusalem, probably the center of regional tourism. When Israel captured traditionally Arab East Jerusalem from Jordan, the action virtually destroyed Jordan's flourishing tourism industry. Israel regards Jerusalem as its "united and eternal" capital and vows never to relinquish control. The Palestinians want East Jerusalem, including the walled Old City with the major Muslim, Jewish, and Christian shrines that are the crux of the tourist trade, to be the capital of a Palestinian state. The international community does not recognize Israel's claim to sovereignty; however, the Walt Disney Company does and identified Jerusalem as the capital of Israel in its Epcot Millennial Celebration, thereby creating a furor in the Arab and Muslim communities.

Among other contentious issues is the fact that more than 180,000 Jews live in settlements on land that Israel continues to occupy in the West Bank and Gaza Strip. Although some concessions were made even in the failed 2000 Camp David talks, the settlements continue to be a highly contentious issue. The Palestinians, who estimate their population at 3 million, say all settlements must go. Most of the international community regards the settlements, created largely by American *baalei teshuva*, or ultra-Orthodox converts, with large infusions of money from New York and Miami, as illegal under the Geneva Conventions, but they are a powerful draw to Orthodox Jewish tourists. The Orthodox, who represent only 10 percent of Jewish tourists to Israel, have discouraged Reformed and Conservative Jewish visitors by insisting that only they are "real Jews" and by attempting to force changes in the legalities of conversion.

Probably the most important issue as far regional tourism is concerned is that of borders and security. Israel's pride in its reputation for tight security is at odds with the needs of affluent travelers who have little patience for interminable border checks. The country that controls the most borders wins in terms of controlling access to other parts of the region as well. The Palestinians want to establish an independent Palestine with sovereign powers throughout the West Bank, including East Jerusalem and the Gaza Strip. They want the borders to be set back to those before June 4, 1967, when the West Bank was under Jordanian control and the Gaza Strip was administered by

Egypt. Interim peace deals gave the Palestinians self-rule in more than 60 percent of the Gaza Strip and about 36 percent of the West Bank. The Israelis refuse to return to the 1967 borders.

There are 3.6 million U.N.-registered Palestinian refugees in the West Bank and Gaza, Jordan, Syria, and Lebanon.[33] They and their descendants are the original refugees from the 1948 war that created Israel, as well as from the 1967 conflict. As the official representatives of all the Palestinian people, the Palestinians residing in the occupied territories take the position that refugees have the right to return. Israel has maintained throughout its entire brief history that those who left in 1948 may not come back. This is the catalyst that ignited the 1970 war between Jordan and Lebanon.

Jordan, Syria, and Lebanon have announced intentions to package regional tours with Israel, but these hang on the fate of the Palestinian refugees. Syria, which stands to gain a great deal from regional tourism, cut itself loose from the Palestinian cause in mid-1999, when it threatened to withdraw support from Damascus-based PLO organizations if they did not negotiate. Egypt, which initiated joint tourism with Israel, was left as the Palestinians' remaining big bat. Egypt's relations with Israel were severely strained by the fingerpointing following the EgyptAir crash in October 1999, two years almost to the day after the terrorist attack at Luxor.

Arie Sommer is a career minister in that he, like Nasser Safieddine in Lebanon, has survived a number of changes of government. The new minister of tourism in Israel, Amnon Lipkin-Shahak, is a retired army general who founded the Center Party in Israeli politics and was rewarded with a cabinet post as a result. Sommer said that there was no problem with the peace process, just "greater potential" with the new government of Ehud Barak in place. However, by the end of November 1999 there was still room at the inn in Jerusalem, where the crucial week between Christmas and New Year's had failed to draw the anticipated rush of travelers anxious to see in the new millennium there. Yehuda Shen, Sommer's deputy consul, estimates that between $12 and $14 million has been spent by the Israeli government to promote Year 2000 travel, totaling about $30 million in conjunction with tour operator coventures. Shen squirmed a bit when pressed to specify the exact rate of vacancy for Christmas week, but finally admitted, "I can't tell you we are officially sold out but it is going very quickly." (Most travel plans for the week were booked months in advance.)[34]

Part of the problem was a spat with the pope, who was unhappy about the siting of a mosque next to a Christian shrine in Nazareth.

The Israelis had anticipated a "large movement" of Christian travelers for the historic week and were hoping that an appearance by the pope would draw in Catholic group tours. Mainstream Protestants were welcomed as well. When the pope delayed his visit because of the mosque issue, the only large groups of Christian travelers still planning to visit were evangelicals, including a thousand-member group shepherded by televangelist Robert Schuler of the Crystal Cathedral near Los Angeles. "I don't know if we can characterize Mr. Schuler as an evangelist," Sommer said, displaying surprising sensitivity for Christian nuance. "He's a Christian pastor with an interest in the electronic media." The preoccupation of some evangelicals with the coming of the millennium as a harbinger of Armageddon concerns security-conscious Israeli authorities.

In tourism circles, a Christmas visit to Jerusalem from the pope, somewhat prematurely announced to the press by Israeli public-relations firms in early 1999, was as keenly anticipated as the coming of the Messiah in others. The pope, unhappy at being used as a promotional tool for tourism as well as at the lack of progress in the peace talks, did not confirm his plans to visit and later announced that he would instead go to Iraq, birthplace of Abraham. This met with a heated response from the Clinton administration, which saw the pope's change in plans as a validation of Saddam Hussein.

In a face-off between the Vatican and the Clinton administration, the Vatican wins. "The U.S. must respect the pope's will to go to the birthplace of Abraham," Sommer said unhappily. "This is a very important site for Christianity." According to Sommer, the volatile peace talks had no bearing on the pope's lack of desire to visit Israel. "I'm not in politics," he said. "The official reason was his health."

In an inauspicious start to the millennium celebrations, the Vatican later accused the Israeli government of fomenting division between the Christian and Muslim communities. Churches throughout the Holy Land locked their doors to thousands of visiting pilgrims the week of November 20 to jolt the Israeli government out of its insensitivity in siting the mosque next to the Basilica of the Annunciation, one of the holiest Christian sites, where the Angel Gabriel announced to the Virgin Mary that she would give birth to Jesus Christ.

Nazareth is a small Israeli-Arab town with a population that is 40 percent Christian and 60 percent Arab. The former government of Binjamin Netanyahu gave the Arabs permission to build the mosque, a preparation for millennial tourism, in order to win reelection. The Christian mayor of the town, Ramez Jeraisy, refused. As the struggle intensified, it polarized the community, where Christians and Muslims had heretofore lived in peace. Christian stores were sacked on Christmas and Easter 1998 and 1999. The local police did not intervene, fueling suspicions among moderates of both communities that the government was pitting one group against the other, much as it was said to encourage the rise of Hamas in the 1980s in order to weaken Yasser Arafat's Fatah movement. (When the pope finally made his visit in March 2000, he apologized to the Israelis for the Vatican's silence during the Holocaust but also stood up for the Palestinians' right to a place in their own homeland.)[35]

Israeli interest in Christian tour groups has increased as the numbers of secular Jews visiting Israel has declined owing to the controversy initiated by Orthodox Jewish rabbis in Israel, who claim that Reformed and Conservative Jews do not qualify. This exemption has prompted many to boycott Israel in their travel plans. Tourism in Israel mimics national politics in more ways than one: Sommer estimates that the decline in arrivals since the controversy began is as much as 30 percent. "For years we took American Jews for granted," he said. "We didn't advertise to their community. Now we're competing." But even advertising is caught on the horns of the political dilemma. "We can't tell them to go because they're Jews," Sommer said. "We tell them to go because it's a great destination."

Today, Shen estimates, 60 percent of Israeli tourism is non-Jewish. "We're losing baby-boomers to other places," he said. "We're using guilt, Zubin Mehta, and the Israel Philharmonic Orchestra; we're working with Jewish organizations who can hit individuals, anything we can. This 'Who is a Jew?' is a problem." Shen says he recently addressed a convention of diaspora rabbis on the subject and pleaded, "Come on, guys. If you want to come to Israel to demonstrate, at least book a hotel package."

Israel also looks to regional tourism to expand its appeal, particularly in the coveted high end. The industry has developed packages with Egypt, its former enemy, in the Red Sea and Sinai areas and looks to develop similar packages with Jordan, Syria, and Lebanon, thematically unified by biblical sites. But these depend on the ever precarious peace, and it is astonishing, in the Middle East, how quickly trade alliances turn back into the conflicts they were intended to heal. In certain cases, to paraphrase Shimon Peres, hotels have not only become more important than military checkpoints, they have become checkpoints.

In the case of the crash of EgyptAir Flight 990 in October 1999, rumors of Mossad (Israeli intelligence) involvement began circulating almost immediately in the opposition dailies, which reasoned that the Jewish state could not pass up the opportunity to do away with the thirty-three Egyptian military officers on board the plane. While Egypt's transportation minister told a parliamentary committee that Boeing, maker of the 767 that crashed, was making a scapegoat of Egypt in an attempt to cover up a mechanical failure that might affect other planes, others theorized that economic competition may have played a part in the disaster.

There are many strings to that bow. Israel is Egypt's closest competitor in cultural tourism, widely regarded as the magnet for "archaeological" tourists who are more affluent than the average Southern Baptist evangelical. The massacre at Luxor knocked Egypt out of first place in the region. Every country involved in the Middle East peace process (with the exception of Syria, which can use Beirut) wants to be the region's airport hub because that is the key to economic dominance. The EgyptAir crash occurred just as Israel's state-owned national airline, El Al, acquired three wide-body Boeing 777s valued at $4 million as well as three or four new, equally expensive A330-200 planes from French Airbus. The purchases were part of a new strategy aimed at shaking off El Al's image as an inefficient and uncomfortable carrier. (El Al has a fleet of thirty-two aircraft that are limited to flying five and a half days a week because of the Jewish Sabbath. Grounding these planes for Sabbath observance has cost El Al at least $60 million a year.)

While the EgyptAir crash was "not a very positive thing," Shen complained that the media overdramatizes such incidents as a "negative by-product of the peace process." "The region is not like Ohio," he said. "This is the Middle East. Things happen in London, New York, and no one pays attention. Civil crimes don't get attention. Political ones do." Shen also pointed out that there is an overabundance of journalists looking for stories in Israel. This is true: the government invites up to 1,500 a year to do "soft stories" on food, wine, and the like.

Shen and Sommer have difficult jobs. The peace process has opened Israel to competition in the region's tourism, and some of the policies that were advantages when the country stood alone are now seen as inconveniences or worse. For example, the government has to step up security because of the expected influx, yet most high-end tourists have no patience with the endless border checks. Israel is now giving its famously intimidating security officers sensitivity training. "No doubt security is the antithesis of travel," Shen said, gazing unhappily into his computer as if it were a crystal ball. Perhaps he was alluding to the fact that, although tourism was a lure in getting the Syrians to the negotiating table, once there the interests of the generals parted company with those of the captains of industry. As journalist Thomas L. Friedman remarked in a *New York Times* editorial in the last days of 1999, "Some serious people believe that Israel should focus purely on the strategic deal—trade the Golan for a wide, U. S.-monitored buffer zone with Syria—and not worry about trade, tourism, or normalization. Syria has very little to trade, and real reconciliation seems unlikely."

When I Hear the Word *Culture,* I Reach for My Gun

At the threshold of the third millennium, the world is in the throes of unprecedented globalization. Many individuals, especially in the developing countries, feel themselves increasingly powerless against the vast forces of global change. Yet along with globalization has come an unprecedented assertion of individual identity.

This rich cultural diversity is not just a treasure we must rejoice in, it deserves to be protected every bit as much as our planet's biodiversity. But more than that, the self-awareness and pride that comes from cultural identity is an essential part of empowering communities to take charge of their own destinies. It is for these reasons that we at the World Bank believe that respect for the culture and identity of peoples is an important element in any viable approach to people-centered development.

We must respect the rootedness of people in their own societal context. We must protect the heritage of the past. But we must also foster and promote living culture in all its many forms. As recent economic analyses have consistently shown, this also makes sound business sense. From tourism to restoration, investments and cultural heritage and related industries promote labor-intensive economic activities that generate wealth and income.

James D. Wolfensohn, Culture and Development
at the Millennium *(1998)*

Proportionately, between Los Angeles and the Irish film community, I believe we have a lower percentage of dives.

*Michael D. Higgins, Irish minister for arts,
culture, and the Gaeltacht (1995)*

SINCE MY EXCURSION to Joensuu in 1990, governments have become increasingly involved in the production of culture, with mixed results. The first claim to accompany most ambitious tourism programs is the vast benefit that will accrue to the host culture, first through the reinforcement of its sense of identity and second through the wealth accruing from the commodification and sale of its various cultural enterprises, such as movies, plays, music, dance, painting, sculpture, video, and performance or other forms of "art." Although World Bank president James Wolfensohn's argument in favor of culture-as-empowerment is a compelling one, it leaves room for more self-serving motives, such as pacifying the population with an "identity" while structuring the region as a neocolonial economy.

It is true that artists need patrons—in fact, art achieved one of its finest flowerings under the Medicis—but it is not true that the bureaucratic culture of governments seeking to assume the mantle of patronage in the twentieth century necessarily represents genuine culture or can create the conditions which nurture it. Nor is it true that art necessarily represents an efficient engine for wealth creation. "Jump-starting" the production of art can actually degrade the product much as mass producing hotels can degrade the environment, with the same consequences in the marketplace. More troubling, the powerful financial incentives presented by governments seeking to promote a favorable national image can subvert art into a propaganda machine which is not only quintessentially antidemocratic but may prove difficult to dismantle; one of the twentieth century's biggest movie enthusiasts was Joseph Stalin.

One of the most peculiar sociocultural phenomena of the 1990s is that of military dictatorships seeking to transform their public images; these despots have become ardent champions of "cultural empowerment," which with a few strokes of the pen can be easily altered to read "bellicose chauvinism" or "neonationalism." The following obituary illustrates one of the more startling twist and turns.

> Dmitri Likhachev, 92, one of Russia's most prominent literary historians and cultural icons[,] who has been described as the conscience of the nation. He spent four years, 1928 to 1932, at Solovki, one of the Soviet Union's most feared prison camps, located in a former monastery on a northern Russian island. After his release, Likhachev gained prominence as a defender of the country's cultural heritage. In particular, he was a vigorous defender of the purity of writings by famed Russian poet Alexander Pushkin. Likhachev headed the Soviet Culture Fund, a privately financed entity dedicated to the preservation of national treasures. The fund was co-founded in 1986 by the late Raisa Gorbachev. More recently, Likhachev was credited with changing Russian President Boris Yeltsin's mind about attending last year's burial service for Nicholas II, the last Russian czar, whose remains were hidden for eight decades after his and his family's execution by a Bolshevik firing squad. Yeltsin initially planned to shun the event but made an

eleventh-hour decision to attend after a talk with Likhachev, a historian at the St. Petersburg Institute of Literature and expert in Russian literature of the 11th through 17th centuries. A few months later, Yeltsin awarded Likhachev the Order of St. Andrew, Russia's highest honor, for his contributions to the development of national culture.[1]

Likhachev's changing status may seem odd when examining the history of such countries as the former Soviet Union in which annoying intellectuals are imprisoned, tortured, or killed as a matter of course. It is not so odd in view of the foreign aid money that flows from the World Bank and other benevolent institutions to former enemies who have invested in the kind of cosmetic surgery that makes them attractive to Western democracies and to tourists at the same time, or in light of the lure of powerful incentives like membership in the European Union and the votes that governments get from boosting the self-esteem of downtrodden minorities by making them a cultural tourism attraction.

Wolfensohn's ringing manifesto for cultural tourism as community empowerment is not, so to speak, art for art's sake. It was given following an Ottawa conference in July 1998 at which nineteen nations, including the United States' closest friends—Mexico, Britain, and Brazil—joined forces to protect themselves from what they saw as the gravest threats to their collective cultures: free trade and the United States. Ministers discussed ways to distinguish culture from ordinary commerce and to segregate their markets from the American entertainment industry. The host country, Canada, deliberately did not invite a representative from the United States, seemingly to prevent that country from imposing its view that Canada and many other countries, for example, France, use culture to erect commercial trade barriers. (Canada and France both limit the number of hours of foreign programming allowable on the national airwaves, something the U.S. entertainment industry has protested periodically.)

Now that Wolfensohn has declared that we are all artists, some of the world's hardest cases have announced their conversion to culture, like drunks at a temperance meeting. Saddam Hussein gave Baghdad its greatest face lift in living memory, laying out new ceremonial avenues and ordering large monuments (to himself) raised at the city's major intersections after the pope announced his intention of visiting Iraq for the millennium. Boris Yeltsin overcame his distaste for attending the repatriation of the remains of the murdered Romanovs. Yeltsin was finally persuaded to cooperate in the highly publicized ceremony as a stimulus for the growth of tourist hotels and restaurants in St. Petersburg.

Fidel Castro, ever the *amigo* of UNEAC, gave the nod to the exportation of Cuban music to the United States in the form of a visit by the pre-Communist-era jazz greats of the Buena Vista Social Club. (Castro's affinity for Cuban culture increased with his drive to clean up prostitution in order to attract a better class of tourist.) Michael Eisner, CEO of the Walt Disney Company, eager to attract wealthier tourists to Disney World in Orlando, Florida, as well as to the new civic auditorium Disney is building in downtown Los Angeles, commissioned a "Millennium Symphony" from two acclaimed contemporary composers, Michael Torke and Aaron Jay Kernis. And even President Bill Clinton, not noted for highbrow interests, declared his White House a champion of cultural tourism after a series of economic-impact studies concluded that cultural activities in the New York metropolitan area had generated $9.8 billion in 1992, mostly from tourists. He also took advantage of the publicity to raise funds for his own presidential library in Little Rock, Arkansas, on the grounds that it would be a tourist draw.[2]

George White, executive director of the Eugene O'Neill National Playwrights Conference, which pioneered artistic exchanges to Russia during the Brezhnev years, claims that the State Department has always used culture as a means of improving its contacts in other countries; in fact, the government paid his salary to direct *Anna Christie* and *The Music Man* in Beijing. White, who has allowed many U.S. playwrights the rare opportunity of developing their work in front of an audience, feels that, paradoxically, with all the heightened interest on the part of government, the cultural exchange has fallen on hard times. Artists cannot find funding for several reasons: many new entities are now competing; the United States Information Agency (USIA), which traditionally sponsored such projects, has dried up; and "a commercial agenda has taken over the political agenda."[3]

No one yet knows the financial impact of cultural tourism nationally, but industry spokespersons estimate that 27 percent of the American public spent "billions" on cultural tourism in 1996. Cultural tourism is believed to attract a better class, that is, people who spend more money. The city of Philadelphia announced that visitors to a Cézanne exhibit spent more than double the average of other out-of-towners. On the basis of this encouragement (and the promise of federal funding), communities such as Las Vegas, Orlando, and Daytona Beach, not otherwise known as cultural centers, are seeking to empower themselves by adding symphony performances and art exhibits to their other attractions. This is well and good, particularly if exposure to art will induce people to behave more civilly in public, but not everyone can be an artist, as witnessed by my excursion to Finland.[4]

There is a danger that popularization will result in a "dumbing down" of art, or that popular behavior will infect art with popular standards. I am reminded of an incident at the Brooklyn Museum of Art, in which small children ran unrestrained up and down the aisles during a concert of serious and demanding music. When confronted by angry audience members, a museum official responded, "The community needs to feel it owns the museum." The voices of the musicians were thus subjected to the voices of badly behaved children. Worst of all, increased government involvement in the arts may also increase their politicization, already high because of "empowerment" issues governing grant subsidies, to levels not experienced since the breakup of the former Soviet Union.

In *The Velvet Prison* (1987), Miklós Haraszti wrote about the situation of artists under a Communist regime:

> If one were to eavesdrop on the conversation of artists and writers as they gather for their mid-morning tea at any of Hungary's country villas reserved for intellectuals, or on the chitchat of high-ranking functionary artists after an official conference, one would be surprised to hear the satisfaction with which they tell each other about their "misadventures" with the state. For censorship is the final glaze that the state applies to the work of art before approving its release to the public.
>
> The old censorship is increasingly being superseded by something altogether new, less visible, and more dangerous. The techniques of the new censorship are fundamentally different from those employed by classical censorship. The heavy-handed methods of the past are pressed into service only when the new ones fail to function properly. That this occurs rarely in Hungary testifies not to the state's liberalization but to the growing success of ever more subtle means of constraint. Traditional censorship presupposes the inherent opposition of creators and censors; the new censorship strives to eliminate this antagonism. The artist and the censor—the two faces of official culture—diligently and cheerfully cultivate the gardens of art together.[5]

Communism was an extreme example of culture sponsored and controlled by the state. Far from suppressing culture, communism spurred its production like any other industry. There were books in the bookstores—by Marx, Stalin, and Lenin. There were symphonies, ballets, and operas performed by huge, state-supported companies, with soul-stirring nationalist themes. Russian constructivist art glorifying the worker inspired Western advertising art. The unsubsidized artists like Alexander Solzhenitsyn, imprisoned in their homes or in Gulags, escaped to the West, along with some of the state's most glamorous stars, like Rudolf Nureyev and Mikhail Baryshnikov. The playwright Vaclav Havel, who became president of Czechoslovakia, declared in *Largo Desolato* that only in prison did he find the freedom to write. Only in prison, where he was once more identified as the enemy, was he free from the seduction of the state.

Today, with the encouragement of institutions like the World Bank, even the West seems to be moving closer to the notion that government is the guardian of culture, with rules that are roughly the same, maintaining bureaucracies that subsidize "native talents" who pipe the tunes of their political masters. Although this process may create more culture, it does not necessarily create better culture. Certainly it has resulted in a good deal of reductionism as large concepts such as one's national history are shoehorned into the prevalent political agenda or trivialized into "performance art" like the travesty in which I participated in Finland. "Transforming" military dictatorships through cultural tourism can aggravate underlying sectarian conflicts, as it did in Ireland when a spate of politically one-sided movies were produced during a vulnerable period in the peace negotiations.

The overproduction that characterizes cultural tourism can also degrade a nation's cultural and historical environment in much the same way that tourism can degrade its physical environment. Of course, like all other forms of production, the production of art requires money; the more money there is, the more opportunity there is, or rather, the more people who have a chance to become visible. This can spur some exceptional artists to produce better work. Witness the difference between Neil Jordan's *Michael Collins* and *Butcher Boy*, his next film, an arresting view of Ireland's class system seen through the vivid character of a child murderer. *Butcher Boy* provides far pithier political analysis than the historical epic. Money can also provide a powerful incentive for the majority to produce nothing but dreck. Most important, the cross-pollination of propaganda, bureaucratic gigantism, and an already rigidly politicized grant infrastructure can ultimately result in a centralized cultural sterilization as opprobrious as Stalinism—and as difficult to get rid of.

Bali

There is nothing new under the sun (particularly, it seems, in the area of political economics), and Ireland's tourism transformation has roots in the postcolonial history of Bali. Both are island cultures, although

Bali is part of the larger nation of Indonesia, which dictates its government policy. Both asserted their independence after centuries of colonial rule. Although Bali's history of cultural tourism is older than Ireland's, both implemented aggressive, highly centralized five-year plans stressing the importance of international tourism as a factor in economic development and laying the foundations of a national tourist policy. Strong leaders, in Ireland's case former prime ministers Charles Haughey and Albert Reynolds and in Indonesia's case former president Suharto, have linked these programs to a need to strengthen a sense of national identity. In both cases, decisions which governed peoples' lives were made far from where those people lived: decisions for the Gaeltacht, which is Ireland's rural tourist Mecca and the sanctuary of the original Gaelic-speaking culture, are now made in Dublin or Brussels, while decisions about Bali are made in Jakarta. Both islands are now suffering the cultural fallout from the aggressive promotion of tourism, which threatens to strip-mine the very cultures it is intended to enrich, and indeed to become a new form of colonialism.

President Suharto's five-year plan for the "new order" Indonesia in 1969 is a good example of how neatly the transformation of military dictatorships through tourism can fit into a nationalist agenda. At the same time, it serves as a model for how turning culture into an object for sale in the touristic marketplace cuts it off from its deepest intellectual roots.

Bali, the crown jewel of Suharto's plan, resembles the west of Ireland, more specifically the communities of the Gaeltacht, in more ways than one. Like the Gaeltacht, since the early 1900s Bali has borne the ambiguous distinction of being a "living museum," that is, a traditional culture insulated from the modern world in which indigenous peoples, whose primitivism was felt to confer upon them exceptional artistic gifts, spend the greater part of their time re-creating bygone days for the privileged onlooker. Exhaustively chronicled by the orientalists, anthropologists, and artists who followed the colonial Dutch army, Bali became an object of exotic curiosity for the first globe-trotters of this century. The Gaeltacht also had its devoted scribes in the Anglo-Irish literati of the Irish Renaissance, which blossomed at the same time. Writers like John Millington Synge and William Butler Yeats, seeking to strengthen their own sense of Irishness, conferred the "noble savage" laureate on aboriginals who, in the end, were far happier to accept central heating and jacuzzis.

In 1908, the same year that the Dutch army overthrew Bali's last raja, the colonial government opened an "official tourist bureau" in

Batavia. Initially centering on Java, the bureau soon expanded its scope to include Bali, then described in its literature as the "gem of the Lesser Sunda Isles." In 1924, when regular weekly steamship service connecting Bali, Surabaya, and Makassar was established through the Royal Packet Navigation Company, hordes of day-trippers descended with motor cars. The number of visitors increased steadily from several hundred in the 1920s to several thousand by the end of the 1940s.

Tourism in Bali came to an abrupt halt with the landing of Japanese troops at Sanur in 1942 and remained extremely limited until the late 1960s because of poor roads, political agitation, and mainland xenophobia. At the same time, just as Haughey did with the Blasket Island of Inishvickillaun, President Sukarno adopted Bali as his favorite retreat and a showplace for state guests. Like Haughey, he attempted to stimulate tourism in the area by facilitating the construction of hotels and airports.

Suharto absorbed his predecessor's work into his own five-year development plan for his new order; he also took over Sukarno's real estate. Banking on Bali's image as a tourist paradise, Suharto commissioned a French consulting firm, SCETO, to draw up a master plan for tourism in Bali, financed by the United Nations Development Program, with the World Bank as executive agency. The SCETO report proposed the construction of a thousand-acre tourist resort at Nusa Dua on the east coast of the Bukit Peninsula along with a network of excursion routes. Proposed at a time when Indonesia was still a tinderbox, Nusa Dua was justified as an attempt to provide jobs and stability to an unstable region.

Tourism became a government priority second only to agriculture. But at the same time, tourists were to be kept strictly quarantined from the natives, who were expected to go on worshiping their gods in prelapsarian innocence—to provide the spectacle for which the tourists were paying top dollar. The Balinese were also isolated from the mainland in a most significant way: while mainland Indonesians for the most part practice Islam or the state-manufactured religion of Pancasila, the Balinese are overwhelmingly Hindu. At a time when Indonesia was undergoing the first of many appalling domestic upheavals over religious differences, to isolate one potentially disruptive religious minority while at the same time giving it a glamorous if cosmetic cultural role had obvious political advantages.

The dilemma facing all social engineers tackling this issue was neatly put by the SCETO consultants.

What happens is that the visitors arrive as individuals with a high standard of living who are more or less frustrated in their own culture and then attempt to idealize a civilization they can only appreciate superficially, identifying it with a Lost Paradise they hope to see preserved. The hosts, on the other hand, only see the exterior trappings of a foreign way of life and are tempted to think of the countries from which the tourists arrive as a sort of Promised Land they must make all efforts to emulate.

Tourism developers are thus caught between the Scylla of preservation, in which the culture must remain closed and avoid contact with the world outside, thus constituting a living museum maintained by regulations and subsidies—and precluding the possibility of developing tourism on a massive scale—and the Charybdis of consumption. Here, tourism is introduced to an area because the way of life and culture of a people are considered a natural resource to be exploited—but after a shorter or longer period of time, the culture will have ceased to exist as such.[6]

In 1971 Suharto designed his manifesto of cultural tourism (which owes a debt to Stalinism): to simultaneously promote culture and tourism so as to ensure that the development of tourism results in a reciprocal development of culture. Thus, if a company intends to invest in the industry of cultural tourism, it should invest not only in the tourism sector but in the cultural sector as well. Western anthropologists like Michel Picard lament the kitschification of cultural traditions as the Balinese, striving to meet the expectations of the tourists, ineluctably forget their own realities.

Other anthropologists disagree. In the eyes of American anthropologist Phillip F. McKean, the wages of tourism revived the interest of the Balinese toward their own traditions, which would otherwise have been forgotten in the struggle for survival. Tourism is thus a means toward the end of a postindustrial society, offering the Balinese the opportunity to profit from what they have always performed for their own satisfaction: their arts, crafts, and religious ceremonials. The Balinese themselves incline toward the more positive view, the official view of their still-repressive government.

In its report SCETO exhorted the Balinese government to attempt a middle path between preservation and consumption by engineering "sustainable tourism" in which tourist resorts would be sited away from residential areas. But given the fact that the chief attraction of Bali lies in its exotic culture, contact was inevitable, if only in previously chosen areas and in carefully regulated contexts. These ultimately make tourism indistinguishable from some of the more repressive forms of colonialism and have produced a powerful backlash. In fact, the attempt to achieve "balanced" or "sustainable" tourism in Bali was not particularly successful. After a promising start in the early 1970s, tourism fell well below expectation in both scale and clientele: instead of well-heeled if corrupt Western capitalists, a plague of hippies descended.

A catastrophic drop in oil revenues in 1983 prompted the government to intervene once more. Officials recanted their xenophobia and made tourist entry visa free. In 1986 Bali was opened to foreign airlines. The number of tourists multiplied from fewer than 30,000 a year in the late 1960s to more than 600,000 in the late 1980s. During the same period, the number of international air passengers rose from 75 million in 1970 to 409 million by 1996.[7]

So although lip service is paid to sustainable tourism, it is clear that from an economist's perspective, fast growth is what makes tourism effective. Even the SCETO consultants had little faith in the success of their plan, predicting that by the end of the five-year plan in 1985, the "cultural manifestations [would] probably have disappeared, but Bali [could] still retain its romantic image and be thought of as a green and sumptuous garden." Today, according to many travel writers, Bali is finished.

> How much more tourism can the island take? How much more traffic? How many more craft shops? How many more Kutas? How many more jets? The answer is that it never stops, the roads are widened, the hotels multiply, the direct flights increase. . . . It is now clear that the unbelievably complex social and religious fabric of the Balinese is at last breaking down under the tourist onslaught. Inflation, freeloading, and other social ills have sprung up, and along with relative affluence have come the breakdown of traditional values.[8]

There is more than a hint of condescension in this notion, which ignores the fact that the Balinese themselves seem to want the traffic. Although today the needs of the visitors are dictating the way of life of the citizens, the real test might be to provide the Balinese with unlimited building materials and see whether they construct thatched huts or stucco houses with central climate control, like their Irish rural counterparts in the "quaint" fastnesses of the Gaeltacht.

Cultural Overproduction in Irish Film

The Irish film industry offers an excellent means to evaluate the success of the proposition that the creation of cultural product, or offering a people the opportunity to profit from what they have always done well, is an efficient engine for the creation of wealth. It is also a good litmus test for determining how powerful, government-sponsored financial incentives can politicize culture and sometimes inflame nationalist sentiment.

Out of the estimated twenty-five to seventy Irish films made annually between 1994 and 1999, relatively few have found distribution and thus a means of becoming visible and creating wealth. The Government Information Service informed me that no figures were available on the ratio of films produced to the ratio of films under distribution, even though two film funds—Section 35 and Section 481—were created to support film projects. Roger Green, chairman of the Irish Screen Commission, said that in order for a film to get such funding, it must have a distributor in place; but who has seen *Divine Rapture* or *Spaghetti Slow*, *Guilttrip* or *Space Truckers*—all made with Section 35 money?

Industry spokespeople will argue that even if a film is shown only in public schools as compulsory viewing, it has found a distributor. That may be true, but it certainly hasn't found a means of creating wealth. When the market is flooded by too many mediocre global brand names, distributors become allergic to the brand. "Not another Irish movie!" groaned a friend of mine whose job it is to view potential acquisitions for a New York–based buyer. When political hay was made of the fact that few of the films made under Section 35 were indigenously Irish, the law was amended as Section 481, which allowed more lower-budget films to be funded by the government. These films, certified by the Irish Film Board, which provides grants for the majority of indigenous, Sundance-level film projects, have found almost no overseas distribution. Now Irish film producers are agitating to get Section 35 restored in the hopes that having more money will enable them to produce films with more commercial value.

But more money means more politics. It is important to remember that few movies of any kind succeed: some sources estimate that the average return on a motion picture investment is 5 percent, less than can be earned from a risk-free Treasury bond. Unless the after-tax revenues of the few successes are sufficient to cover the many failures, the risk to taxpayers' (and voters') money is considerable: in Ireland, the red faces over *Divine Rapture* and other failures was caused by the threat of dire fiscal embarrassment, which eventually caused Finance Minister Ruari Quinn to intercede. (In fact, close scrutiny of movie accounting would not make either finance ministers or taxpayers very happy.)

The pressure on already timid bureaucrats to make the safest choices is thus tremendous. This may result in either an interpretation of commerciality that would make a Hollywood Z-movie producer blush or in choosing a respectable failure with "value-added" politics, as witnessed by the spate of IRA-themed movies described in Chapter 6. Neither schlock nor toeing the party line offers much room for cultural experimentation; and without that freshness the hope of making any splash in distribution markets abroad is very slim indeed.

Irish filmmakers are divided in their opinions of Section 35 and on whether it created an Irish renaissance in film. "Our industry would collapse overnight without Section 35," argued Kevin Moriarty. But even the bullish Moriarty, who oversaw the expansion of Ardmore, cautioned that overproduction is as dangerous as underproduction. "In the eighties in America, people overexpanded to the point where any blips in the business took them under. We're not looking to expand overnight. The development process should take years."⁹

"There was too much activity," said producer-director-writer Jim Sheridan, whose films *In the Name of the Father* and *My Left Foot* are credited with putting Ireland on the moviemaking map along with Neil Jordan's *The Crying Game* and Pat O'Connor's *Circle of Friends*. "Something like Section 35 would be better advised to develop a small number of production companies that are (a) financially responsible, and (b) creatively capable."¹⁰

Sheridan is proof of the argument that the best things develop slowly. Today in his late fifties, he went through a full career in the theater before switching to film, working as artistic director of the Project Arts Center in what is now Temple Bar but was then just another dark, dirty, dangerous Dublin neighborhood. A friendly man of short but sturdy stature usually clothed in football (soccer) jerseys, he was part of the movement toward a working-class, socially conscious theater. In the early 1980s, unable to make a living in local theater, he left Dublin for New York to try and do it there. In New York he eked a precarious living at the Irish Arts Center but was unable get enough recognition to do more universal work.

Life changed considerably after Miramax Pictures backed him to direct his own screenplay of *My Left Foot*, based on *Down All the Days*, the memoir of quadriplegic writer Christie Brown. The film, which is as much a paean to life in the impoverished but cheerful back streets of Dublin as it is a testament to Brown's own courage and his loving family, made being poor and Irish seem attractive, as did the boisterous good humor of Alan Parker's *The Commitments*, about a Dublin soul band. Suddenly the Irish had an international identity as something other than murderous thugs, an image that Sheridan reinforced by following *My Left Foot* with *In the Name of the Father*, which put a human face on the convicted IRA pub bombers known as the Guildford Five and starred Daniel Day-Lewis, of *My Left Foot*. The London *Evening Standard*'s Alexander Walker, not usually a fan of IRA-friendly films, gave it a good review because of its even-handedness, a favor he did not accord to *Some Mother's Son*, produced by Sheridan and written and directed by Terry George, who also wrote *In the Name of the Father*. Suddenly the IRA was box office, and Hollywood came courting Sheridan, who had been ignored when he was living in America. But *Some Mother's Son* did not do as well as the partners' earlier film, a fact some attribute to a neglect of dramatic content in favor of political polemic.

Today, Sheridan makes relatively few movies for a director of his stature, preferring to work behind the scenes by godfathering other projects. He spends most of his time in Dublin in a large, comfortable but not extravagant house in the middle-class suburb of Ballsbridge, within walking distance of his favorite pub. Sheridan has never lost his sense of being part of the streets he celebrates. He likes to give interviews in his oversized kitchen, an amalgam of Ireland and California, with herbs growing in the greenhouse windows and scripts piled on the pine table. His brother Peter is one of his protégés. The younger Sheridan is the literary one of the duo. A theater director whose biopic on the late Irish playwright Brendan Behan never made it into production, Peter explained, "This spate of activity could develop into something phenomenal, like the Irish Literary Revival of the 1890s. But we need a substructure for people to learn, grow, and develop, something like a National Film Academy."[11]

What Ireland got instead was "the king of the Bs," Roger Corman. Director-producer John Boorman (*Excalibur, Hope and Glory, The General*), who has been making movies in Ireland since 1969, and his partner and attorney Kieran Corrigan set up a mutual fund to establish a film studio for Corman in Galway, Higgins' seat and the home of the Irish Film Board. Although Corman is an extremely competent low-budget producer and is credited through his willingness to exploit young talent with "training" such fine directors as Jonathan Demme, he is best known as Hollywood's leading producer of schlock. Corman, who said he decided to locate in Ireland to get around GATT restrictions in the European film market, received a subsidy of $1.7 million from the Irish government to build and equip two soundstages, over considerable grumbling from Irish producers who felt that Ardmore, finally in the black after years of struggle, deserved the assistance more.[12]

Galway is not only Higgins' home base, it is also the heart of the

Gaeltacht, whose preservation is part of his ministry. Here, in mountain fastnesses and stony burrens, Irish language and culture have lived for centuries, insulated from change by conditions that are often as desolate as they are beautiful. As part of the prerequisites of the subsidy, Corman said that Higgins "suggested" he hire only Irish speakers, who have been sidelined in the rapid economic development that overtook the rest of the country. With yet another generous government subsidy, he paid them about $450 a week, probably more than any Corman trainee ever earned in Los Angeles. To fulfill his mandate, Corman is also required to send out company correspondence in both English and Gaelic. Although Gaelic sounds a lot like Yiddish, he said, "It's a little difficult" to translate titles like his first effort, *Trained to Kill*, starring kickboxer Don "The Dragon" Wilson, into Gaelic.

Although Ireland has exported a few successful plays to London and Broadway, its greatest cultural success so far is *Riverdance*, a dance, folk song, and light show that is, by definition, apolitical. It is an interesting paradox that the Irish, who were so skillful at public relations for the peace, have yet to translate their epic history and storytelling skills into a major commercial movie. While stories like *The Crying Game*, a distinctly quirky comedy about an IRA hit man who seeks redemption at the hands of a transvestite, have had their successes, the larger canvas remains slippery.

Part of this is an old story, told in the history of the Abbey Theatre, which, after a promising birth in the fires of the Irish Renaissance in the 1920s, failed to rise because its intense chauvinism became parochialism early on, limiting its creative field to patriotic expressions and turgid domestic dramas or "mammy" plays. "To find a universal story of a small culture that will appeal abroad is very, very difficult," Jim Sheridan noted. Noel Pearson, who is trying to beat his own illustrious track record as a theater producer (*Dancing at Lughnasa, An Inspector Calls, Translations*) by making movies, said, "We've become too inward-looking, too obsessed with our Irishness. My God! We're getting like Canadians." Part of the problem is new: the intense politicization that is part of using government funds to create. Although a hit movie on the subject of the Troubles may be what the Irish want, they may have made it impossible for themselves to make one.

St. Petersburg: Show Me the Money

As in all enterprise in today's Russia, the development of cultural tourism in St. Petersburg has devolved into a sorry tale of promises not kept and finance gone astray. When the dingy gray Iron Curtain came tumbling down in 1989, real-estate developers rushed into St. Petersburg to see whether they could restore it to its former glory as the Venice of the North. Erected almost four hundred years ago by Peter the Great on the backs of muzhiks who died building it, the city is strung on a necklace of glittering canals and boasts an embarrassment of rich waterfront buildings by some of Europe's best classical architects. The international business community, eager to find a more livable city than Moscow in which to base their Russian operations, cast a hungry eye on these potentially gorgeous living quarters. But because of the glaring absence of anything resembling property law, everybody waited for the other guy to put his money down.

Unlike many Russian cities, St. Petersburg had a preservation-minded city council intent on cultivating tourism and keeping wildfire high-rise development out of its historic center. One investment which was considered fairly safe was the large-scale museum restoration promoted by an array of government agencies to establish St. Petersburg as an art mecca and bring in tourist dollars, which, the reasoning went, would set the ball in motion for other investors.

When Peter began building his city in 1703, it was to provide a Baltic port from which his cherished navy could launch a sea war against Sweden. But the legendary monarch, who was known equally for his barbarism and his progressivism, looked toward Europe, particularly France, for alliances that would transform his xenophobic, medieval country. Peter fell in love with the airy vistas of his "window on the west," forsaking Moscow in 1713 to make St. Petersburg his new capital. The Italian architects he hired adorned it with magnificent palaces and granite quays built at breakneck speed at the cost of thousands of workers' lives.

The palaces, which form the museum system today, were designed to outshine those of Peter's archrival, the Sun King, Louis XIV. In order to keep their positions at Peter's court, his nobles had to finance the construction of the rows of palaces that still line the banks of the Neva River on either side of the Winter Palace, now part of the Hermitage Museum. Under the patronage of Peter's daughter, Elizabeth I, the Italian baroque master architect Bartolomeo Rastrelli built the Winter Palace, the Stroganov Palace, and the Catherine Palace at Tsarskoe Selo, which became the favored retreat of Catherine the Great and for many centuries the summer home of the royal family.

Catherine completed Peter's great work, and under her stewardship St. Petersburg became one of the world's most brilliant capitals.

Its streets were made familiar through the novels of Pushkin, Turgenev, Dostoyevski, and Tolstoy. It reached its apogee as a crucible for literature, theater, music, and ballet, as well as a center for the haute monde in the late nineteenth and early twentieth centuries. Under the glittering surface, however, social upheaval fermented. St. Petersburg had also become the industrial center of Russia, largely because of the Putilov (now Kirov) armaments plant, the Russian equivalent of Germany's Krupp. The large and dissatisfied proletariat captured by Dostoyevski made the city a haven for secret revolutionary societies of all hues. A petition from the St. Petersburg dockworkers to the tsar precipitated the revolution of 1905; and it was the workers, soldiers and sailors of the city who again shook the world in February and October 1917 and initiated the Bolshevik revolution. Though it had lost much of its glamour, St. Petersburg remained the economic and cultural rival of Moscow which replaced it as the country's capital under the Communist regime in 1918.

During World War II, the city (now renamed Leningrad) was cut off from the rest of Russia by the fall of the fortress of Schlusselberg to the Germans. For two years Leningrad withstood daily shelling and air raids by three German armies while work in the armaments plants carried on. The museum curators waged an equally fierce and courageous battle to save the city's treasure of artworks, shipping them to Siberia or hiding them under the mosaic floor of St. Isaac's Cathedral. After the war even Stalin's government recognized the value of this artistic patrimony and financed the reconstructions of Peterhof, Pavlovsk, and Tsarskoe Selo. After the war, successions of Soviet bureaucracies camped out in the palaces, rendering them unfit habitation for humans let alone some of the world's great art.

When the city, once again known as St. Petersburg, first became attractive to international business concerns in the early 1990s, restoring the royal museums became a state priority—and a popular vehicle for drawing in Western funds. The World Bank, the World Monuments Fund, the Metropolitan Museum of Art, UNESCO, and Britain's Prince Charles were among the many potential saviors.

Among the large-scale restorations launched with high hopes and public monies were the Stroganov Palace, Mikhailovsky Castle, and the Hermitage. Although the Hermitage was in better shape than the Mikhailovsky, which has endured no less than seventeen tenants since its resident royals were forced to vacate in 1917, it had no climate control. After six years' worth of restorations, and the expenditure of millions of dollars, public and private, it still had no climate control.

Although this defect ultimately poses an even greater threat to its priceless collection than the Germans did in World War II (St. Petersburg is built on a swamp), a World Bank official whom I interviewed on the efficacy of the bank's cultural funding programs in 1998 snapped that "climate control is not high on our list [of priorities]," a remark that betrays serious financial misjudgment as well as ignorance of art conservation.[13]

The asperity of the World Bank is explained by the embarrassing fact that the bank had to cancel its contracts with the Hermitage for nonperformance around the same time that large sums of money loaned to Russia went missing in early 1999. The complications attendant on the large museum restoration projects illustrate how "culture" can become a beard for graft. Fourteen million dollars were spent without even addressing the problem of climate control at the Hermitage, probably the single most pressing conservation issue in St. Petersburg. Tom Blinkhorn, lead operations specialist for the World Bank's St. Petersburg project, claimed the project was not going forward because of "procurement difficulties." An investigation of the Bank of New York, which allegedly has laundered World Bank funds misappropriated through Russia, commenced shortly after our interview.

Initially, these massive projects were state financed, but when the Chechnya war reignited in 1994–96, state funds for cultural institutions dried up or was diverted to jazzier efforts such as the 1994 Goodwill Games. In some cases, such as the $50 million restoration of the Church of the Saviour of Spilled Blood, a multimillion project was halted by protracted ownership disputes. (Built on the site where Tsar Alexander II was assassinated by a bomb in 1881, this Russian Revival landmark's 24,000-square-foot mosaic floor, reputed to be the largest in the world, was gutted under Stalin's stewardship and used for storing theatrical props.)[14]

There are many legitimate logistical problems which would make such restorations herculean tasks under the most benign of circumstances. Engineer Elena Kalnitskaya, director of the Mikhailovsky, joked that it would take her more than three times as long to restore the castle as it took to build it—nearly a decade—largely because the original plans are lost in the mists of revolution, and the castle has been rebuilt many times. She also had to function as a mini–United Nations in order to synthesize "input" from seventeen different subcontractors representing almost as many nationalities owing to the fact that so many different countries had inside tracks through other business deals. But Russian museum directors are nothing if not skilled at working under adverse conditions, and they are craft-conscious and ardent conservationists. Over at the Stroganov, architect Nina Smolnikova figured out how to install climate control in the 250-year-old building without damaging the historic structure and decoration. The engineers found an existing web of heating channels running from the basement to the attic, with floor grates in each room. A thorough cleaning of the network allowed an air-conditioning unit in the attic to control both temperature and humidity by forcing air downward through a system of fans, a simple solution that could have been adapted to the Hermitage as well.[15]

It was axiomatic that lack of funds exacerbated many problems typical of restoration in St. Petersburg. Instead of careful phasing that minimized demolition, projects tended to proceed in fits and starts, and infrastructure repairs collided with delicate interior work. However, these problems did not disappear when the funds appeared, thanks to the World Monuments Fund and private enterprises such as the Stroganov Foundation, which collected upward of $500,000 on art tours publicized in the pages of *Vogue*. (These extravaganzas boasted lavish dinners at the palace priced at $10,000 a head.) In fact, the problems only seemed to get worse.

When Lehr International, a New York–based engineering firm with projects in several Russian cities, took on the risky and unprofitable infrastructure repairs at the Stroganov in a bid to enter commercial real-estate development in St. Petersburg, it found that "long-standing alliances" more than doubled its estimated costs. In one instance, the Stroganov ended up paying four times more than Lehr's estimate for new boilers because of a particularly cozy relationship between Russian contractors. But, like masochists in love with a sadist, the fundraisers for the Stroganov insisted that such expensive complications must be accommodated in order to keep local "interests" involved. While the engineer in charge pointed out that Russian firms are only useful for getting help with the Russian authorities, the attorney for the Stroganov Foundation insisted coyly that the Russians were the best. "We can't come in like a bull in a china shop and say 'We're Americans. We know how to do it right.'" The Hermitage restoration, halted by the World Bank in 1999, was estimated at some $400 million.

In its preoccupation with restoring the glories of its past, St. Petersburg appears to have forgotten the present. Beyond the city's historic center, most of its 5 million population live in stark, six-floor walk-ups. Designed during the Stalin years to fall apart after four decades and make way for a new generation of structures, they have reached an advanced state of decay made all the nastier by their having been conceived as workers' paradises.

During a visit to St. Petersburg, I lived in one of these superannuated utopias on Moskovsky Prospekt, the main road to the airport. My hosts were the best elements of Russian culture personified: Sascha, a physicist who is active in city politics, and Mascha, his wife, a geologist and one of the leading architectural experts on St. Petersburg. Part of a growing wave of Russian homeowners, they purchased the rights to their four-room apartment with a few hundred dollars borrowed from American friends under a new Russian law allowing tenants of formerly state-owned buildings to purchase their dwellings. But there is no co-op board or superintendent here. The cracked and sagging concrete stairs are kept clean (or not) by residents. There is no hot water in the kitchen. In order to wash the dishes, Mascha must carry warm water from the bathroom, where a thin trickle is supplied by a temperamental gas tank above the tub. Water for drinking or cooking comes from bottles or through a two-cup filtration system perched on the edge of the kitchen sink—the water in St. Petersburg is highly contaminated by *E. coli* bacteria, as I learned to my regret after brushing my teeth with tap water.

In their early sixties, Sascha and Mascha are members of the old intelligentsia. Like most Russians their age, they live on pensions—a combined total of some sixty dollars a month, supplemented by Mascha's part-time work as an archivist. On autumn weekends they cycle ten miles to their *khollektivnuye*—cooperative garden—to dig for potatoes. Though the open-air market near their subway stop sells all manner of foods, the prices, pegged to the tourist population, are beyond their reach (an ice-cream costs two dollars, the same as it does in New York). Dinner in a restaurant is out of the question. They could rent out one of their rooms, but Sascha is afraid to advertise it. He worries that the ad will attract the attention of the local mafia, known to scare elderly residents out of their apartments and take possession. (This, too, is just like New York.) In the new Russia, possession is the full ten-tenths of the law. Sascha and Mascha eke out their pensions by taking in the occasional paying guest like me. Saving what they can, miraculous as that seems, they hope one day to renovate their apartment—or at least replace the wiring and install a toilet that flushes properly.

Sascha and Mascha cannot afford to partake of any of the pleasures of the new St. Petersburg, and they are too proud to allow themselves to be taken out. In a courtyard behind the Nevsky Prospekt, not far from Pushkinskaya, where trendy squats are springing up in a movement similar to the development of New York's Soho and Lower East Village, a large international group of students mingles in Russian folk dancing and hip-hop with the ubiquitous, amiably drunken Finns. A gang of black-clad Russian youths rumbles in around 11; but instead of fighting, they join the group of dancing students. When I tell this story to Sascha and Mascha, who are waiting up for me like any parents, Mascha's ice-chip Tatar eyes light up.

"No fighting?" she asks, unbelieving.

"We just danced," I say.

Mascha grabs my hand. "Next time you take me there," she says. And in the middle of her unrenovated kitchen, she dances.

Western optimism to the contrary, the rising tide will not lift all the boats in St. Petersburg. People like Sascha and Mascha, who are the backbone of Russian culture, seem destined to live out their lives worlds apart from the newly opulent St. Petersburg of hotels, restaurants, and museums. With government and world financial institutions failing to show as much commitment to housing and infrastructure improvement as it does to developing tourism, the city is likely to resemble itself at the time of the tsars—glittering palaces along the river and public concourses with fermenting slums behind them.

Understanding Reinvented as Consumption

culture (kul'cher), n. [Fr.; L.cultura< colere; see CULT] 1. the cultivation of soil. 2. the raising, improvement or development of some plant, animal or product. 3. the growth of bacteria or other micro-organisms in a specially prepared nourishing substance, such as agar. 4. a colony of micro-organisms thus grown. 5. improvement, refinement, or development by study, training, etc. 6. the training and refining of the mind, emotions, manners, taste, etc. 7. the result of this refinement of thought, manners, emotion, taste, etc. 8. the concepts, habits, skills, arts, instruments, institutions, etc. of a given people in a given period; civilization.

Webster's New World Dictionary of the American Language

While more and more is said about the virtues of culture and its quasi-religious powers, the fuzzier its definition becomes. In the New Age of cultural tourism, "culture" can be orange picking at the Orlando Science Center or belting back beers at a shebeen in Soweto. It can be touring the prisons of St. Petersburg—or its palaces. Increasingly, however, as marketing becomes more and more targeted, the same populations do not do both. Culture includes high art in its parameters but sometimes in conjunction with low life, as in the Rio All-Suite Casino Resort exhibit of three hundred years of Romanov treasures, or the display by the chairman of Mirage Resorts, Steve Wynn, of French Impressionist masterpieces at his showcase casino, Bellagio. *Culture* expresses a general reverence for history but also a tendency to airbrush out its unpalatable particulars, like the minimalist chic of many Holocaust memorials in Berlin.

Some manifestations of the ahistoricity of the new tourism-promulgated "culture" are merely amusing, like the federal government's attempt to expunge the negative image of the Mustang Ranch, a legendary bordello near Reno, by reopening as an "interpretive center" for the Wild Horse and Burro Adoption Center. Others, like the totality of what has come to be called "Shoah business," are infinitely more troubling. Increasingly, these commemorations of the Holocaust are coming to replace the thing they are memorializing: it may be just a matter of time before some concentration camp sites which have filed for bankruptcy are taken over by real-estate developers and supermarket chains.

In 1990 the municipal leadership in Berlin was trying to figure out how to reinvent the city following the initial thrill when the Wall came down on November 8, 1989. In particular, the leaders were anxious to relocate the seat of government for postunification Germany back to Berlin from Bonn. The city suffered from schizophrenia. What had survived World War II and communism had mostly been ripped down to wipe out the past. The East Germans had demolished the old Royal Palace and built apartment blocks on the site of Hitler's chancellery. In West Berlin, theaters, cinemas, shops, and hotels vanished along with any trace of Gestapo and SS headquarters. Many Berliners regretted the wholesale trashing of their history and planned to restore the interior of the Reichstag for the new German parliament, along with Pariser Platz, Potsdamer Platz, and the imperialist splendors of the Esplanade Hotel. Not to be outdone, the state of Bavaria announced that it had found an investor to turn the site of Hitler's official summer residence at Berchtesgarden into a tourism complex plus documentation center.

Two major "commemorative" projects got under way. One was designed to be the ultimate Holocaust memorial; the other a new historical museum to improve Germany's image. Each came, curiously, to resemble the other in that each was designed to attract rather than to repel tourists.

Chancellor Helmut Kohl commissioned the historical museum after the closure of the history museum on Unter den Linden because it was a repository of Communist kitsch unlikely to draw crowds to the new, liberated East Berlin. Kohl, clearly cognizant of the reservations of his neighbors in the E.U. regarding the reunification of Germany, was reputed to have offered ten million dollars to the Holocaust Memorial Museum in Washington, D.C., to devote a section of the museum to the democratic rebirth of Germany, a rumor the German government denied. Kohl wanted a museum that would reveal the Germany that existed before Hitler, the Germany of Bismarck and Goethe and Schiller, that would "take back" German history to an older, nobler Germanness, that of the Enlightenment.

Originally, Kohl conceived of an elaborate complex that would be designed by architectural superstar Aldo Rossi to cover the entire public gardens near the Reichstag at a cost of $550 million; but with East Germany to pay for he couldn't afford Rossi and settled for renaming the arsenal the German Historical Museum. The museum opened in December 1994 with an exhibit entitled "Witnessing German History," a locution perhaps deliberately shared with Holocaust exhibits, which attempted to draw strong parallels between German and American history in their "pursuit of happiness": democratic enlightenment. The exhibit was scoffed at by critics, who labeled it "Nationalism Lite" and decried its amnesia with regard to Germany's military history from Frederick the Great through the First World War to Hitler himself.[16]

Ironically, plans for the proposed Holocaust memorial came in for the same critical treatment, leading many to conclude that the best way to commemorate the unspeakable is silence. Spearheaded by a brash talk-show host-turned-entrepreneur named Lea Rosh, the project resembled a really bad Hollywood epic. Rosh's idea was for a vast underground Jewish star chamber or series of chambers that would be entered through concentration-camp gates reading *Arbeit Macht Frei*. Fortunately, it was scrapped by the Berlin Senate when it was dragged in to the tune of four million dollars, an amount which was matched by Bonn. The two cities, after much wrangling, appointed a jury to select twelve "internationally known" artists to submit designs for which they paid $35,000 each, in addition to some five hundred designs that were submitted in open competition.

The designs, exhibited in a show which became a fiasco, walked a precarious line between minimalism and deconstruction, and kitsch. They included a gigantic silo for the blood of six million Jews; a field of six million glass shards; a monumental oven to be kept fired day and night; a Ferris wheel hung with deportation freight cars; and a sea of salt tears in which a steel block corroded. Rosh opted in favor of a

108,000-square-foot tombstone in which the names of millions of Holocaust victims would be engraved, surrounded by eighteen boulders from Masada, the biblical site where besieged Jews died to the last inhabitant defending themselves from Roman legions. Kohl vetoed the tombstone when it excited a scandal between Jews and Germans, the last thing his administration needed.

Ten years after the initial burst of triumphalism, the plans to resurrect Berlin have been only partly realized, owing in part to the tension between its two histories. The difficulty, as one acute observer remarked, lies in preventing the *lieux de memoir* (literally, "places of memory"; in French, *lieu* means "reason" as well as "place") from being turned into places where people walk through the experience of victimhood on their way to shopping or a nice lunch—precisely what a tourist attraction requires. Conversely, the line between "documentation" and nostalgia at Berchtesgarden can be very thin: *Hitler*, by German filmmaker Hans-Jürgen Syberberg, contains some appealing footage from Hitler's home movies.

The novelist John Fowles remarks in *The French Lieutenant's Woman* on the Victorian mania for categorization: once the Victorians labeled an experience or a human being they didn't have to think about it anymore. Understanding had been reinvented as consumption. This is what so many of the new "memorials" designed for tourists to "commemorate" experiences in which for the most part they did not participate, feel like: a way to get rid of the experience, to say, "Oh, yes, we saw that." They do not linger in the mind or in the heart, like walking through the camps themselves; or seeing Alain Resnais' documentary *Night and Fog*; or, rarest of all, talking to someone who was there. When I was sixteen I walked through the Anne Frank House in Amsterdam with her father, Otto. He didn't say very much, just showed us the marks he made on the wall as the children grew. But to this day I remember the quality of his silence.

The publicity generated by "Shoah business" has spawned a host of imitators all over the world: the word *culture*, in cultural tourism, has come to imply a culture of victimization. One interesting example is in South Africa, where the township of Soweto, ground zero in the battle against apartheid, is trying to draw white tourists into its ambiance by marketing local shebeens, or speakeasys. The hope is that the shebeen, a local South African term that is actually Irish in origin, will be a brand name tourists will recognize from the global franchising of the Irish pub. Thirsty visitors thus combine an "education" in colonialism with their need to indulge in excesses not tolerated at home.

Shebeens, like pubs, have been hubs of black social life and township culture for most of this century. (Irish country pubs, for most of the colonial occupation, were like the "hedge schools" taught by renegade priests, places where the Irish language that was banned for a long time by the British could be spoken and sedition preached.) During the darkest period of apartheid, when booze and business were alike forbidden to South African blacks, the shebeens were gathering places for both activists and drinkers. Like the pubs, they became symbols of defiance to white rule. Like the pubs, they were also the cradle of township music and gave such international South African stars as jazz trumpeter Hugh Masekela and singer Miriam Makeba their first airings. Like the pubs, their entrepreneurs often have long rap sheets as revolutionaries: the driving force behind the shebeen circuit is a Soweto liquor-store owner named Chris Mhlongo, a student activist who participated in the 1976 uprising which left 140 people dead and more than 1,000 injured after a week of bloody street fights between youths and security forces.[17]

The shebeen is a variation on "roots" tourism: cultural tourism based on a specific history or ethnicity. While the marketing of the shebeen is geared toward attracting white tourists into black South African neighborhoods, roots tourism generally targets diaspora populations like Irish Americans, Jewish Americans, or African Americans. Almost by definition, roots tourism focuses on a history of oppression: slavery, the Potato Famine, the Holocaust. While these histories are real and important, particularly to how these populations got to the New World, their marketing places them on one end of the scale as a variation of the Victorian ghost story told by a cozy fireside to emphasize the comfort of the home and on the other as engines for nationalism.

In Vietnam, war tourism is the main attraction. The tourist highlights in Ho Chi Minh City include excursions to the Chu Chi tunnels forty-five miles to the southeast. The tunnels, a seventy-five-mile underground maze which was one of the best-known battlegrounds of the Vietnam War, today offer a platoon of young men and women in Vietcong costumes who stage attacks for the benefit of the visitors. Visitors are greeted by a sign reading, "Please try to be a Chu Chi guerrilla," and are asked to don black pajamas, pith helmets, and old rifles before entering the tunnels.

Another attraction, the Museum of War Remnants, which displays captured weapons and catalogs the atrocities of the war, changed its name from the Museum of American War Crimes recently, when more American visitors started coming. Many of the new American visitors are Vietnam veterans seeking closure to their war experience: one American tour operator uses a global positioning satellite to pinpoint old battlegrounds for clients. In Hue, the ancient capital and the theater of the heaviest fighting of the Tet offensive, streetside kiosks tout visits to Khe Sanh, Dong Ha, Marble Mountain, and China Beach. Even the site of the My Lai massacre has practically been turned into a theme park, with a cemetery, museum, storytellers, and a memorial reading, "Forever hate the American invaders."

About a third of the $22.6 billion that foreign companies have invested or promised to invest in Vietnam since the late 1980s is tourism-related. A little to the east of the country, in the infamous Golden Triangle composed of the intersection of Burma, Laos, and Thailand, drug lords are cashing in on the boom by switching from the opium business to the casino business as visa rules loosen on the Mekong Delta between Laos and China. Inevitably, we can expect to see a lot of art from the Golden Triangle.

In Poland, the famous meeting hall where Lech Walesa, Adam Michnik, and the other leaders of Solidarity gathered in the heady days of the strikes has gotten in the way of a glittering $5 billion development package of hotels, offices, a marina for luxury yachts, and a theme park. Poland is wooing the world's leading expert on labor problems, Donald Trump, as its major investor for the project. The developers plan to make the building into a museum and move it outside the gates to attract tourists.

Perhaps the most stomach-churning example of "cultural tourism" is an excursion to St. Petersburg's notorious Kresty Prison, where for twice what they would pay to see the beauties of the Hermitage, Russians and foreigners alike can gape at the diseased and overcrowded inmates as if they were animals in a zoo. The prison is named both for its cruciform shape and for the days when criminals were punished by crucifixion. A crumbling hulk built in 1892 to house three thousand prisoners in cells measuring 6 feet wide and 12 feet long, it now holds more than ten thousand inmates, of whom at least six hundred have active tuberculosis. The prisoners are crammed together, with up to fourteen in one cell.

In Restoration England and prerevolutionary France, the wealthy often toured prisons and madhouses as a form of amusement. Today prison director Alexander I. Zhitenov offers more socially acceptable reasons for inviting tourists: "openness," a rudimentary approach to privatization, and a deterrent to a life of crime. A thirteen-year-old visitor seemed to think the tour was fun. Some exhibits deal with the rape system used by guards and prisoners. And the guides sell souvenirs: small, ugly models of prisoners and their jailers that the inmates make by chewing their stodgy black bread into a dough, then model and paint. If this is what the "concepts, skills, habits, arts, instruments, institutions, etc. of a given people in a given period" has boiled down to, we have survived the Cold War only to face our own decadence.[18]

Whatever the new, elevated notions of tourism may be, statistics illustrate that shopping is what concerns tourists most. In 1995, in northeastern Philadelphia, the Cézanne exhibit was far outgunned by the 215-store Franklin Mills outlet, which drew almost six million tourists of all nationalities, twelve times the draw of the museum exhibit and four times the 1.5 million visitors to the Liberty Bell, for decades the state's top tourist attraction. In San Marcos, Texas, the estimated 4.2 million tourists at two outlet centers far exceeded the 2.9 million visitors to the Alamo. Pigeon Forge, Tennessee, a hamlet composed of two hundred outlet shops, drew a million people more than the number who visited the Great Smoky Mountains National Park nearby.

While shopping is a perfectly respectable passion on its own, culture suffers in the marriage of culture and tourism, particularly with regard to knowledge. In a 1997 dinosaur exhibit at the Museum of Natural History in New York engineered as a "product-launch" for Steven Spielberg's new science-fiction thriller *The Lost World: Jurassic Park*, the dinosaurs were largely Spielbergian fakes. Mercedes-Benz, the show's main sponsor, included a model of its first U.S.-made car, the M-class sports utility vehicle, among the exhibits. For all the lip service paid to culture, the degradation of knowledge is becoming increasingly acceptable. In Los Angeles, the Museum of Jurassic Technology (no relation), is made up of inspired fakes. A journalist who took a bus tour of New York counted at least a dozen inaccurate or made-up "facts" in the guide's presentation, an experience replicated at Ephesus and other tourist traps the world over. In Prague, tourists will buy a Franz Kafka T-shirt but will not read his books because they are too difficult.

Increasingly popular are tourist treatments of the culture of celebrity, like Tinseltown Studios, a theme-park and dinner-theater complex near Disneyland where what appears to be the supporting cast of Nathanael West's *Day of the Locust* pays admission to be treated as stars. It is a fairly safe bet to say that none of the visitors who plunk down their forty-five dollars to be Princess Di or Barney or their idol of choice for the night will ever be famous on merit. Why should they even try, when a mere forty-five dollars buys red-carpet treatment, a swarm of fans, and paparazzi clamoring for interviews and autographs—even, if one wins sufficient acclaim from one's friends and relatives, an "Academy Award" for being edited into scenes opposite Tony Perkins in *Psycho?* Ogden Entertainment, which owns Tinseltown, is betting cleverly on the cheapening currency of celebrity in these anti-elitist times. While its fundamental appeal is the same that prompts people to show their guests home videos, it also resonates with those who ask, "In a culture where Monica Lewinsky can be a celebrity, why can't I?"[19]

"Roots" Tourism: Culture and Nationalism

Marketing techniques have increasingly tied the larger concept of culture to the smaller concept of identity. The shebeen, for example, is an effort to overcome the segregation preserved in other areas of African tourism. While the north coast of Africa, including Egypt, the "cradle of civilization," has universal appeal, along with Morocco and Tunisia, black visitors from other countries tend to cluster around areas like the stone forts and castles of Ghana, testimonials to the slave trade. Safari tourism, reengineered as the more palatable "ecotourism," with its upscale trappings offering a fond tribute to the days of empire, attracts the descendants of colonials, the Ralph Lauren-in-the-bush set who are to be found in other areas of *frisson* travel as well.

The original, unburnished colonial relationship is still apparent in the least-developed places where ecotourism flourishes and is perhaps preserved by it. In Bwindi National Forest, Uganda, a game warden and eight foreign tourists were killed by tribesmen in March 1999 after farmers were evicted from a park in favor of the silverbacked mountain gorillas that foreigners will travel far to see. Although rebel Hutus claimed credit for the murders as a way to punish Uganda for aiding Congolese rebels by crippling its tourism, it is unclear where the original land dispute left off and the claims of the Hutus began. The local Bwindis who were making money as porters and drivers for tourists tracking gorillas said that they would go back to farming and timbering, their original way of life, if they had any choice in the matter.

In Israel, roots tourism geared toward strengthening the Jewish identity of American visitors has tripped over itself as relations between Reformed and Orthodox Jews have become increasingly testy. The question, "Whose identity is it, anyway?" arises in the face of the many different kinds of Jewish identity—as many as there are Jews; and the tradition of intellectual dissent is strong in all of them. Marketing for one group has resulted in the exclusion of the others: Reformed Jews have voted with their feet and refused to visit Israel. Non-Orthodox travelers, who represent 90 percent of visitors, are inconvenienced by the strict kosher and sabbath observance laws which now govern restaurants and tour operators. Women in general are repelled by the harassment from Orthodox men and women, who harangue them to cover themselves in public. The West Bank settlers to whom much of the hardening of party lines can be traced, and who have caused so much of the disruption and delay that has characterized the peace process, are largely roots tourists who came, stayed, and became more Israeli than the Israelis themselves, permanently affecting the political process.

In Ireland, which likes to compare itself to Israel, it is too early to say whether roots tourism will have the same effect. Certainly, Ireland is attempting to re-create itself as a homeland for the Wild Geese who scattered during the famines, political persecutions, and pandemics of unemployment that have marked so much of the country's history. Its genealogical roots tourism is attracting large numbers who visit once to trace their Irish ancestry, come back, and ultimately buy homes. But the majority of these appear to be retirees who are unlikely to become political agitators, although they may, like the Miami–Tel Aviv shuttle contingent, be very active in fundraising. The younger visitors who stay are not, as a rule, searching for their identities but for jobs in the booming economy, or, in the case of the lucky few creative artists, for tax amnesty. (In Ireland the earnings of artists are tax-free.) There is a high degree of competition for jobs as well as for school places, and even Irish Americans are reporting a fair amount of hostility from the natives. "Great hatred, little room" was Yeats's summary of his homeland. It is unlikely, with that reception, that too many Wild Geese will stay to become hawks.

The "Big Idea" of Tourism

"Optimism is the engine for change."

Nerea Abasolo, communications director,
Guggenheim Museum, Bilbao

While much of the Big Idea of tourism, that is, tourism married to democratic ideology, has created a cultural product that one would travel far to avoid, there are undeniable success stories: one great advantage of artistic "overproduction" is that the greater number of artworks churned out increases the statistical probability of a good one. The Irish have produced *Riverdance*, a great touring moneyspinner which is the dance equivalent of *Cats*, as well as some travel-worthy playwrights, including Colm MacPherson. Their music industry, although becoming a bit too familiar, is thriving. Some fine small films have been produced by a number of countries, notably the surprising *West Beirut*, a delicate coming-of-age story completely free of politics.

One masterpiece has been produced, the Guggenheim Museum in Bilbao, Spain. Designed by architect Frank Gehry with the nobility of a galleon in full sail, the structure has been called the great building of the twentieth century and credited with transforming the Basque region in which it is set (where former IMF president Michel Camdessus makes his summer home). Along with the Getty Center in Los Angeles and other leading museum projects, promoters of the arts hope that the Guggenheim will represent a return to the great cathedral-building epoch of the Middle Ages, with art substituting for religion.

Like Belfast, the Basque area of northern Spain was once a center for heavy industry, notably shipbuilding. Like Belfast, as these industries declined, the Basque region fell into a depression which was roiled by the decades-long terrorist campaign of the ETA separatist group. Almost as old as the IRA, the ETA has its roots in the Spanish Civil War, when the central Spanish government gave the three Basque provinces of Alava, Guipuzcoa, and Vizcaya their autonomy in return for their support. A new offensive abolished this autonomy in 1937. The Basques, hard and wily warriors who have resisted every attempt at dominance from the Romans onward, continued to fight for the Loyalists and against any government that threatened their independence.

In 1991, as the cultural bandwagon was gathering momentum, the Basque regional administration agreed with the Guggenheim Foundation to build a museum at a cost of between $100 million and $140 million. The Guggenheim's collection is so immense that only a fraction of it can be displayed at its flagship Fifth Avenue museum in New York, and the museum has franchised itself to Berlin and Seoul as well as to Bilbao.

Almost all the construction was done by Basque companies, who used the project to showcase impressive skills in marrying their traditional building techniques with advanced technology. The building has been an outstanding success, attracting three times the expected number of visitors when it opened in 1997 and adding $160 million to the Basque economy. Bilbao is justifiably proud of its triumph and has undertaken other major architectural projects with such international stars as Sir Norman Foster and Cesar Pelli.

Gehry himself has been tapped to design a project that will offer yet another opportunity to convert a declining port city into a great tourist attraction. The architect is attached to a proposal to develop Fort Sherman and other areas of the former Panama Canal zone as the United States hands over its military bases. But to date, Gehry has expressed only limited enthusiasm for the project. Perhaps he is aware of one of the pitfalls of cultural tourism: a great idea usually works best on its first airing. Amador, one of the main areas of a projected resort investment of some $400 million, is an all but beachless strip of land overlooking one of the world's premier shipping lanes. Panama has a major image problem to overcome as well. Although it is peaceful today, its global brand name is still Noriega. Conservatives in the United States fear that the canal zone, which was also a key base for U.S. regional antinarcotics missions, could destabilize again once the bases are gone. Crime is high, and the isthmus is particularly vulnerable to takeover by drug lords from neighboring Colombia, who have hijacked helicopters by posing as tourists. The solution of the Panamanian government is to attract more tourists, using the cosmetic skills of none other than Irish director John Boorman to sell the country in his adaptation of John le Carré's spy novel, *The Tailor of Panama*.[20]

In an excellent example of how the selling of culture now works, the Panamanian government is quick to sing the praises of Panama's cultural offerings but slow to fund a promotional budget. Out of a total budget of $17 million (according to industry sources), or $12 million (according to Ireola de Cordoba, head of the Panamanian Institute for Tourism, which functions as Panama's ministry for tourism), only $2 million goes into the vital job of publicizing Panama's heritage. The rest goes to the salaries of institute employees (372 according to de Cordoba: 600-plus according to industry sources). Tourism professionals, perhaps a little envious, describe these as nepotistic appointments: de Cordoba is a school chum of Panamanian president Mireya Moscoso. While the country teeters on the edge of civil unrest, in part because of the large number of service jobs lost through the canal handover, the serious money goes into offshore banking and construction, viewed as popular vehicles for money laundering. Panama is working hard to shed its "image" as Colombia's cleaner, so we may be hearing a great deal about its culture for the foreseeable future. However, Boorman, a shrewd director with a mind of his own, has portrayed the culture of the country as . . . a money laundry.

The End

Elizabeth Bates has been to Rome
And looked at the statues there;
Elizabeth Bates has scaled the Alps
And sniffed at the mountain air.

Elizabeth Bates has winced at Nice
And quibbled at gay Paree,
And lifted her delicate eyebrows at
Indelicate Barbary.

Elizabeth Bates has "done" the globe
From Panama back to the States,
But all she saw on the way around
Was Miss Elizabeth Bates.
Milo Ray Phelps, New Yorker (December 21, 1929)

NEW YORK CITY, New Year's Eve, 2010. Times Square is filled not with holiday-makers but with an ugly mob. The neon ticker tape on the Morgan Stanley building shows the still-cascading slide of the stock market. The theaters and restaurants and shops are not only shut but shuttered, with trigger-happy security forces on guard. Hundreds of inexperienced riot-trained police, supplemented by plainclothesmen, force the crowd into rigidly controlled, too-narrow paths of movement. Parents with children in their arms eye the toys in the windows which have gone unsold because everyone in finance got pink-slipped and jobs in tourism dried up six months later. Unemployment has leaped from 10 percent to 30 percent and is still rising, for New York gave up its manufacturing base in the twentieth century. The only other jobs left are in the arts, whose constituents, adept at back-stabbing, have turned themselves into a new form of KGB.

Food prices, driven by shortages occurring all over the world as people sell off their land to work in tourism, have risen to highs not seen before in the developed nations. The oil cartel, sensing weakness in the West, has driven fuel prices up as well. In Harlem, embittered minorities who have had their hopes raised by empowerment programs are already looting shops, provoked by representatives from a diversity of terrorist organizations. The police have closed off access up above 110th Street and are trying to keep unrest from spreading, but what is left of the middle or "professional" class in Manhattan is mad as hell and not taking it anymore from rich foreigners who have made their housing unaffordable. The focus of this middle-class anger is the Disney Store, filled with unaffordable toys. When the first autographed Yankees bat thuds against the glass, the frightened rookie cops roll in, cracking heads left and right. Children fall and are trampled. The mob surges back. Mayhem spreads to the neighboring streets, and troops of reserves are called in. And so the police state arrives in America . . .

This is, of course, a hypothetical scenario. (Another one, borrowed from novelist Robert Stone, is that a shadowy Middle Eastern group, possibly Islamic, possibly Israeli, sets off a bomb in Times Square in retaliation for a similar incident at the Dome of the Rock in Jerusalem.) However, it illustrates many of the dangers attendant on making the world "safe" for tourism: a one-trick economy that becomes susceptible to any external shock; social division; and an overly muscular security force pumped up to protect tourists and the companies that profit from them. It is difficult to see how this combination might serve the advance of democracy but not at all difficult to see how the social controls that foster tourism might also serve the interests of repressive regimes or, indeed, of multinational corporations, for whom such controls optimize the opportunity for delivering a good bottom line.

When tourism collapsed in Egypt in 1997, it threatened the government of popular president Hosni Mubarak. Gama'a al-Islamiyya, an Islamic militant group that had been waging a violent campaign since 1992 to oust Mubarak's secular government, focused deliberately on tourists, trains to Southern Egypt, and Nile River cruisers before striking at Luxor, the ancient Thebes and site of Tutankhamen's tomb as well as other top tourist draws. Tourism was, and still is, Egypt's main foreign-currency earner. Its receipts are Mubarak's weapon for staving off a devaluation similar to Mexico's. Periodically the IMF has pressured Mubarak to devalue in order to spur exports, but the president, who fought to raise the average Egyptian's income from $581 in 1981 to $1,200 in 1999, has resisted in order to avoid inflation and widespread civil unrest.

In October 1999, two weeks before EgyptAir flight 990 crashed into the Atlantic corridor just north of New York City, the Mubarak government rejected yet another call for devaluation from the IMF, asserting that tourism receipts, which had recovered after the Luxor massacre, would compensate for the shortage in U.S. dollars caused by rising imports. Foreign-exchange assets of Egypt's state-owned commercial banks have been used to finance the balance-of-payments deficit while the central bank allowed its own reserves to fall, also prompting criticism from the West. Research by a Western investment bank contradicted statements made by Egyptian tourism authorities: the investment bank pointed out that although the annual number of tourists visiting Egypt rose by 36 percent in the first six months of 1999, it had yet to reach pre-Luxor income levels owing to deep discounting by hotels and cruises. Ayden Nour, Egyptian Tourist Authority director for the Eastern United States and Latin America, maintained that it had and that there was no more discounting. Nour also said that Cairo and other Egyptian cities were booked to capacity for Christmas week and that he did not expect the crash of the plane to affect bookings. (Turkey made the same response when PKK leader Abdullah Ocalan was captured and the country's summer tourism was almost wiped out.)[1]

For any country, but particularly for one as strategically important as Egypt, to become so dependent on tourism runs the risk of exacerbating underlying economic problems if tourism falls off, thus inflaming nationalist sentiment, and possibly becoming a target for terrorism by competing powers. It is difficult to see how this plan is a recipe for peace. The mysteries surrounding the EgyptAir crash aroused both anti-American sentiment and anti-Israeli sentiment almost immediately and will probably continue to do so as long as any mystery remains. It is by no means certain that a satisfactory answer will ever be made: the crash of TWA Flight 800 (also a Boeing plane) remained unsolved until 2000.

When the interests of a multinational corporation like Boeing become an integral part of U.S. foreign policy because of that company's immense strategic and economic significance, the choices are all difficult ones. On November 30, 1999, U.S. regulators initiated a "special audit" of Boeing planes after a string of assembly-line problems which date back to 1997, ranging from a tool left behind in one widebody jet's fuel tank, to widespread use of substandard insulation strips to line cockpit walls, to improperly tightened bolts and parts that failed a federal flame test. Special audits are conducted when a specific problem or problems comes to the attention of the FAA. This audit was characterized by the *Wall Street Journal* as an "extensive audit of Boeing's manufacturing practices." Boeing has lost market share since 1997, when it came under unfavorable scrutiny for speeding up its assembly line in order to meet an anticipated surge in orders due in part to the decade's expansion in global tourism. In the mid-1990s, hoping to deal the coup de grâce to its greatest rival, French Airbus, Boeing attempted to corner the narrow-body plane market by selling a new version of its 737 to several large American carriers at steep discounts. Making any profit on the deal was contingent on slashing production costs, but the rush of new orders clogging the assembly line caused costs to soar instead. In 1997 the company had to halt production of the 737 and 747 and delay deliveries, angering clients and causing it to post its first annual loss in fifty years. Boeing's last special audit occurred in 1998; this one concerned missing fasteners in 737 tail assemblies, supposedly a factor in at least one crash.[2]

If Boeing's special status as a diplomatic bargaining chip was used in order to conceal an internal problem, the diplomatic consequences could be severe: Egypt's powerful nationalism was affronted by the American assertion that the Egyptian pilot crashed the plane deliberately in a peculiarly Islamic suicide. Other nations, sensing that commerce and diplomacy are now one to the United States, may fight back using the same weapons. The unkindest cut for Boeing in recent years came from a former ally. El Al, the Israeli national airline which formerly flew only Boeing jets, announced plans in 1999 to split a wide-body order between Boeing and Airbus. Ironically, the deal clinched by the Clinton administration on Boeing's behalf with the Saudis in 1993 may have resulted in Airbus's victory in 1999. The blow was a harsh one to already embattled Boeing: observers at the failed 1999 World Trade Organization talks in Seattle—Boeing's corporate headquarters—noted that there were Boeing machinists in the ranks of demonstrators.[3]

Using tourism to achieve peace and democracy is what historian Robert Conquest calls a Big Idea; and in Conquest's analysis Big Ideas are something to be wary of. Big Ideas are utopian by definition and offer a millenarian solution to all human problems, like MEMTA and its talismanic appreciation of the year 2000. Making the world safe for tourism is essentially big business tricked out in ideological robes, Nelson Rockefeller tailored to transnational megamergers. Whether it will become, in Conquest's lovely phrase, one of the rogue ideologies that has savaged and trampled humanity in the twentieth century remains to be seen. But in its own way this Big Idea may show how capitalism,

having "triumphed" over communism in the last decade of the twentieth century, ended up imitating its victim: its one-size-fits-all approach
increasingly resembles the "central planning" of Stalin's Soviet Union
which resulted in, among other things, the complete dismantling of its
agricultural system.[4]

"Empowering" communities or countries by promoting their cultures at the same time you destroy the way of life that produced these
cultures—farming, fishing, mining—is illogical to say the least. In country after country (Turkey, Thailand, and Uganda, to name a few examples) farming in particular is the product of generations of land
ownership that has structured whole societies. The destruction of these
networks by hotel or ecotourism developers has uprooted entire villages
and sent the populations into the cities. In many developing countries
these in turn have metamorphosed into megalopolises without infrastructure or other facilities; Jakarta, which in 1999 experienced social
unrest approaching revolutionary levels, is by some counts now the
largest city in the world. In Turkey, as I have noted, the displaced rural
population has had a tremendously politically destabilizing effect, seed-
ing the growth of obstreperous Islamic fundamentalism. In Thailand,
calamitously, tourism has fed the exponential growth of the underage
sex industry. In Uganda dispossessed farmers who do not want to work
as drivers or porters in the tourist industry have struck back at the
tourists they perceive to have deprived them of their birthright. This
one incident, though isolated, gave disproportionate power to its per-
petrators, who virtually shut down tourism. With such power at stake,
the terrorists' "success story" will probably inspire others.

Finding a way not to disrupt patterns of land ownership which are
the essence of identity could be the most serious problem tourism faces
if it is truly to be a force for peace and democracy. Agritourism
(tourism based on cultivated land rather than wilderness), such as that
developed in France, Italy, Germany, parts of Latin America, and the
western United States, is one answer. The forward-looking government of Turkey also recognizes the need to prevent further exodus to
the cities and is including agritourism in its arsenal, although it may
be too late for areas like Antalya, where a whole generation has left the
land and the remainder sniffs at farming jobs as being low status.

At the same time, agriculture and agritourism are threatened by
countries like the United States and Latin America, which, under the
umbrella of the World Trade Organization, want to eliminate export
subsidies and do away with other big farm supports. The European
Union and Japan, backed by Korea, Norway, and Switzerland, have

asked the World Trade Organization to preserve subsidies and to recognize the "multifunctional role" of agriculture in preserving rural life,
that is, agritourism. (The countries which wield the most power in the
European Union, France and Germany, receive the majority of the farm
subsidies.) It may be that the loss of land and of the deep social roots
that come with land ownership is an inexorable process, with multi- and
transnational corporations replacing the old colonial powers; but if that
is the case then displaced populations will probably continue to resist it
by whatever means they can, and they will be justified in doing so.

Kofi Annan, secretary-general of the United Nations, has called
for a global compact between business and the United Nations in
which that organization could play a role in "help[ing] corporations to
act in accordance with internationally accepted principles of human
rights, labor standards, and environmental protections." If we take Disney's preemption of diplomatic solutions to the division of Jerusalem
at the Epcot Millennial Celebration as an example, it is difficult to see
how such a compact would work. Would the United Nations sanction
Disney for trampling on the human rights and labor standards of the
Palestinians? Why would Disney expose itself to sanctions which might
seriously impede it in its business? Indeed, why would Disney ever
want to be a part of such a compact, if not to use the United Nations
for its own PR? If so, the only way the United Nations could "help"
Disney behave responsibly would be to remove the U.N. name from
the enterprise, and thus no compact.[5]

Perhaps the United Nations could play a role in the preservation
of land ownership, which plays a part in human rights, labor standards,
and environmental protections. But Annan has joined the United
States and Latin America in calling for an end to all farm subsidies on
the grounds that this would help poor farmers in the developing world
who cannot compete with subsidized imports. Agriculture is a ticklish
issue, which divided the riot-torn 1999 World Trade Organization talks
in Seattle. There is a clear understanding among the European Union,
the Japanese, and the Germans, the French, and the Italians (the high
end of the industrialized world) that agricultural production and agritourism are highly desirable assets and represent not only the breadbasket but also a large portion of the cultural patrimony of a fully
"developed" country. It would be ironic if, in the twenty-first century,
overinvestment in tourism created food shortages, agriculture turned
out to be even more hotly competed for than information technology,
and farmers, far from looking down on themselves as being of low status, looked down on investment bankers instead.

Ireland, the most successful example to date of using tourism as a fast-growth model, has managed to diversify its tourism into a base of related jobs, notably information services like telemarketing and banking services. Ireland has an advantage in its English-speaking base that other countries, such as Cuba, do not. The financial and lending institutions that underwrite tourism would be wise to put some of their resources into intensive language training in any non–English speaking country. Even Ireland's technological industry, as it seeks to parlay itself into the Silicon Valley of the twenty-first century, will face stiff competition from those of other English-speaking countries such as the United States. Keith Dawson, a Boston-based Internet consultant who tracks Silicon wannabes, counts eighty-eight companies worldwide, seventeen in the United States alone. There are ten Silicon Prairies, three Silicon Mountains, one Silicon Island, two Silicon Bayous, and two Silicon Swamps. The overseas competition includes Silicon Fen in Cambridge, Scotland's Silicon Glen, Wales's Cym Silicon, Israel's Silicon Wadi, Switzerland's Silicon Valais, and India's Silicon Plateau.[6]

Whether the economic benefits resulting from tourism ultimately compensate for the cultural cannibalism that goes with the fast-growth model is a big, open question. The industry is making some tentative efforts to regulate itself, largely in the area of ecotourism. Michael Seltzer, acting chair of nonprofit management for New York University's Robert J. Milano Graduate School of Management and Urban Planning Policy, describes one such experiment in an organization called Business Enterprises for Sustainable Travel, which is in the planning stages under the chairmanship of Connie Higginson of American Express. The group of industry leaders draws upon the resources of the International Commission for Monuments and Sites, the predecessor of the World Monuments Fund, through which it expects to communicate with the industry worldwide. One of his pet projects is a Galapagos Islands tour operator which is setting up a foundation to aid local conservation efforts. The bottom line for the operator, Lindblad Special Expeditions, is that passengers whom it informs through aggressive marketing of the benefit their holiday has brought to the locals will want to take other ecotours in other parts of the world. "If you want to make money, this is the high end," Seltzer observes.[7]

Seltzer, a former VISTA worker and Ford Foundation scholar, stressed that these efforts, though intended to preempt government regulation, are not explicitly self-regulatory on the part of the companies themselves. "Efforts like these begin to show that companies are prepared to be good corporate citizens," he said, adding that such measures preempt efforts like that of the Indonesian government a few years ago to set aside a proportion of tourism profits to give back to the community, a move that sounds suspiciously like a tax. "Our intent is to surface those solid practices which are in the industry already"— preserving the environment, enhancing culture, and adding to the economic and social well-being of the communities themselves. A success story he hopes to patent in other hotels is the program of day classes in hula, lei-making, and Hawaiian culture at the Kaanapaali Beach Hotel on Maui. "You can't just lie on a beach all day," he said. "A growing part of the travel population now wants to learn about where they are."

More to the point, some organizations are developing programs which are a form of workfare for tourists. In exchange for a modestly priced travel package, the tourist actually enters into the life of the community by working as a farmer, for example, or a language teacher. While these programs face certain limitations in the usefulness of labor performed within the timespans of most vacations, this is a creative idea and worth pursuing.

It is difficult to see how these efforts, laudatory though they are, will mitigate the enormous growth projected for travel by the U.N.-affiliated World Tourism Organization, also infelicitously acronymed WTO. (The confusion may be less than accidental as the words *democracy* and *free trade* are used interchangeably in discussing tourism.) "That's a very tough question," Seltzer said. "Of course we already have places like Cancún. Nobody can do anything about that. The newer resorts hopefully will avoid these mistakes, now that NGOs are being invited to the table."

It is estimated that more than double the current number of international arrivals will burden airports within twenty years, from 612 million international arrivals in 1997 to 1.6 billion by 2020. Along with telecommunications and information technology, tourism is expected to be the main economic driver for the new millennium. As the Internet becomes increasingly popular as a means of self-booking, *frisson* travel is expected to balloon as well. Ironically, tourists now seek to re-create the hardships of historical travel in safe and insular environmental packages, perhaps a sign that consumption has gone as far as it can go.[8]

Africa is now the tabula rasa of the industry, where the mistakes of the past have a chance to be wiped clean. It is also regarded as the region of greatest opportunity as it is reachable by plane in four hours from Paris and contains much of the world's most pristine, high-end, ecotourism. Perhaps not entirely by coincidence, the United Nations, with U.S. ambassador Richard Holbrooke, focused its attention on Africa in the year 2000.

Mozambique is an example of "self-regulation," where the government has granted the local tribes exclusive rights to set up ecotourism: however, tourism in Mozambique was wiped out by catastrophic floods in early 2000. South Africa, where tourism is viewed as a major part of the economy, is another beacon: the government there has set up an investment fund for supporting local NGOs. But these efforts, as even Seltzer admits, represent "a very small part of the continent." And, he says, ecotourism is how many land-rights abuses occur because of the autocratic governments that still exist in most of Africa. "You can't create ecotourism at the cost of local livelihoods," he says. "Uganda doesn't yet have a strong civil society. For businesses to do the right thing not only for themselves but for the whole community, you have to have existing community institutions."

There are many persons of goodwill like Michael Seltzer and Scott Wayne of the WTTC working in the industry today, and the potential for doing good certainly exists in the swarm of opportunities that any big business turns up. The vision of corporate good citizenship is a tantalizing one, but the invisible hand is very strong. A wise philosopher once said that it takes a very long time to create and a very short time to destroy, ergo, the battle between good and evil is always a losing one; but that is no reason not to engage in it. The histories of companies such as Standard Oil, American Express, and Boeing make very clear who will win in a conflict of interests: the story of Orson Welles and Nelson Rockefeller is a good example. It takes an exceptionally strong artist or idealist to complete good work under the extraordinary pressures created by these opportunities, as evident in the making of *Michael Collins* or in some of the Russian Orthodox church restorations, which have spotty completion records and were said to be driven by oil interests using them as "charities" through which to spirit funds out of the country tax free.

Some of the business dealings that go on under the guise of "culture" ain't too refined, like money-laundering or the kind of corruption that blew open the European parliament in 1998–99, when it was "discovered" that some $10 billion of the E.U. budget had disappeared through fraud, incompetence, or "error," some of which was laid at the door of the Tourism Commission. Artists must also ask themselves whether they wish to lend their talents to creating a new norm of pseudo-art or pseudo-culture that in time could consume the real thing. Or, as the SCETO consultants in charge of the Bali five-year plan put it, "The cultural manifestations will probably have disappeared [that is, at the term of the Master Plan, by 1985], but Bali can still be thought of as a green and sumptuous garden."[9]

This is of course nothing new. Hollywood, still the pinnacle of endeavor for so many countries struggling to "emerge" by creating or stimulating their film industries, is a metaphor for the consumption of cultural identity in the twentieth century. It has succeeded to the point where it has consumed itself and now must look to the cultures of other countries for fresh material, thus reversing the process that began in the early years of the century with immigrants going to the movies to learn the manners and mores of America. This process created a broad enough audience to create wealth and, packaged with the ideas of freedom and opportunity, eventually sold to the rest of the world. We may be looking at a more complex and less successful business in the twenty-first century. Movies that create wealth and movies that preserve cultural identity are, generally speaking, very different creatures: as Jim Sheridan aptly remarked, it is very, very difficult for a small culture to create a story with universal appeal.

While the gale of creative destruction rages on, there is as yet no clear-cut evidence that prosperity brings peace. The Basques, who with the Frank Gehry Guggenheim at Bilbao have enjoyed an unprecedented run of prestige and material betterment in the 1990s, decided to end their cease-fire in the last week of November 1999, just as Northern Ireland reached a tentative power-sharing agreement between Republicans and Unionists. The Basque peace process up to that point had closely followed upon Northern Ireland's: in fact, Gerry Adams visited the Basque region as a negotiator. Dwindling popular support was believed to be the main factor in the ETA's decision to call its campaign to a halt in 1998; however, the militant minority has managed to keep the conflict alive for the past thirty years. Some observers felt the resumption of hostilities was a bluff to keep political pressure boiling for a crucial election in March 2000. If this is so, it does not bode well for either the Basque or the Northern Irish peace. As *New York Times* reporter Tina Rosenberg acutely remarked in an article about so-called "free" elections in Cambodia, where dictator Hun Sen was worried about losing tourism to Angkor Wat, the mouse has learned how to make the good doctor bring it cheese.

This is not to say that tourism should be abandoned as a foreign-policy instrument. It seems to have played a considerable role in getting the Syrians to the negotiating table, at least, although once there the interests of tourism and trade and security diverged. But its claims should be moderated and the invasion of its PR into matters of state strictly modified. Certainly, there is no strong evidence to support the notion that multinational corporations should be given tax breaks, government funding, or a voice in foreign policy decisions because their corporate endeavors advance the cause of peace.

One company has almost single-handedly promoted the idea of tourism as democracy onto the policy map and into the public view. From the end of World War II, American Express sold foreign travel as an extension of the Marshall Plan, a way in which ordinary Americans could help the economy of the Western world. Through creating, funding, and placing its executives on the boards of such organizations as the WTTC, MEMTA, the World Monuments Fund and the World Monuments Watch, Rebuild Dubrovnik, and Businesses for Sustainable Tourism, the company has continued to maintain that travel is a "social, political and economic force . . . a powerful instrument of helping foreign nations gain much-needed dollars." Through these not-for-profit organizations and its foreign-exchange dealings, the company has nurtured strong affiliations with the World Bank and the United Nations. Former executives are now statesmen. Even if former CEO James Robinson III still wanted to form a government agency to deal with Third World debt problems he wouldn't have to: it exists in the form of American Express.[10]

Historically, however, the record suggests that the democratizing potential of tourism has been used by powerful corporations like American Express to advance their own interests: in 1986, when Robinson floated the idea of his government agency, the greatest threat to the bottom line of American Express was the prospect of loan defaults to less-developed countries like Mexico, Brazil, and Argentina. Today, Reebok and other global brand name companies are now getting involved in such human rights issues as the plight of refugees. But given the example of how American Express encouraged tourism in Croatia at Serbia's expense, the premise is a shaky one. Business is inevitably driven by its own narrow investment interests. How many refugees can a business handle without cutting into its profit margin? What if a company like Reebok assists the Hutus and forgets the Tutsis?

Corporations are not democratic institutions, and any peace dominated by their concerns will not be democratic either. Conquest quotes a well-known American Marxist literary critic, Fredric Jameson, who claims that Stalinism was a "success" because it "followed its historical mission to force the rapid industrialization of an undeveloped country." Tourism has claimed the same ground for itself in the post-glasnost era. Conquest observes that Jameson's statement is fallacious on several grounds which hold true for tourism as well: "The advances were far and away smaller than claimed; the gigantism of enterprises was a grave distortion, as was pointed out to the Stalinists by (for example) Western automobile manufacturers; and Soviet-style industrialization was by world standards an anti-innovative dead end."[11]

The study of history may be for depressives, but Conquest points out something else which should be taken to heart by all policymakers, particularly those involved in substituting tourism for more traditional forms of foreign aid. "After the economic disaster of collectivization there were two possibilities: to admit failure and change policy, even to relinquish total power; or to pretend that success had been achieved. The latter course was chosen. In fact the Idea, contradicted by reality, coped by denying it. As a result, for the rest of the Soviet epoch the country lived a double existence—an official world of fantasy, of happiness, grand achievements, wonderful statistics, liberty and democracy, and a reality of gloom, suffering, terror, denunciation and apparatchik degeneration."[12]

Bearing in mind the fact that aid for the world's poorest nations has fallen by as much as 40 percent in the past ten years, a significant portion of global stability now depends on an industry which is notoriously skittish. Projections for the continued and perhaps exponential growth of tourism rest on two legs: the nest eggs of retiring babyboomers and the discretionary income generated by the decade-old bull market. However, while growth in world tourism more than tripled in 1999, it fell short of expectations, mainly because of the failure of the millennium to stimulate travel. The policymakers had better be right. If the economy turns down, the mob in Seattle has given us a brief glimpse of what the alternative might look like.

The free movement of people, enshrined in the Treaty of Rome and celebrated by Robinson as a learning instrument for forgetting national differences and living together in a global economy, is indeed a cornerstone of a free society; but its mirror image is something else, the restless surging of uprooted populations foreseen by Rebecca West as the most pernicious of the century's evils. It would be a stunning epiphany on the nature of capitalism if globalization, the engine of utopia in the second half of the century, were to create the same condition as the catastrophic wars of the first.

When the final days of the twentieth century wound down, I took my place among the vast and diverse crowds surging through the streets of Manhattan and contemplated West's definition of the seed of fascism: rootlessness. I was assaulted by familiar Christmas carols sung by children who didn't know the music, a gift from one of the city's cultural programs. "Does anybody know the difference anymore?" asked the bemused, urbane woman next to me, a native New Yorker of several generations with neatly cropped white hair and the kind of anonymously expensive cloth coat which is the uniform on the Upper East Side. "Are any of these people New Yorkers?" I am a tourist here myself, a stranger in my own city. So many of the faces are blanks. So few respond. So many are restlessly in search of an identity to try on like this year's fashion, a virtual life, someone else's culture. Like children jaded with new toys, it takes little to turn their tempers ugly. Jangling oddly with West's words and the distortion of the familiar tunes is a small notice I clipped from the *New York Times*, which, perhaps reluctant to hurt business, buried it in the Sunday paper. It is a State Department warning advising Americans to stay away from large holiday gatherings and celebrations throughout the world, based on "credible targeting information" possibly related to planned attacks by Islamic fundamentalist Osama Bin Laden.

Of course "nothing happened" on December 31, 1999, in the sense of a definable act of terrorism. Something more insidious *did* happen. The ferment that accompanied the turn of the last century was conspicuously absent. Instead of crowding into the streets, people stayed home and watched the distant spectacle on television. The same kind of social control that makes the world safe for tourism constricts it considerably, not only in less developed countries. Some social critics even argued that governments used the fear of terrorism and other Y2K-related disasters as a form of social experiment to frighten their citizens into passivity. While tourism as an engine of growth is the product of good times, the machinery that produced it is not so benign when times are bad.

Rebecca West, writing perceptively about the rise of fascism in Europe between the world wars, identified rootlessness as "perhaps the most real distress of our age." Describing Luccheni, who assassinated Empress Elizabeth of Austria in 1898, she could be describing a dispossessed rural living in Istanbul or Johannesburg or Cairo today:

> He belonged to an urban population for which the existing form of government made no provision, which wandered often workless and always traditionless, without power to control its destiny. . . . The long servitude in the slums has left this kind of barbarian without any knowledge of what man does when he ceases to be violent, except for a few uncomprehending glimpses of material prosperity. He therefore can conceive of no outlet for his energies other than the creation of social services which artificially and unnaturally spread this material prosperity among the population, in small doses that keep them happy and dependent.[13]

Notes

Chapter 1 The Democratization of Travel

1. Fletcher, in Eric Newby, *A Book of Travellers' Tales* (London: Collins, 1985), 109.
2. Montagu, in Newby, *Book of Travellers' Tales*, 117–118.
3. Richard Montagu, *The Life and Adventures of Mrs. Christian Davies* (London, 1740).
4. Sévigné, in Newby, *Book of Travellers' Tales*, 115.
5. Gray, in Newby, *Book of Travellers' Tales*, 124.
6. Henry James, *Daisy Miller* (Oxford: Oxford University Press, 1985), 113.
7. Quoted in Cynthia Enloe, *Bananas, Bases, and Beaches* (Berkeley: University of California Press, 1990).
8. Peter Z. Grossman, *American Express: The Unofficial History of the People Who Built the Great Financial Empire* (New York: Crown, 1987), 82–83.
9. Twain, in Newby, *Travellers' Tales*, 165.
10. Grossman, *American Express*, chap. 6.
11. Ibid., 182.

Chapter 2 "Little Rockiefeller"

1. Information on Nelson Rockefeller is from Cary Reich, *The Life of Nelson A. Rockefeller*, vol. 1 (New York: Doubleday, 1996). Cary Reich's untimely death came before the completion of volume 2.
2. Mark Twain and Charles Dudley Warner, *The Gilded Age: A Tale of Today* (New York: Meridian, 1994), xxi.
3. Reich, *Life of Rockefeller*, 222.
4. Ibid., 240.
5. Ibid., 455–467.
6. Grossman, *American Express*, 249–255.
7. Through BCCI, Clark later played a role in perhaps the strangest chapter in the history of American Express. In 1989 the U.S. attorney-general's office ran a money-laundering crackdown called Operation Polar Cap, which exposed an international scheme by Colombian cocaine traffickers to move drug profits out of the United States to banks in South America. The U.S. government filed suit against nine major U.S. banks, including Citibank, the Bank of New York, BCCI, Republic National Bank of New York, and the American Express

Bank. Early in the decade, American Express had purchased the Trade Development Bank in Geneva from Republic National's owner, the renowned
Edmond Safra. When Safra, whose family had been in banking for generations, discovered that he did not fit within the corporate culture of American
Express, he quickly severed his ties but agreed not to compete with that company for five years. When the time was up, he founded the bank that became
Safra Public Holdings, causing fierce resentment among top American Express
officials, who orchestrated a smear campaign against him. Through a series of
largely obscure articles in international publications, Safra's name, a highly
respectable one in banking circles, was linked with, among other things, BCCI
and the Iran-Contra affair, largely through a client account for a Swiss trading
company called Shakarchi which was undergoing an overlapping investigation
for laundering drug money from secret police as well as for drug lords worldwide. Nothing was ever substantiated. American Express, headed at that time
by James Robinson III, later issued a public apology to Safra, who was a devout
Jew and a donor to Jewish causes, and paid $8 million to Jewish charities of
his choice. Safra died in 1999 in a fire in his heavily guarded penthouse in
Monte Carlo, under circumstances that remain mysterious. See Bryan Burrough, *Vendetta: American Express and the Smearing of Edmond Safra* (San Francisco: Harper Collins, 1992), 172–239; see also *Wall Street Journal,* 12/6/99.

8. Reich, *Life of Nelson Rockefeller,* 427–431.
9. Matthew Lynn, *Birds of Prey: Boeing v. Airbus and the Battle for the Skies*
(New York: Four Walls, Eight Windows, 1998), 60.
10. Ibid., 48.
11. Geoffrey de Havilland, *Sky Fever: The Autobiography of Sir Geoffrey de Havilland* (1979), cited in Lynn, *Birds of Prey,* 24.
12. Henri Ziegler, president of Aerospatiale, quoted in Geoffrey Knight, *Concorde: The Inside Story,* cited in Lynn, *Birds of Prey,* 77.
13. Lynn, *Birds of Prey,* 63.
14. Keith Rockwell, *Journal of Commerce,* 5/27/94, 1–A; Colin Narbrough,
Times (London), 4/2/94, Bus. sec., 9; Thomas L. Friedman, *New York
Times,* published in the *Houston Chronicle,* 2/17/94, A–1.
15. Financial Staff, *Guardian* (Manchester), 2/18/94, City Page, 17; Friedman,
New York Times, published in the *Houston Chronicle,* 2/17/94, A–1.
16. Lynn, *Birds of Prey,* 1–9; interview, Matthew Lynn, 10/30/98; Richard
Weintraub, *Washington Post,* 2/17/94, B–11.
17. Financial Staff, *Guardian,* 2/18/94.
18. Alden Hatch, *American Express: A Century of Service* (New York: American
Express, 1954).

Chapter 3 The Biggest Business in the World

1. *World Tourism Organization Yearbook of Tourism Statistics,* 49th ed. (Madrid:
World Tourism Organization, 1995), vol. 1. Unless otherwise indicated,
all figures are in U.S. dollars.
2. Leonard J. Lickorish and Carson L. Jenkins, *An Introduction to Tourism*
(Oxford: Butterworth and Heinemann, 1997), 12.
3. *World Tourism Organization Yearbook of Tourism Statistics.*

4. See Daniel Yergin and Joseph Stanislaw, *The Commanding Heights* (New York: Simon and Schuster, 1998), 79.

5. Ibid., 126.

6. Amartya Sen, *Poverty and Famines: An Essay on Poverty and Deprivation* (Oxford: Clarendon, 1981).

7. Amartya Sen, "Development Strategy and Management of the Market Economy," 267–271.

8. World Bank, Tourism Sector Working Paper (Washington, D.C., 1972).

9. Peter Waldman, "Egypt's Tourism Rises as Violence Ebbs," *Wall Street Journal*, 1995; Mark Husband, "Egyptian Militants Drop 'Failed' Armed Campaign," *Financial Times* (London), 4/28/99; Mark Huband, "Egypt Devaluation Seen as a Priority," *Financial Times* (London), 10/28/99; interview Ayden Nour, director for the eastern United States and Latin America, Egyptian Tourism Authority, 11/22/99.

10. Interview, Carolyn Cain, tourism specialist, IFC, 2/4/99. Unless otherwise indicated, all further Cain quotations from this source.

11. Interview, Ian Christie, lead Africa specialist, World Bank, 2/12/99. All further Christie quotations from this source.

12. "Indonesia: Bali Tourism Project," World Bank Project Completion Report (Washington, D.C., 6/5/85).

13. Yergin and Stanislaw, *Commanding Heights*, 152–153.

14. Bryan Burrough, *Vendetta: American Express and the Smearing of Edmond Safra* (San Francisco: Harper Collins, 1992), 208–210, 221, 284–285.

15. Jon Friedman and John Meehan, *House of Cards: Inside the Troubled Empire of American Express* (New York: Putnam, 1992), 202–203.

16. Interview, Ian Christie; *Wall Street Journal*, 1/26/99.

17. *Los Angeles Times*, 8/27/99, 9/3/99; *Wall Street Journal*, 10/22/99.

18. Memorandum of the President of the International Bank for Reconstruction and Development to the Executive Director on a Country Assistance Strategy of the World Bank Group for Lebanon (Washington, D.C.: 1/7/97), 6; Kerry Dolan, "Kings, Queens and Dictators," *Forbes*, July 1998; Interview, Nachib Rachid, director of corporate communications, Solidère, Beirut, 5/24/99.

19. Interview, Carolyn Cain.

20. Lickorish and Jenkins, *Introduction to Tourism*, 41–42.

21. *Wall Street Journal*, 1/26/99; *Financial Times* (London), 3/21/00.

22. John le Carré, *The Tailor of Panama* (New York: Ballantine, 1996), 75–76.

23. *Far Eastern Economic Review*, 1/13/94; *Caught in Modern Slavery: Tourism and Child Prostitution in Asia*, conference proceedings, Ecumenical Coalition on Third World Tourism, Bangkok, 5/1–5/90; James Petras and Tienchai Wongchaisuwan, "Thailand: Free Markets, AIDS, and Child Prostitution," *Z Magazine*, September 1993; interview, Carol Smollensky, director, ECPAT-USA, 1/22/99; Margaret A. Healy, "Child Sex Tourism," *International Law Journal* 18 (1995): 1852, 1865.

24. Lilian S. Robinson, "Touring Thailand's Sex Industry," *Nation*, 1/11/93; Enloe, *Bananas, Bases, and Beaches*.

25. Margaret A. Healy cites a list of sources for Rajanasathian's remarks in "Child Sex Tourism."

26. Petras and Wongchaisuwan, "Thailand"; Thomas Von Mouillard, "Sex Tourism Arives in Cuba," *Ottawa Citizen*, 3/13/93, R–5.

27. Thailand position paper in *Caught in Modern Slavery*.

28. Indian position paper in *Caught in Modern Slavery*.

29. World Bank, *Global Commodity Markets*, Series 1, quoted in *Financial Times* (London), 2/3/99.

30. Polly Patulla, *Last Resorts: The Cost of Tourism in the Caribbean* (New York: Cassell, 1996), 91.

31. Interview, Carol Smollensky, director, ECPAT-USA, 1/22/99.

32. Patricia Goldstone, *Nation*, forthcoming.

33. Bill Rolston, "Reformation and Sectarianism," in John Darby, ed., *Northern Ireland* (Belfast: Appletree Press, 1983), 200–201.

34. Yergin and Stanislaw, *Commanding Heights*, 154.

Chapter 4 Have I Got a Country for You!

1. Harff, cited in Yohanan Ramati, "Stopping the War in Yugoslavia," *Midstream*, April 1994, 2–3. See articles by Judy Dempsey and Guy Dinmore in the *Financial Times* (London), 3/20–31/99, on Israel's reluctance to bomb Serbia.

2. Harff, cited in Ramati, "Stopping the War," 2–3. Merlino's book is called *Les Vérités yougoslaves ne sont pas toutes bonnes, à dire* (Paris: Albin Michel, 1993).

3. Interview, James Harff, director, Global Communications, 3/3/99. Unless otherwise noted, all Harff quotations are from this source.

4. Interview, David Finn, founding partner, Ruder Finn, 3/1/99. Unless otherwise noted, all Finn quotations are from this source. Interview, Joel Carmichael, editor in chief, *Midstream*, 3/2–3/99.

5. See David Finn, *The Way Forward: My First Fifty Years at Ruder Finn* (New York: Millwood, 1998).

6. Jack O'Dwyer, "Jack O'Dwyer Public Relations Directory," newsletter (New York, 1998).

7. Tina Rosenberg, *New York Times Sunday Magazine*, 6/30/98.

8. O'Dwyer, "O'Dwyer Public Relations Directory."

9. Dan Burstein, *Euroquake: Europe's Explosive Economic Challenge Will Change the World* (New York: Simon and Schuster, 1991), 54–55.

10. Interview, Gregg Anderson, North American head, New Zealand Tourist Board, 4/5/99.

11. Rebecca West, *Black Lamb and Grey Falcon*, vol. 1 (New York: Viking, 1964), 231.

12. Interview, Nazli Weiss, Rebuild Dubrovnik Fund 3/5/9. Unless otherwise indicated, all Weiss quotations are from this source.

13. Stuart Ewen, *PR: A Social History of Spin* (New York: Basic, 1996), 161; see also Edward Bernays, *Biography of an Idea: Memoirs of Public Relations Counsel* (New York: Simon and Schuster, 1965), 57–61.

14. Edward Bernays, *Propaganda* (1928), quoted in Ewen, *PR*, 164–165.

15. Walter Lippmann, *Public Opinion* (1922), quoted in Ewen, *PR*, 158.

16. Ibid.

17. Interview, Cord Hansen-Sturm, director, MEMTA, 2/16/99. Unless oth-

erwise indicated, all Hansen-Sturm quotes are from this source.

18. Interview, Peggy Bendel, PR representative, SATOUR, 4/16/99.

19. Interview, Cord Hansen-Sturm.

20. National Association of Manufacturers Executives Conference (Philadelphia), *Public Relations Proceedings*, 10/19/43, 2.

21. Finn, *Way Forward*, 168–170.

22. O'Dwyer, "O'Dwyer Public Relations Directory."

23. Interviews, John Ruggie, assistant to the secretary-general, United Nations, 4/6/99, 11/19/99.

Chapter 5 Tourism Under Castro

1. Armando Valladares, *Against All Hope* (New York: Knopf, 1986), p. 216; interview, John Kavulich, U.S.-Cuba Trade and Economic Council, 11/24/98. Unless otherwise noted, all Kavulich quotations are from this source.

2. The Paris Club is one of the ad-hoc intragovernmental groups that determine the eligibility of debtor nations for foreign loans. "Potemkin villages" were the "villages"—theatrical sets really—built in the Soviet Union by Joseph Stalin to convince visiting journalists that the Russian peasants were well housed.

3. Robert Quirk, *Fidel Castro* (New York: Norton, 1993), 771–772.

4. Christopher Baker, *The Cuba Handbook* (Chico, Calif.: Moon Travel Publications, 1997), 73–79; interview, Dr. Gunther Rau, president and CEO, FERI International.

5. Baker, *Cuba Handbook; Financial Times* (London), 11/17/98.

6. Quirk, *Castro*, 317.

7. Interview, Myra Saldivar, sales manager, Havana Libre, 11/6/98. Unless otherwise indicated, all Saldivar quotations are from this source.

8. *Wall Street Journal*, 8/7/95.

9. Ibid.

10. Quirk, *Castro*, 128.

11. Ibid., 281.

12. Andres Oppenheimer, *Castro's Final Hour: The Secret Story Behind the Coming Downfall of Communist Cuba* (New York: Touchstone, 1992), 319–355.

13. Quirk, *Castro*, 385.

14. Interview, Kerry Dolan, reporter, *Forbes*, 11/21/98.

Chapter 6 Ireland

1. Interview, Senator David Norris, Irish Senate Foreign Affairs Committee, 11/23/99. Unless otherwise indicated, all Norris quotations are from this source.

2. Stephen O'Shea, "Dublin Rediscovered," *Harper's Bazaar*, July 1995.

3. *Financial Times* (London), 10/1/99.

4. *New York Times*, 3/12/97.

5. Interview, Ruth Croke, PR and Marketing Executive for the Irish Industrial Development Authority (IDA), 8/23/00.

6. *Wall St. Journal*, 11/6/95.

7. Ireland Operational Plan for Tourism, 1989–1993 (Dublin: Ministry for Tourism, 1993), 9.

8. Ron Brown, speaking at Foreign Policy Association, New York, 3/20/96 (my notes); *Financial Times* (London), 9/23/99.

9. Interview, Nicholas O'Neill, film producer, 10/10/95.

10. Interview, Gregg Anderson, North American head, New Zealand Tourist Board, 4/5/99.

11. Interview, Alexander Walker, film critic, *Evening Standard* (London), 6/27/96.

12. *Irish Times*, 5/18/96.

13. *Federal News Service*, 11/16/95.

14. Patricia Goldstone, "Psst! Ya Wanna Revolution?" *Premiere*, September 1996.

15. Interview, Morgan O'Sullivan, 10/11/95. Unless otherwise indicated, all O'Sullivan quotations are from this source.

16. Interview, David Cullen, stockbroker, 10/15/95; "Report on Financial Incentives for Film Production in Ireland," Media and Entertainment Group, Arthur Cox Law firm, Dublin, 1993–1995.

17. Interview, Jim Sheridan, film director and producer, 10/15/95; interview, Kevin Moriarty, CEO, Ardmore Studios, 10/6/95.

18. Interview, Sean McGrath, realtor, 10/15/95.

19. Interview, Michael D. Higgins, Irish minister for arts, culture, and the Gaeltacht, 10/9/95. Unless otherwise indicated, all Higgins quotations are from this source.

20. Interview, Karen Millett, manager, Investment Marketing Services, MIGA, 2/4/99. Unless otherwise indicated, all Millett quotations are from this source.

21. Patricia Goldstone, "Construction Compromises the Irish Countryside," *Metropolis*, May 1996.

22. Figures are from the Irish Hotels Association publications.

23. Goldstone, "Construction Compromises the Irish Countryside."

24. Frank McDonald, "The Ribbon That's Strangling Ireland," *Irish Times*, 9/15/87.

25. Goldstone, "Construction Compromises the Irish Countryside."

26. *Financial Times* (London), 9/22/98, 11/13/98, 3/1/99, 6/10/99.

27. *Financial Times* (London), 3/23/99.

28. Ibid.

29. *Financial Times* (London), 10/4/99.

30. Ibid.

Chapter 7 The Middle East

1. Interview, Cord Hansen-Sturm, director, MEMTA, 2/16/99. Unless otherwise indicated, all Hansen-Sturm quotations are from this source.

2. Economist Intelligence Unit, *Travel and Tourism Analyst No. 6* (London, 1997).

3. Amy Dockser Marcus, "Israel Moves to Build Tighter Economic Ties to Arab Neighbors," *Wall Street Journal*, 1995.

4. Interview, Akel Biltaji, Jordanian minister of tourism, 6/1/99. Unless otherwise indicated, all Biltaji quotations are from this source.

5. *New York Times*, 11/24/99.

6. Interview, Christian Ibrahimchaw, hotelier, 5/23/99. Unless otherwise indicated, all Ibrahimchaw quotations are from this source.

7. *Development of Turkish Tourism* (Istanbul: Association of Turkish Travel Agencies, 1999), 29, 34–35.

8. Statistics are from the Turkish Ministry of Tourism.

9. *Wall Street Journal*, 8/96.

10. Interview, Ahmet Tan, minister of tourism, Turkey, 5/14/99. Unless otherwise indicated, all Tan quotations are from this source.

11. *Financial Times* (London), 9/8/99.

12. Interview, Gaye Carmikli, director, tourism division, Nurol Holdings, 5/14/99. Unless otherwise indicated, all Carmikli quotations are from this source.

13. UNICEF and EcoSoc findings reported in position paper of Indian Steering Committee for *Caught in Modern Slavery: Tourism and Child Prostitution in Asia*, conference proceedings, Ecumenical Coalition on Third World Tourism, City here, 5/1–5/90.

14. Interview, Bertan Tolkun, 5/16/99.

15. Interview, Kurt Johnson, head chef, Antalya Sheraton, 5/17/99. Unless otherwise indicated, all Johnson quotations are from this source.

16. Interview, H. Reza Elibol, manager, Antalya Sheraton, 5/17/99.

17. Interview, Nancy Ward-Thomas, head of British Women's Association, Antalya, 5/17/99.

18. Interview, Arthur Nazarian, minister of tourism, Lebanon, 5/21/99. Unless otherwise indicated, all Nazarian quotations are from this source.

19. Interview, Nasser M. Safieddine, adviser to the minister and director general, National Council of (Lebanese) Tourism, 5/20/99.

20. Interview, Christian Ibrahimchaw.

21. Interview, Faysal Mikdashi, director of the Civil Aviation Authority for Lebanon, 5/20/99.

22. Interview, Denis Chagnon, director of public information, ICAO, 8/19/99. Unless otherwise indicated, all Chagnon quotes are from this source.

23. Interview, Rebecca Prechsler, FAA Press Office, 8/18/99; interview, White House Press Office, 8/19/99.

24. Interview, Margaret Schmidt, deputy director, State Department Near Eastern Affairs Press Office, 9/3/99.

25. Conversation with M. and Mme. Haffar, 5/22/99.

26. Interview, Wissam Ezzeddine, television producer, 5/19/99.

27. Interview, Wahith Chbat, hotelier, 5/22/99.

28. Interview, Mohamed El-Sarji, filmmaker, 5/23/99.

29. *The Middle East on a Shoestring* (Hawthorne, Australia: Lonely Planet, 1997), 404.

30. Ibid.; Ministry of Tourism (Jordan).

31. Interview, Nikos Xitos, general manager, MAICO, 5/28/99.

32. Interview, Arie Sommer, consul tourism commissioner for Israel in North America, 9/9/99.

33. "Final Status Issues," *Los Angeles Times*, 9/99.
34. Interview, Yehuda Shen, deputy commissioner for tourism for Israel in North America, 11/22/99.
35. *Financial Times* (London), 11/27–28/99.

Chapter 8 When I Hear the Word *Culture*, I Reach for My Gun

1. *Los Angeles Times*, 10/1/99.
2. *The Economist* (London), 7/6/99; Patricia Goldstone, "St. Petersburg," *Metropolis*, March 1996; *New York Times*, 12/6/96.
3. Interview, George White, executive director of the Eugene O'Neill National Playwrights Conference, 12/10/98.
4. *New York Times*, 4/24/99.
5. Miklós Haraszti, *The Velvet Prison* (New York: Basic, 1987), 7–9.
6. Michel Picard, "Tourism and the Uses of 'Balinese Culture' in New Order Indonesia," *Review of Indonesian and Malaysian Affairs* (Summer 1990).
7. World Bank, "Indonesia: Bali Tourism Project," Project Completion Report (Washington, D.C., 6/5/85).
8. B. Dalton, *The Bali Handbook* (Chico, Calif.: Moon Publications, 1999), 35–36.
9. Interview, Kevin Moriarty, CEO, Ardmore Studios, 10/6/95.
10. Interview, Jim Sheridan, film director and producer, 10/15/95.
11. Interview, Peter Sheridan, theater director, 10/9/95.
12. Interview, Roger Corman, film director, 10/21/95.
13. Interview, Tom Blinkhorn, World Bank Lead Operations Specialist, St. Petersburg, 2/25/99. Unless otherwise indicated, all Blinkhorn quotations are from this source.
14. Goldstone, "St. Petersburg."
15. Ibid.
16. Jane Kramer, "The Politics of Memory," *New Yorker*, August 1995.
17. *Wall Street Journal*, 6/30/98.
18. *Los Angeles Times*, 10/17/99.
19. *New York Times*, 11/13/99.
20. *Financial Times* (London), 11/2/99, 7/1/99.

The End

1. Interview, Ayden Nour, director for the eastern United States and Latin America, Egyptian Tourism Authority, 11/22/99.
2. *Wall Street Journal*, 12/1/99.
3. *New York Times*, 12/1/99.
4. Robert Conquest, *Reflections on a Ravaged Century* (New York: W.W. Norton, 2000).
5. *Financial Times* (London), 12/6/99.
6. *Wall Street Journal*, 11/29/99.
7. Interview, Michael Seltzer, director, Businesses for Sustainable Travel, 12/9/99. Unless otherwise indicated, all Seltzer quotes are from this source.

8. *Financial Times* (London), 12/6/99.
9. *Bali Tourism Study Report to the Government of Indonesia*, 6 vols. (Paris: UNDP/IBRD, 1971).
10. Peter Grossman, *American Express: The Unofficial History of the People Who Built the Great Financial Empire* (New York: Crown, 1987), 254.
11. Conquest, *Reflections on a Ravaged Century*, 149.
12. Ibid., 96.
13. Rebecca West, *Black Lamb and Grey Falcon* (New York: Viking, 1941), 9.

Acknowledgments

Writing this book launched me into an unknown world, and I would like to thank all those who helped me find my way. First and foremost, I owe my editor Judy Metro my greatest thanks for her championship over a long and at times frustrating process, and for giving me the opportunity to embark on this adventure. I would also like to thank the Publications Committee at Yale University Press for putting their faith in me, my agent Joe Regal for his support, and senior editor Patricia Fidler for carrying on after the departure of Judy Metro. Thanks as well to manuscript editor Susan Laity for making what is usually a very ticklish process extremely enjoyable.

Many political, business, and economic thinkers gave generously of their time and insights in interviews in six different countries. I would like to offer special and heartfelt appreciation to Dr. Akel Biltaji, minister of tourism, Jordan; Carolyn Cain, International Finance Corporation, Washington, D.C.; Joel Carmichael, editor of *Midstream;* Gaye Carmikli, vice-president in charge of tourism, Nurol Holdings, Turkey; Denis Chagnon, chief information officer, International Civil Aviation Organization, Montreal; Ian Christie, lead Africa specialist, World Bank, Washington, D.C.; Kurt Johnson, executive chef, Sheraton Hotel, Antalya, Turkey; Dr. Elena Y. Kalnitskaya, director, Mikhailovsky Museum, St. Petersburg; John Kavulich, U.S.-Cuba Trade and Economic Council, New York; Geoffrey Lipman, former president of the World Travel and Tourism Council, London; Faysal Mikdashi, director-general of civil aviation, Lebanon; Karen Millett, general manager, Multilateral Investment Guarantee Agency, Washington, D.C.; Kevin Moriarty, chief executive officer, Ardmore Studios, Dublin; Arthur Nazarian, minister of tourism, Lebanon; Sen. David Norris, Irish Senate Foreign Affairs Committee, Dublin; Ayden Nour, director, Egyptian Tourist Authority, eastern United States and Latin America, New York; Margaret Schmidt, deputy director, U.S. State Department Near Eastern Affairs Press Office, Washington, D.C.; Michael Seltzer, executive director, Business Enterprises for Sustainable Travel, New York; Ismail Serageldin, vice-president of special programs, World Bank, Washington, D.C.; Carol Smollensky, director, ECPAT-USA, New York; Dr. Ahmet Tan, former minister of tourism, Turkey; and George White, executive director of the National Playwrights Conference, New York.

I would also like to thank filmmakers Wissam Ezzeddine, Jim Sheridan, and Morgan O'Sullivan as well as film critic Alexander Walker of the *Evening Standard,* for their special creative insights.

My deepest personal thanks go to Dan Burstein, senior adviser to the

Blackstone Group and author of *Euroquake, Yen!* and *Road Warriors,* for giving me the benefit of his encyclopedic knowledge and experience. Scott Wayne of the World Travel and Tourism Council was and is a font of information. Cord Hansen-Sturm kept me entertained. Stephen Walt, Evron and Jeane Kirkpatrick Professor of International Affairs, John F. Kennedy School of Government, Harvard University, and Darra Goldstein, chairman of Russian at Williams College, gave graciously of their time. I would also like to thank my translator in Cuba, Patricia Oakes Leigh-Wood, for her excellent Spanish and for her company. In Turkey, Bekir Cumurcu provided invaluable help and introduced me to my favorite teenager, his son, Adam. In Turkey, my thanks also go to Leyla Ozhan, counselor to the Ministry of Tourism.

In Lebanon I have many people to thank: first, Dr. Hicham Hamdan, former Lebanese ambassador to the United Nations, for his advice, reassurance, and many, many phone calls on my behalf. I would also like to thank Mme. Boushra Haffar for her gracious hospitality and support. My host, Christian Ibrahimchah of the Hotel Alexandre, and Philippe Asseily were also of great help; and I owe Wissam Ezzeddine a special thanks for introducing me to the Rotarians of Beirut.

One of the greatest pleasures of travel is the opportunity to form odd and wonderful friendships. I met so many people along the way who surprised and delighted me. My gratitude and love go to Ali Awwad "Taxi Day and Night," Joumana and Raymond Maalouf Chalfoun; Kevin Thomas; Bertan Tolkun; Kurt Johnson; Prof. Emel Ozcan; and the "UNIFIL boys." A safe journey and a happy homecoming to you all.

Last but certainly not least, I must thank those dear friends at home who sustained me through the difficult times: Bonnie Burstein and Douglas Quaid Corey, Ellen Bollinger, Jeffrey Bolton, Benita Cohen, Ali, Moshgan, and Sam Amir-Ebrahimi, Patricia Goldhammer, Male and Siegfried Jauernick, Merrill Lishan, Jack Morgan, Galip Ozbek, and Mary Sunshine. This book would not have been possible without you.